The Mediumship
of
Arnold Clare

Leader of the Trinity of Spiritual Fellowship

by

Harry Edwards

Captain, Indian Army Reserve of Officers. Lieutenant, Home Guard.
Parliamentary Candidate North Camberwell 1929 and North-West
Camberwell 1936.
London County Council Candidate 1928, 1931, 1934, 1937.
Leader of the Balham Psychic Research Society.
Author of
The Mediumship of Jack Webber

Published by THE PSYCHIC BOOK CLUB
144 High Holborn, London, W.C.I (1942)

New Edition 2019 published by

Saturday Night Press Publications
England.
snppbooks@gmail.com
www.snppbooks.com

Format of this edition © SNPPbooks

ISBN 978-1-908421-35-7

www.snppbooks.com

Cover by Ann Harrison @ SNPP

FOREWORD

APART from the report by Mr W. Harrison of the early development of Mr Arnold Clare's mediumship, the descriptions of the séances, the revelations of Peter and the writing of this book took place during the war years 1940-41.

As enemy action on London intensified, the physical séances ceased and in the autumn of 1940 were replaced by discussion circles. The first few circles took place in the author's house before a company of about twenty people. It was soon appreciated that the intelligence (known as Peter), speaking through the entranced medium, was of a high order and worthy of reporting. So these large discussion groups gave way to a small circle held in the medium's house, attended by Mr and Mrs Clare, Mr and Mrs Hart, Mrs Edwards and the author, an occasional visitor and with Mrs W.B. Cleveland as stenographer.

The procedure at these circles would be that in normal white light Mr Clare would enter into a trance state. His Guide, Peter, taking control, would discourse upon the selected topic answering all questions fluently and without hesitation.

Frequently, during these sittings, the air-raid sirens would be heard and the local anti-aircraft guns would be in action. At such times Peter would be asked if he wished to withdraw; and invariably he would reply, "No, it is not necessary, there is no imminent danger to you." Not on any occasion was the work interfered with; and Peter would continue to talk and answer questions without concern, in spite of the drone of enemy aeroplanes, the noise of gunfire, the bursting of shells and falling shrapnel.

It may be said that no other work dealing with an involved subject of this nature has ever been compiled under such unusual conditions. It is difficult to conceive a normal mind giving forth an uninterrupted smooth flow of wisdom upon (at times) involved and sometimes technical matters, without being disturbed by the external threat of imminent danger.

Peter's work will be all the more appreciated as one can recognise the need for calm and placid conditions for trance work. For Peter to have continued under these circumstances to explain and in a manner within our capacity to understand much that hitherto had been incomprehensible, pays an eloquent tribute to Mr Clare's mediumship and Peter's ability to hold the control.

.　　.　　.　　.　　.

The purposes of this book are threefold, and it has been divided into three parts.

The first section presents a brief history of the mediumship to date, personal notes and the records of the phenomena produced through the mediumship. The second section is devoted to Peter's explanations of the manner in which phenomena are produced, the nature of the forces employed and the mechanics of the operations. An effort has been made to relate authenticated records of phenomena, through mediumships past and present, to the explanations.

The third section indicates an avenue of philosophy for the governing of human conduct towards a more enlightened and spiritual outlook on life. The basis of this philosophy is the demonstration of the truth of individual survival of the ego after the physical body has been discarded.

This last section is the most important; for without it the first two are purposeless. The spiritualisation of mankind has ever been the aim of the realm spiritual. To those who ask "What is the purpose of a levitation or a materialization?" here is the answer.

.　　.　　.　　.　　.

Physical mediumship and spirit control such as that of Mr Clare is very rare. During the past fifty years the number of outstanding physical mediums the world over can be counted on the fingers of two hands.

I considered I was most fortunate and privileged to have been so closely and intimately associated with Jack Webber for the last two years of his life—he passed to the higher life at the end of March 1940. My book, commemorating his mediumship with the infra-red photographs[1] obtained, was published in July 1940, three editions being published within the first twelve months.[2]

Three days after the passing of this gifted medium, a message was received from him by means of the direct voice through another medium. This medium and the sitters present were not aware that Jack Webber had passed on. The message was, "Tell Mr Edwards I will direct him to another medium." Possessing a somewhat sceptical mind, I did not place any reliance upon this message, even though on past occasions my scepticism had received some shocks through other prophetic messages coming true.

Yet four weeks later, by special invitation, I sat in the private home circle of Mr Clare (referred to by Mr Harrison) when again I received a further message from Webber.

My further experiences with Mr Clare are narrated in the pages that follow: this work is the result of these experiences.

I ask the reader's indulgence for these personal remarks, For I consider I have been fortunate beyond expression in being associated almost continuously with two such great mediums. I may add, further, Jack Webber's Guide once told me that my association with him had long been planned and that various experiences I had been through were merely preparation for my association with the work of the Spirit people. He told me of this preparation and training, citing instances that were very personal and only known to myself. Indeed, some of these I had temporarily forgotten, but they possessed great significance when related to the whole story.

Part of this training was my direction into severe political controversy. My having contested two parliamentary elections and several London County Council elections, was for the purpose of developing an analytical mind and a faculty for fighting for causes. Indeed, these resources were called in to being several times when Webber's gifts were challenged. Peter, too, has referred to this, and though it is not strict evidence I record it for what it is worth.

One of the criticisms I anticipate is that the records in Part I are not corroborated by more independent testimony—that they are my own narration and those of friends associated with the medium.

1. Many of these photographs are used as examples in this book. (AH)
2. *The Mediumship of Jack Webber*. Rider & Co. (and snppbooks.com, 2019)

This weakness was early anticipated, and arrangements were in being for independent people of note to be invited to séances to record their experiences. The report by Mr Colin Evans was the first of these.

Unfortunately, war conditions prevented the continuance of physical work. In this connection I may say that Mr Clare is engaged upon highly technical work for the Admiralty; and his duties often keep him away from home for varying periods. This strain and the uncertainty of his free hours were also contributory factors to the cessation of physical séance work, for it will be appreciated by all knowledgeable persons how essential for successful issue are regular sittings.

This criticism, however, will be offset by several factors. The first is that the characteristics of the described phenomena are similar to those recorded with every other physical medium who has been subjected to severe tests.

That the sitters on the various occasions were experienced sitters, accustomed to séance-room work, who would quickly have questioned any action that was inconsistent with experience. Further, their faculties, being trained to note every change, slight sound or unorthodox movement, would have noted at once any suspicious activity.

Other considerations of some weight are that Mr Clare is not a professional medium and up to the time of writing has never, to my knowledge, profited financially from his mediumship. When sittings were given to the public the whole of the proceeds were devoted to the church organising the sitting, and when sittings were held at my house and a small charge made, the whole amount was given to the funds of another church. When sittings have been held by the medium or his associates and a small charge made (generally no more than half a crown), the entire proceeds have been devoted to some charity, or fund, associated with the Spiritualist movement.

Those immediately associated with the medium spend the major portion of their free time in voluntary service with Spiritualist churches and in the development of their own spiritual gifts. They also assist in Mr Clare's further development.

Both Mr and Mrs Clare have given years of voluntary service as honorary officers to Spiritualist churches, giving all their services freely and, actually have been considerably out of pocket in consequence.

Thus there can be no profit motive to prejudice the reports. If it is assumed for argument's sake that the phenomena were not as reported, it would mean that there had been a conspiracy involving a fairly large number of people. This would be an assumption which would incriminate not only the writer and those associated with him, but many more who are respected leaders of Spiritualist activity.

There are further considerations. The structure of the revelations in the second part indicate an intelligence that has provided a tenable thesis for psychic phenomena, from the explanation of the simplest process to the most intricate, in a manner never before attempted. Thus, when the reader views the whole structure, from the phenomena to the explanations, as one picture; it is hoped it will be found to bear the impress of truth as a comprehensive, consistent, tenable recording, and that in no way is it at variance with previous experience or reason.

However, the responsibility is the readers to accept the records as a true statement of fact or to brand all connected with the mediumship and this book as either exceedingly simple dupes or unscrupulous rogues, as they will.

HARRY EDWARDS.

Balham Psychical Research Society,
11 Childebert Road,
London, S.W.17.
August, 1941

CONTENTS

CHAPTER IX
THE ETHERIC REALM

CHAPTER X
THE DEVELOPMENT OF PHYSICAL MEDIUMSHIP

CHAPTER XI
THE FUNCTIONS OF THE GUIDES AND CONTROLS

CHAPTER XXI

THE PURPOSE

Influence of phenomena—Christ and phenomena—the lead provided—perspective of phenomena—and value—mission of superior intelligences—another John the Baptist—limitation of guidance—importance of the séance room—parallel of the time of Christ—the disciples' special instructions—similar procedure of today—linking of effort—future growth—rebuilding the church—back to the séance room—spiritualising humanity through knowledge—and the simple mind—more implications of survival—the Purpose—and influence of the Spirit—the laws—harmony—the mission—the universal purpose. . . . 230

LIST OF ILLUSTRATIONS AS SKETCHES

LIST OF ILLUSTRATIONS AS PHOTOGRAPHS

Arnold Clare - The Medium

PART I

CHAPTER I

THE MEDIUM, ARNOLD CLARE

ARNOLD CLARE was born of Suffolk parents at Felixstowe, in 1901, where his father owned a hand-made basket business.

Arnold went to school until he reached the age of 12, when he took up employment in a grocery establishment. At the age of 15 he went to sea under sail; and shortly afterwards, during the World War and at the age of 15½ joined the Royal Navy.

His first war service was spent in destroyers and light cruisers on ocean convoy work; and with the Dover Patrol.

In 1917 his duties took him through the Mediterranean to Mount Athos, where he was engaged for a time on shore duties in the wireless station.

It was here at Mount Athos that Mr Clare, not yet 17 years of age, met a personality who influenced his life from that time onwards.

At one of the monasteries he met a Greek Father, named John, who could speak English fairly well. He was an old man, and a strange friendship grew up between them. Arnold spent much of his free time at the monastery, listening to the wisdom from the lips of the old monk. One can perhaps picture the venerable white-haired and bearded monk and the young sailor discussing mysticism and philosophy amid the background of the stone ruggedness of the monastery. Mr Clare does not remember much in particular of the old man's teachings, but does remember that he was greatly impressed at the time by their profundity. Before leaving Mount Athos John said, "I won't say good-bye, my son; we will meet again."

Mr Clare's service in the Middle East did not end there. He went overland to Baku on the Caspian Sea, where his duties took him on board a Russian ship, the Emile Nobel. His naval service on this ship lasted for nine months.

The ship was navigated by a Russian captain between whom and Mr Clare grew up a close friendship. One day the captain took him home to tea, and this visit was to prove the forerunner of many more. One evening, after tea, the family drew round the fire, the captain on one side, his wife on the other, and his two daughters and Arnold completing the fireside circle.

The wife would play a mandolin and then commence to talk in a strange tone in Russian. Though he did not know it then, Mr Clare was at his first séance, for at that time he had no idea of spirit intercourse and did not recognise the trance state of the lady.

Mr Clare often joined the circles they held—for, as he says, there was nothing else to do—but he was not greatly interested in any of them since the language used was unintelligible to him. One night, however, the lady ceased speaking Russian and spoke English in John's voice. Here was a peasant type of lady, who knew only the local patois, speaking English in a voice and with an intonation unmistakably John's and reproducing his natural inflexions. Still Mr Clare did not appreciate the significance of the phenomena which he was witnessing.

"I told you, my son, we should meet again," said the voice, and each evening, while the circle was held, John would speak and continue his teaching from the point at which he had left off in Mount Athos. John told his listener that he had work to do and that he was being prepared for it. Mr Clare says today, that not knowing of the meaning of survival, he did not realise the meaning of John's words or even that he had passed on since he had left Mount Athos. So natural was the conversation that he did not think he could be "dead".

The time came for Mr Clare to leave, though neither he nor the captain had any knowledge of this as yet. On what turned out to be the eve of departure John said: "I must now say farewell for a little while." Mr Clare thought this meant that John would not be speaking again for some time, but the next morning surprise orders started him on his homeward journey. This was in 1919.

Mr Clare tells how in the excitement of coming home, and during post-war activity, he lost sight of the intimate meaning of John's teaching. He was engaged on wireless work at a Government station; and about this time met Miss Vera Lawson, who later became Mrs Clare.

They have three sons: Stanley, aged 18, now serving in the Army; Tony, aged 17; and Pat, aged 11 years.

One day Mr Clare picked up an old magazine and read an article by Conan Doyle. This described an Egyptian bronze vase with inscribed figures around the edges. Conan Doyle speculated as to its use and thought it might have been used of old for divination with a pendulum. This article so impressed Mr Clare that he wondered, "Why have a bronze vase, why not do without?" So taking a sheet of paper he wrote the letters of the alphabet around the edges; and tying his collar stud on to a short length of thread, held it over his letter chart. The stud moved as if propelled by a persistent force and spelt out the word "John".

Mr Clare tried automatic writing for a time and found that information was given to him on topics he knew nothing about. He did not attach any great importance to them; and they have not been kept. At the same time he had many other interests and the automatic writing was only engaged in spasmodically as a means to pass an idle hour.

At the age of 28, Mr Clare sought an extension of Government service and went to the medical officer for an examination. The doctor told him he could not be passed fit as he was suffering from tuberculosis. This was a great shock; and the doctor was asked if he would agree to consider the examination as "off the record", and to study Mr Clare's condition at a future date. This the doctor agreed to do.

Mr Clare went home and gave Mrs Clare the doctor's report. He says he then commenced to pray as he had never prayed before and continued doing so nightly. As the nights passed so he became conscious of the presence and personality of John. He received the impression that he was not to be unduly alarmed, that he would be made well, and that he had work to do.

Two months later Mr Clare again went to the medical officer and he was given a clean bill of health.

From this time onwards Mr Clare sat in solitude every night whenever possible, from half an hour to an hour, mainly around midnight. It was in this way he primarily developed those powers of which this book speaks.

It will be seen that the pattern of "John" is interwoven through Mr Clare's life, that the development of his spiritual gifts took place in spite of himself, and that the spirit people associated with him gradually directed his life for the work they had to do.

Mr Clare's association with Spiritualist Churches began with the church at Scarborough where he was a Vice-President; he followed this by commencing a healing circle at a Winchester church, of which he later became hon. secretary. Coming to London in 1933 Mr Clare continued his solitary development: It should be noted he was averse to trance work; and when he undertook services for churches would not allow himself to be a trance subject. During the latter part, of his solitary development he again felt the presence of John. One particular physical reaction he noted was that he felt incapable of movement for the time being.

At this time Astrology became his hobby and he lectured on this topic a number of times in London.

In 1937 Mrs Clare and he joined the Balham Spiritualist Church; and he became hon. secretary in 1939. During these two years he conducted healing circles in the church and was intimately connected with all its branches of activity, giving addresses, clairvoyance, psychometry as well as healing.

At this time a small home circle of church members was sitting privately for the development of a Mr Edwin Twitchett, who showed signs of physical mediumship. The Guide of this circle directed that Mr and Mrs Clare should be invited to join. Knowing of Mr Clare's aversion to trance work they said they did not think he would join. The Guide replied, "You ask him, and he will come." Mr and Mrs Clare were thereupon approached, and they consented. This circle had been sitting weekly for eighteen months and signs of movements were being observed. Mr Twitchett, however, left the circle, which carried on in the hope that he would return. Subsequently, on New Year's Eve, 1938, Mr Twitchett agreed to return, and a sitting was arranged for that night.

At this time the sitters were a Mrs Sheppard, Mrs Shelston, Mr and Mrs Clare, and two others.

On that New Year's Eve, Mr and Mrs Harrison were at tea with Mr and Mrs Clare when the telephone bell rang, and a message given that Mr Twitchett could not attend. Mr Clare felt that no matter what happened, the sitting should take place. It did, and that night Mr Clare's physical mediumship functioned for the first time. There were apports and Mr Clare's Guides made themselves known.

The story is continued by Mr Harrison, but this chapter must not end without recording Mr Clare's gratitude and thanks to his wife for her unfailing help and courage through all the days of trial, for her unbounded patience in the circles, and her energy for the work. This culminated in February of 1941, when Mr and Mrs Clare opened their own church, "The Trinity of Spiritual Fellowship".

To inaugurate a new centre of devotional activity during the topsy-turvy conditions of this war year denotes both courage and confidence; and, to date, the new church has shown every sign of making progress.

Finally, the author desires to express his personal thanks to Mr Clare for his ever-ready willingness to give up so many hours of his all-too-limited home time for the purpose of this book. Never on any occasion was this co-operation refused, nor has any effort on his part appeared too great to render whatever service he could.

One afternoon, when Mr Clare's second son, Tony, was thirteen years old he was in his room, and commenced to draw upon a sheet of paper. The drawing of Brother Paul was the result. Tony says that while the time he appeared to take over the drawing appeared very short, he was surprised to find, when he had finished, that evening had set in. He did not attach any importance to the drawing and put it away, without saying anything to his parents.

It was some time later, when Brother Paul first made himself known through his medium to the developing circle. On his first appearance he startled Mr and Mrs Clare with the statement that they had a picture of him in their house. They said they had no knowledge of it, but Paul said there was such a picture and they were to ask their son for it.

Returning home, they asked Tony if he had any picture, and he went to his room and returned with the drawing.

A peculiar characteristic is the squared nature of the drawing; and a decided technique is shown by the effect of light and shadow imperceptibly produced by the shading of the squares. Paul said that he had impressed Tony to draw it and it could be regarded as a reasonable likeness.

The author has seen other drawings made by Tony, and their undeveloped technique bears no comparison to the drawing of Paul. He has never produced a similar picture either before or since. It appears from Tony's uncertainty as to the way or manner in which he drew the picture—he says he does not remember having a

FIG. I
Brother Paul, Chief Guide to the medium, as
drawn under the unusual conditions described,
by Tony Clare.

rubber—that he was inspired in his effort, being in a state of natural semi-trance, unknown to him at the time. It is definitely stated that the technique employed is far beyond his normal accomplishment and indeed when he tried to copy this drawing he could not do so with success.

THE HEALING OF MRS CLARE

As Peter's discussions were drawing to a close, Mrs Clare was taken ill and entered hospital, where she underwent a surgical operation. An unexpected complication set in, and the medical authorities decided that it would be necessary to set Mrs Clare's body in plaster of Paris for nine months. She was moved to a country hospital for this purpose.

The matter was discussed with Peter on the Sunday evening of the day Mrs Clare was moved to the country hospital. It appeared that Mr Clare and his sons' minds were a little upset that the spirit healers had not been able to avert the trouble and restore Mrs Clare to health. On the evening in question, Mr Clare being in trance, his sons raised the issue.

Peter replied that so far no effort had been made to ask for spirit assistance. The matter had been regarded casually; and it had been taken as a matter of course that spirit healing would be given. Peter seemed to resent this, but a request by the sons being made for help, Peter agreed they would see what could be done in the matter.

That very night Mrs Clare, in her new hospital, felt the change taking place within her; and when on the following morning a specialist arrived from London to undertake the plaster of Paris casing, Mrs Clare surprised him by asking if she could sit up. The specialist knew this should have been impossible. Mrs Clare, however, not only sat up, but stood up and walked about the ward. In a short while she was home and able to walk about fairly normally. Without doubt, there is definite evidence of another "miracle" healing, the direct result of spirit intervention.*

---

* A further work dealing with the science of healing, spiritual and magnetic, has already been commenced by the author with the collaboration of and explanations by Peter.

CHAPTER II

OBSERVATIONS ON THE RESTRICTION OF MEDIUMS

IN recording the psychic manifestations received through the mediumship of Mr Arnold Clare, criticism is anticipated from those who deem that the most rigorous control of the medium's body is essential before supernormality is proved. There would be justification for such criticism if the events reported were limited to the immediate proximity of the medium's body; also were there no other factors such as light, time and other evidential data to determine beyond all doubt that supernormal energy and activity were present.

With modern physical mediumship, the technique of the spirit operators (who are masters of ingenuity) provides far more intelligent "tests" proving supernormality than the most inquisitorial fettering of a medium's body by means of ropes, wires, cottons, sticking-plaster, electrical gadgets, adhesive tapes, cages, etc., so dear to certain types of minds associated with psychic research.

Obviously, the way to obtain the greatest proof of spirit activity is to give the medium and the spirit operators comfortable and amenable conditions in which to work. If the conditions under which the sitting is held are hard, unnatural, and foreign to the spirit-people, no one should blame the medium or the operators if phenomena are scanty or absent. One of the most important factors contributing to success is that the medium's mind should be confident and sure of successful issue, happy and without any mental strain or anxiety. Mediums, as a rule; are more sensitive than ordinary people and therefore the preliminaries before a sitting should take into account the psychological reactions of the medium to the conditions, if any, to be imposed.

A professional medium who demonstrates his gifts in order to secure a living is more or less bound to submit to being restrictively controlled. Most professional mediums welcome and invite some form of "reasonable" control, though at times there will be differences of opinion as to the interpretation of reasonable control. There is also the professional medium whose outlook is selfishly limited to financial advantage and is not concerned with any scientific approach, no matter in how friendly a manner this may be introduced. A reason for this is that the medium is aware of the harm that has been caused to other mediums by research groups imposing conditions involving strain to the physical body. He therefore regards investigators as enemies rather than "understanding friends". There is one justification for this attitude of mind since a number of physical mediums have had their gifts impaired whilst others have suffered physically from the strain imposed—I know two physical mediums, still with us, who suffer from continual internal haemorrhage, the result of undue strain.

Another important contributory factor to success or non-success is in the nature of the sitters themselves. There is a vast difference between a circle of alert-minded yet cooperative sitters and a circle of people mentally obstructive and non-co-operative. When Jack Webber sat for "test" séances where extra-restrictive control was employed, or at séances where the hard, non-co-operative mind predominated, it invariably followed that the operators found it much harder to manifest phenomena. When they did appear, they were spasmodic, jerky, with time-gaps in between each action—so different from the continual free flow of activity at a normal séance.

Few words are more ambiguous or less understood than the word "conditions" as applied to psychic matters; yet it is of paramount importance for successful results for all present to attain to harmonious mental co-operation. The scientific mind that regards the universe as matter only has to learn the importance of the reality of the dimension of thought before it will make progress in comprehending the realm of spirit activity.

There is the type of medium of which Margery (Mrs Crandon) is perhaps the finest example, who had no need to demonstrate for financial profit, yet was willing to undergo every kind of restrictive and humiliating control—short of crucifixion—such as may at times be devised by the investigators. So much thought has been devoted to the various ways in which the human body can be deprived of the independent muscular action that it seems that the science of the control of mediums has become more important to the investigators than the phenomena itself.* Margery knew the potency of the forces used through her mediumship, and knew also that when she surrendered herself to those exacting conditions she was in constant danger of injury to health, if not to life, as the following may indicate.

From U.S.A. *S.P.R. Proceedings,* page 357:

"I, Grace V. Reuter, certify that I assisted at the disrobing of Margery, and thoroughly examined the dressing-gown in which we wrapped her, after which I controlled her hands until she was led into the glass cabinet on a floor two stages higher. There she was wired in the glass cabinet, hands and feet, so that any movement of the extremities was impossible. Her head was bound to the ceiling of the cabinet with a thick rope which fastened around her neck so that she could not move her head without danger of suffocation. (Page 372). The psychic is clad in a single garment, (kimono) stockings and shoes. She and her garments are examined by a woman at the request of the Commission before and after the sitting. In bright light now, there are tied around the Psychic's wrists and ankles long pieces of No.3 picture wire. The part going round the limb is protected against cutting the skin by rubber tubing. All knots are either made, observed in the making, or tested by the Commission. A leather collar is padlocked around the Psychic's neck by a Commissioner and the key kept in his possession. The Psychic is now conducted by a Commissioner into the red-

---

* According to the *Proceedings of the American Society for Psychical Research* volumes dealing with "The Margery Mediumship", Margery (with the consent of her husband, the late Dr. Crandon) permitted herself to be used without any restraint. Baron von Schrenk Notzing visualised a special kind "of psychic laboratory, furnished for all kinds of experimental psychology and psychophysics.

Registration should of course be made independent of the sense organs, which are subject to deception, and should, as far as possible, be transferred to physical apparatus. A self-registering balance, the full use of photographic and electrical aids (such as photographs with ultra-violet light), the use of various degrees of brightness of light and spectrum colours, thermometers, and other specially constructed instruments may find their place in such an institute. Other apparatus of a more physiological kind would be necessary for investigations of the medium's organism."

One can well imagine the reactions of a sensitive medium to such an environment, and his or her shrinking from placing either himself or herself in a hypnotic or trance state at the mercy of psychic "vivisectors'. It would be hard to imagine conditions more prejudicial to satisfactory issue than these.

lighted séance room and there seats herself in a Windsor chair in the Richardson plate glass cabinet. The ends of the wrists and ankle ties are now threaded through and round fused closed-ring eye-bolts on the floor and through the sides of the cabinet respectively. They are securely tied, observed in the tying, or inspected by the Commission and the ends threaded through American Railway Express lead seals and sealed by a member of the Commission. Heavy twine is tied by a Commissioner to the leather collar in knots peculiar to himself and the other end is similarly tied to a fused eye-bolt in the roof of the cabinet. The excursion for the feet is not over six inches. The excursion for the hands is not over two inches; for the head not over six inches forwards, nine inches sideways."

It has been truly said that mediums who so voluntarily place themselves at the discretion of investigators enter upon a martyrdom as great as that of any other of our fellows who have sacrificed themselves for the sake of posterity.

There remains yet another class of medium, in which Arnold Clare may well be placed, that self-sacrificing body who do not profit materially from their mediumship. They regard their gift as of a spiritual or divine nature to be used for the comfort of the distressed and for the enlightenment, by teaching, of man's present materialistic conduct of life. Such mediums do not demonstrate purely for the scientific mind, they are not concerned with it; and are quite indifferent to the approval of any Society or group. (My first request to Mr Clare to agree to sitting for infra-red photography was refused, mainly for the above reason; and that he only wished to serve those who sought his help in a spiritual sense.)

The position should therefore be clear, that one cannot expect every physical medium to suffer indignities freely for the glory of a halo from any particular society. The number of such societies and groups who seek to investigate phenomena thus far exceeds the number of mediums available, and few societies will accept the evidence of another society, insisting upon their own research. The demands upon a medium for "a series of test sittings" become more and more numerous as his mediumship is established. Thus, the attitude of physical mediums is better understood when at times they refuse to agree to submit themselves to "tests"; and are content to put up with the opprobrium they receive when they also refuse to be "tested" by any society wishing to investigate their powers.

It would, however, be most unreasonable to reject *authenticated* reports of phenomena, simply because mediums have not been willing to sit in almost strapped nudity. When they state that they are not willing to be treated with so much suspicion, they are quite within their rights.

Each case of mediumship should be treated individually, and the proof that supernormal action takes place should be considered according to the nature of the evidence the operators are able to provide. I do not hesitate to emphasise that these remarks should be taken as expressing, on behalf of mediumship, a plea for a more discriminating and intelligent outlook than that of the rope and straitjacket.

Before evidence is submitted to illustrate how supernormal action is provable without restriction, a few general remarks concerning physical mediumship will not be out of place.

Before any person is able to demonstrate in public as a physical medium, a wealth of labour and sacrifice has been necessary. As a rule, a number of years (in Jack Webber's case ten years, in Mr Clare's twenty years) are devoted to developing the psychic faculties. This means that for at least one, probably two nights every week, the potential medium and a number of friends sit for an hour or so with the utmost regularity. It may be that for years no movement is observed, and so far as the persons themselves are concerned, both potential medium and the sitters, they may be just wasting their time.

There are in Great Britain thousands of such circles sitting week after week and year after year, but it is only very rarely that the circle produces a medium able to demonstrate publicly. In addition to the weekly sittings, the medium devotes a part of each day preparing himself for future use. He lives an abstemious life, avoids excesses, and creates for himself a code of rules as spiritual as he can.

After the passing of years of endeavour, phenomena may at last become noticeable, perhaps only raps, or the slight movement of a trumpet. When these signs are obtained the development settles down in earnest, and, as a rule, several more years of continual sitting week by week follow before the medium is able to demonstrate outside his home circle. Actually, the development is never complete, and continues even after the mediumship has been acclaimed.

As the mediumship becomes known, the medium's real trials commence. He is importuned on all sides by people who desire to sit with him and observe the phenomena or receive help and comfort from the "return" of their relatives and friends. As the medium makes himself available, so does he immediately become the centre of suspicion. "Is he honest?" "Is he a fraud?" etc. The medium may feel he would like to obtain a "certificate of honesty" and submits to "tests" in the manner described already. If he succeeds, he finds many more societies seeking further tests; and the author has known an established research society impugn a mediumship in order to force the medium's hands and induce him to agree to a series of sittings for experimental purposes.

The medium also has to face the ever-present danger that some irresponsible person will flash a light on him during a séance or interfere in some other manner with the activity taking place. At the time of writing one medium known to the author lost both his gift and his sight on such an occasion; another well-known physical medium recently passed over after an interference of this nature; and numbers of others have been seriously ill from ignorant and ill-conceived interference.

Reverting to the mediumships under review, the following are examples of what is intended by the mediumship being able to prove itself, without fettering restraint.

Mr Arnold Clare uses a fairly large plaque, measuring 25 ins. by 14 ins. This plaque is, as a rule, freshly painted before each sitting with luminous paint, to give maximum luminosity. The degree of light from this plaque will illumine an object four feet away, and ordinary 10-point type (slightly, smaller than used for this book) can be read at a distance up to three feet, so that it will be noted that any article lying on the top of the illuminated surface would be seen very clearly indeed. At times, with Mr Clare's sittings, this plaque lies on the floor, illuminated side uppermost. Over the bright surface ectoplasmic material is cast. In appearance it looks like a spider's web, very fragile and almost transparent. This substance is lying perfectly flat, without a crease, on the plaque. Sitters can thus observe the web-like substance become animated at the edges only.

There is no question of the whole piece being shaken or moved, the edges only assume life, and move and form prehensile projections, like small fingers. They come and go. As they build up, it is noticeable that they cease to be transparent and appear dark and opaque. These protuberances grip the edge of the plaque and draw it towards the medium. The plaque stops, the protuberances loosen their hold and take a fresh grip on the sides of the plaque, which is then moved in a controlled manner sideways, forwards, backwards. The whole material is withdrawn, whisked back; and a second later again cast over the plaque, lying on it perfectly smoothly. As it rests on the plaque, so immediately is the plaque gripped and moved about the floor. Clearly here is observable supernormal activity, judging by the rapidity of movement, the sureness of the cast, the animation of a transparent web-like substance into solid fingers or claws, the controlled and ordered movement of the plaque. The word supernormal is used to denote an action that cannot be imitated under the same given conditions by human means. In the incident just described, it is asserted that man cannot produce the same effect under any conditions, even given the use of mechanical means or by the employment of electricity, magnetism, or any other force we know.

A further supernormal performance is demonstrated when the plaque is held about two to three feet from the floor, the illuminated surface shining downwards upon a length of ectoplasmic material stretching from the medium towards a trumpet about four feet away. The material, being of a whitish colour, is very clearly seen in the illumination from the plaque against the dark colour of the linoleum. The substance becomes animated, its farthest extremity extends towards the small end of the trumpet, and grips hold of it firmly. Whilst this is taking place the flaccid diaphanous-looking material twists together tightly, but only from the trumpet to where it reaches the floor in front of the medium. Then, using the end of the twisted material near the medium as a point for leverage, the twisted material, now rigid, raises itself up on the end (nearest the medium) with the trumpet held in perfect alignment. All this in clear light. This position is maintained for a second or two before the trumpet falls to the floor. These and other still more remarkable incidents are described in the records that follow.

It should be noted that Mr Clare's trumpets are not of the light aluminium kind, but are made of celluloid and insulating tape. They are 33 ins. long and weigh 7½ozs., and to lift up this weight the tension on the small end of the trumpet is equivalent to 3½ lbs., from the point of the fulcrum, about three feet away.

Jack Webber's mediumship was also proved by visible and audible demonstrations, as for instance the removal of his stitched-up coat while his hands were held; the instantaneous putting on of white light immediately before and after phenomena. Details of all these will be found in the volume *The Mediumship of Jack Webber,* as well as such other examples as: the time factor in a number of varied acts of phenomena; the act of switching on white light immediately after such activity as the photographing of expanses of ectoplasmic materials; the movement of trumpets and objects in distinguishable red light and a number of other acts of phenomena reported and verified.

Jack Webber was controlled by various methods: ropes, cottons, seals, etc., but not so restrictively as by those imposed upon Rudi Schneider or Margery, yet no one, on the evidence, would dismiss the reports as being valueless because the medium was not so controlled. Neither should any reasonable mind, taking into account the testimony accompanying the reports of Mr Clare's mediumship, refuse to accept the fact of the phenomena simply because Mr Clare was unfettered.

In this presentation of further evidence of spirit activity, the sceptic should remember that if a certain incident appears to partake of the "miraculous" as being contrary to, or outside the range of, ordinary human experience, such incident may well be only the extension of experiences already noted and recorded by responsible and reputable observers. It is suggested that to reject such an incident on the ground that it is of novel or supernormal character would indicate a negation of the scientific outlook on the critic's part.

It would seem only reasonable to accept fearlessly all problems presented fairly and not to reject the implications arising therefrom without careful investigation of the evidence, past and present. In this world, governed by the Cosmic law of evolution, will be found problems untold in scope and number for probing investigation and analysis: they will only be solved satisfactorily if implications arising are faced without fear of consequences.

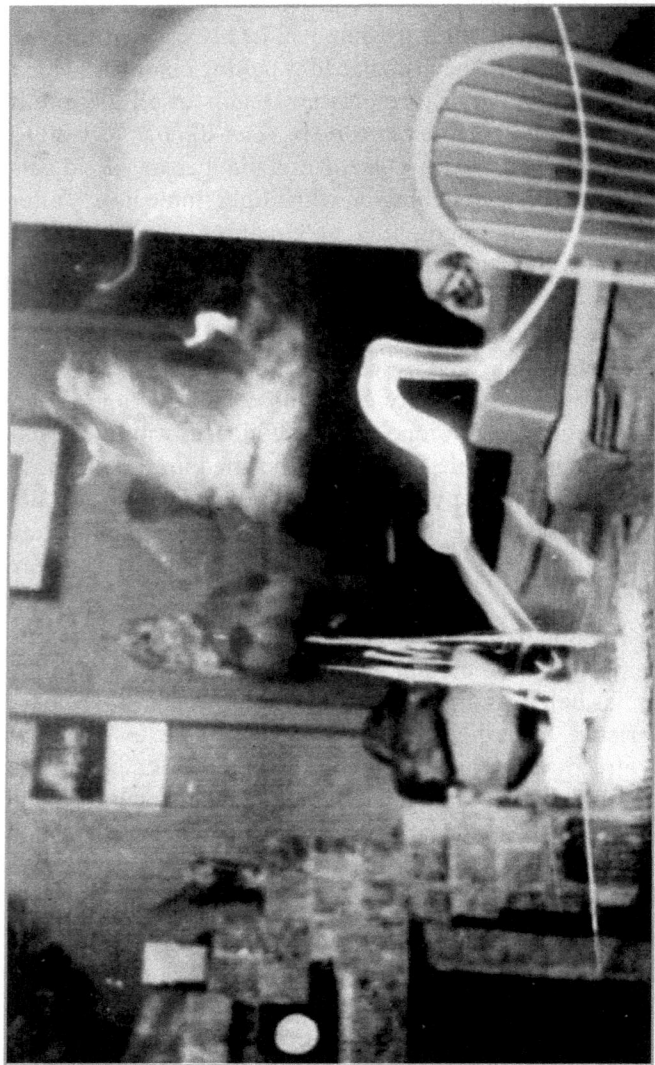

PLATE 2

The mechanism used for conducting "direct voice" to the trumpet. The conductor which conveys the etheric sound waves is housed in an insulation, which protects it from external etheric bombardment (See Chps;. XV and XVII.)

Photograph by Mr. R. F. Bounsall.

CHAPTER III

THE PHYSICAL MEDIUMSHIP OF ARNOLD T. CLARE

(By William E. Harrison, President of the Balham
Spiritualist Society)

ON the table, as I write, lies a queer assortment of twenty different articles: an auctioneer's hammer, pieces of ivory, a lion's claw, numerous coins, an arrow, a small carved cross, a locket, three small carved images and other things difficult to describe. All of these things came into my possession in the séance room through the mediumship of Arnold Clare; and surveying them again my mind goes back to the early days of this circle.

We often hear how those who have developed the gift of physical mediumship sit for many years patiently awaiting the first movement of the trumpet; but in the case of this medium the story is quite different and the rapidity with which the range of physical phenomena developed was almost startling.

My first contact with the circle was in June 1939: At that time Mr and Mrs Clare, with two other ladies, had been sitting for only a few months and each week I had been told of their progress, now they had had levitation of objects, strong psychic breezes and their apports.

One evening I was invited to the circle and in a small box-room at the top of the house, bare of all furniture except five chairs, I witnessed for the first time the things of which I had been told. The medium was secured to a small arm-chair by tapes bound very securely round his wrists, and then for over an hour there occurred the levitation of three trumpets, gramophone records being put on and taken off by invisible hands, and the appearance of two small apports (medallions) for the two ladies. But for me the most impressive event was the transportation of an object from my home about a mile away to this little room.

This is how it happened.

On the afternoon of that day my wife was sewing. She was using a thimble which was afterwards put away in a needle-work basket.

Later in the day she required the thimble again but could not find it anywhere.

At the séance in the evening, Peter, speaking through Mr Clare, mentioned the loss of the thimble and said: "We will now return it to you to take home to your wife;" and sure enough through the trumpet came the thimble right into my hands. The thimble was the one belonging to my wife which had been "lost" that afternoon and was easily identifiable by me through its special marking. Mrs Harrison was not present and was amazed and surprised to find that I was able to return it to her from the séance room. Perhaps I should add that Arnold Clare had not been in my home for more than a week previous to this sitting.

Discussing the matter later with the Guide, he said they had chosen this way of proving to me how they were able to transport objects over distance, knowing that if something from my house was removed to a distance it would give me confidence in the apport phenomena.

At a much later date a similar happening occurred to another circle visitor. In this case a small feather was removed from a hat in a locked wardrobe at her house, and much to the lady's astonishment was presented to her in the circle being held almost a mile away.

During the next six weeks I visited the circle on two other occasions and witnessed the phenomena of the trumpet. The latter was always under perfect control, the movement being "clean" and rapid.

So far I had heard no voices, and although a few attempts had been made at the production of ectoplasmic structures, nothing definite or recognisable could be observed.

However, the apports were most prolific during this period, and quite frequently ten or twelve articles and coins would appear and usually were put in the sitter's hands through the trumpet.

In each case the trumpet would be levitated ceiling-high and remain stationary for perhaps a minute. The article would then be heard rattling in the trumpet. This latter would travel to a sitter and the object would be placed in his hand.

No sittings were held during August owing to holidays, and then, with the advent of war, Mr Clare was able to devote only a very limited amount of time to the work.

From September 1939 to January 1940 only four circles were held. Two of these were held in my house, and it was quite obvious from the commencement of the first circle that the rest period had produced no adverse effect upon the phenomena. In fact, the first of these circles was one of the finest demonstrations of physical phenomena that I have witnessed.

There were only four of us: Mr and Mrs Clare, and Mrs Harrison and myself. We sat in a semi-circle around the fireplace, almost touching one another, and in the small confines of this space all the following took place: levitation of three trumpets at once; a sewing-machine in the corner of the room moved into the circle, unlocked itself, the handle turning continuously for some minutes; oranges were taken off the sideboard and put in the writer's jacket pocket, one each side; a clock and two photographs were taken from the mantelpiece and transferred noiselessly to a table the far side of the room.

A child Guide who announced himself as "Little Peter" spoke through the trumpet for the first time and amused us with his chatter. He seemed to be able to speak quite clearly and easily, and the childish intonation was particularly noticeable. This was really the first time I had heard a voice through the trumpet in this circle.

Formations of ectoplasmic substance which assumed various shapes were shown us.

The "rushing winds" reminiscent of the Pentecostal séance recorded in the Bible were much in evidence this night, and there were a number of apports.

One of these latter, a small Eastern jug-shaped object, was given to me. I held it for a few minutes and was told by the Guide to put it back in the trumpet. On doing so it disappeared. A little time later it was returned to me filled with a most exquisite perfume.

Perfume had always been splashed about in small amounts in previous circles, but this was the first time I had seen any considerable quantity.

These or similar happenings were repeated at the following three séances, at one of which the circle was made of up fourteen people and eighteen apports were distributed to the various sitters.

At this séance, January 6, 1940, the Guide said there were to be no more visitors as a further period was required for development.

As a result of this, a sitting with Peter for discussion on the matter was held when only Mr and Mrs Clare and Mrs Harrison and I were present.

Peter stated they were not satisfied just to keep repeating the same manifestations, and they sought to develop the phenomena with the object of obtaining direct and independent voice. He stated they wished to build figures that could walk about, talk with sitters, and were capable of holding sustained conversations. Mrs Harrison and I were invited to join the group, which was to remain as now constituted (four of us) and meet weekly.

We were given to understand that the apport phenomena would cease and they would only be allowed on special occasions, and in fact for a few weeks we were not to expect any phenomena at all.

For a few weeks we sat quietly, usually for one and a half hours, and most of the time was spent in talking with Peter and John on various aspects of the work and spiritual problems. It is my one regret that these talks were not taken down by a shorthand writer, as they were deeply interesting, but many of the questions discussed have since been reported by Mr Edwards at special circles.

During our talks I had referred to the subject of book tests and John promised to try this. The following week, John said I had a book called *Sunwich Port* in my library, a small brown book. I could not recall this book at all.

However, he insisted that it was there and that on page 22 at the top I should find these words: "Why should you think my father wanted your bed?"

On returning home I immediately looked for the book, and sure enough I found W. W. Jacobs' book, *At Sunwich Port,* a small brown book which I had not looked at for twenty years or more. Eagerly I turned to page 22 but was disappointed at not finding the words quoted. I dismissed the matter, but two or three days later thought of it again and somehow felt impressed to look at page 122, and there found the sentence exactly as quoted.

Saying nothing of this to Mr Clare, I went to the circle the next week and John referred to his mistake in the page and said he was glad I had looked again and found the words and that the impression which I had felt so strongly to turn to page 122 had come from them. I asked for another example of this work and he quoted a passage which I wrote down verbatim from page 39 of Renan's *Life of Jesus,* which was in my possession and which was perfectly accurate.

Although most of these evenings during the next eight weeks were spent in talking, there were periods when attempts at independent voice occurred. Usually it was Little Peter whose voice was heard saying one or two words fairly clearly and from different parts of the room—sometimes over the medium's head, sometimes directly in front of our faces, at other times at the back. Usually, towards the end of each séance, the last ten or fifteen minutes were devoted to a full operation of the phenomena, rapid levitation of trumpets and sometimes furniture, Guides speaking through trumpets, scent and slight attempts at materialisation.

The independent voice did not seem to develop very well and although several efforts were made by others to talk in this way, the only one who succeeded was Little Peter; and as no progress was made the Guides decided to concentrate for a period on the production of ectoplasmic structures with a view to building up full-size figures.

The various formations were manipulated by the operators with astonishing speed and skill, and were frequently shown to us on the illuminated side of the slate, which clearly showed the fine texture of the substance.

At this particular period (on the Guide's suggestion) a rope was introduced into the circle and for some weeks the medium was securely tied to the chair by the Guides. The roping was accomplished swiftly in the dark and at the end of the séance they also did the un-roping.

Sometimes in the course of the séance the medium would be un-roped and Mrs Harrison and I would be roped together by these invisible hands. Frequently they would leave the ropes tied in all kinds of fancy knots and we often found it difficult to unravel them, an illustration of the strength which had been used in the tying process. However, this practice was discontinued as the ladies thought it might be dangerous.

By this time materialised figures were beginning to build up very clearly and Peter was very active in these manifestations, building up three or four times, showing himself in profile in order that we should see his pointed beard and gradually moving away farther from the medium each week and ofttimes speaking a few words to each of us.

Another Guide who then frequently made an appearance, but whom we had not contacted before, was Abdul, an Egyptian, and he it was who was mainly responsible for this part of the work. It is certain that from the time Abdul came on the scene the materialisations became much clearer and stronger and were able to move about to a far greater extent.

About this time the Guide suggested it might be advisable to hold a few public séances, inviting eight people, so that they could judge the effect of their work. Accordingly, several of these circles were held, and at each one of them the phenomena produced usually commenced without delay and carried on continuously for one and a half hours.

It was quite obvious that these few weeks of development had helped the work considerably. As various records of these séances show, the voice communications were clearer and conversations prolonged. The materialised figures were able to get well away from the medium, frequently twelve to eighteen feet away; and the control over the phenomena by the spirit operators was excellent.

After these efforts I suggested to the Guide that perhaps it would be possible to produce the phenomena in a subdued light. We had a long discussion about this and finally Peter said that if we were prepared to sit for some time without results it should be possible. He stipulated that the light required should be "ice-blue", and eventually we managed to get the required shade of light and began the sittings, with a light sufficient for us to see one another clearly.*

These sittings commenced in June 1940, and for the first four weeks nothing happened, excepting that we could see the trumpets rocking backwards and forwards on the floor where they stood-then in two successive weeks they were knocked on to the floor and constant effort was made to lift them, but only on one occasion did they succeed in moving one trumpet to a foot off the floor.

We had now reached the middle of August and Peter, in his weekly talks, forecast many of the dangers which threatened us as a result

---

* "Professor Ochorowicz employed with success a faint blue light. So did Paul Gibier, the Director of the Pasteur Institute in New York." from von Schrenk Notzing: *Materialisations*.

of war conditions, saying that he thought it would be impossible to meet regularly in the weeks ahead and also that it would be wiser to abandon these sittings in the light for the time being. As we know, the September blitz on London started the following week, and from that time only a few circles have been held at intervals.

I am sure that under normal conditions, and given a sufficient time for development, much of the phenomena now obtained in darkness could be witnessed in a subdued light to the complete satisfaction of all who may be sceptical of séances held in the dark.

SPIRIT WRITING

During the sittings of the home circle in March and April 1940 the Guide was asked whether he thought it possible that if a pencil and paper were provided in the circle written messages could be given. Peter agreed that it could probably be achieved, and at least was worth trying.

Accordingly, a small writing-pad was laid on the floor of the circle together with a pencil; and at the first sitting we heard the pencil scratching over the paper, which was then torn off the pad. Eagerly we awaited the end of the circle to see what had been written and found that two pieces had been detached from the pad—on one was written, "John greets you" and the other "God bless you all, Peter".

One was heavily written (John's), whilst Peter's was much more lightly scrawled.

This seemed a good start, and for some weeks we never failed to put the pencil and paper in the circle, and each week we received two or three different messages. Some were messages of affection from our own loved ones—two were sentences foretelling developments in the war both of which turned out to be correct with regard to developments in the East. "Little Peter" seemed to be delighted with this method of communication and never failed to write some simple message which he sometimes accompanied by a drawing. One of these drawings is particularly good, having regard to all the difficulties under which it was accomplished.

The drawing is of a flower (intended for a carnation) with a 3-inch stem and leaves, against which leans a small ladder. At the foot of the ladder is drawn a small elfin figure. The remarkable part of the drawing lies in the fact that it was drawn in the dark and yet not one line overruns another—it is perfectly spaced in every way and is right in the centre of the page. Had it been drawn in full light it could not have been spaced more perfectly. Anyone who has tried to write in the dark will appreciate the remarkable result achieved by "Little Peter" under these conditions. The drawing took little more than five

FIG. 2
A drawing in the dark by a spirit child control
(Little Peter) during a seance.

minutes and was the only one received that night; and during the time it was being done we could hear the pencil working at what seemed incredible speed. To hear the pencil moving over the paper naturally gave rise to the thought, "If we could only see it working" and the wish was expressed to Peter. At the next sitting he promised to try to show us this phenomenon illuminated by the slate.

The following week he kept his promise. The illuminated slate was lifted sufficiently to allow the light to spread over the floor immediately in front of it for about a foot. In this lighted space the spirit operators placed the pencil and pad so that we could see them quite easily. Slowly the pencil was raised by what appeared to be two small prongs or pincers which slowly moved the pencil point to the blank paper. The pencil then began to move over the paper rapidly until a sentence was written and then the sheet of paper was detached from the pad. It was most fascinating to watch the movement of the pencil over the paper. After this we were given the opportunity of watching the experiment several times and in all cases the procedure was exactly the same.

We thought this method of message-giving very helpful and in the later séances, where visitors were invited, a number of people received messages from their spirit friends which can be truly called "Letters from Heaven".

THE GUIDES AND CONTROLS

The chief spiritual leader of this circle is Brother Paul, a monk, who one evening gave an account of the many years he had spent when on earth at Beaulieu Abbey. Many of the details we afterwards verified on a visit to Beaulieu in 1939. Paul finds much difficulty in coming into the earth conditions and it is only when conditions are exceptionally good that he speaks for any length of time.

He has on occasion materialised and sometimes given a blessing at the close of a circle in direct voice (through the trumpet).

Most of the talking is left to Peter who, as he has often said, finds it easy to work through the medium and so becomes the second-in-command and the mouthpiece of Paul, as he never fails to remind us when giving some lengthy discourse on spiritual things.

Peter is a most interesting personality and I have never known him avoid a question; his replies are usually given without the least hesitation and always to the point.

He has materialised many times and usually appears at least once in a physical circle and always, makes a point of showing his short, pointed beard. I have never heard him speak much of his earth life, but he has stated he passed over more than a hundred years ago. When Peter is occupied in the physical work; he leaves the medium in the control of John.

I have always liked the personality of John, it has a certain similarity to that of Peter and yet there is a subtle difference. He has a keen sense of humour and is quick at repartee; and whilst he will talk on general things, can seldom be drawn into a deep discussion.

These three Guides are the only ones I have ever known to control the medium, and each one seems to give the impression of acting as a medium for the other. Indeed, this is the idea which Peter has frequently mentioned when we have discussed the work that takes place on their side. Each one is a link in that ever-ascending chain of the angel ministry.

Farther down the ladder we have the invisible helpers; and in this circle we have Simba, the African. When Simba first manifested in the circle things were moved with great power and speed. He it is who is mainly responsible for the rapid swirling of the trumpets and other objects and levitation. Peter has often said Simba has a heart of gold but a simple child-like mind and takes a great delight in displaying strength and power in the movement of these things.

He, too, has a great deal to do with the production of apports which, Peter states, he does in conjunction with the "little people" (Peter's favourite expression for nature spirits and those lower down in the scale of evolution).

Another helper who used to be more in evidence in the early days but who does not come forward so much now is Pedro, a one-legged sailor. There is never any mistake when he appears, because he pads around the room exactly as a man with a stump would do. He is usually accompanied by "sea breezes", and sometimes the rushing cold wind has been so violent that it has billowed the curtains.

We heard little of Pedro after Abdul carne on the scene, and apparently, he receded into the background when the work of materialisation was pushed forward. Certainly, Abdul made a tremendous difference in this aspect of the work. He (Abdul) was able to show himself very clearly, and frequently the jewel in his headgear was easily visible and the swarthiness of his skin most apparent.

The perfume which is always a feature of the phenomena, we were told, was produced by the power of an Indian girl and though most often reminiscent of parma-violet, other distinct perfumes have been given. On one occasion a small potted-meat jar was filled for us and the contents kept for many months without losing strength.

The other personality is one whom all sitters very quickly come to know: "Little Peter", who passed over in early life. Sometimes he used to bring with him a little girl who, he said, was his sister. Little Peter was always full of fun and mischief and fond of pranks. One night he took a packet of cigarettes out of my pocket and told me I should find them in my overcoat which was outside the room in the hall—and after the circle that's where I found them.

On another occasion he told me to hold my wife's handbag very tightly over the clasp, as he wanted to get some of the things out. Within a minute or so, although I held the bag tightly and I know it was not opened, a comb and a small pair of scissors were taken from the bag and put into my wife's hands. Many instances similar to this could be quoted and we had only to suggest to him that something was beyond his power and he would constantly try, until he succeeded.

He often attempted to materialise, and although we could always see his small figure the face was never sufficiently clear, but he certainly was the most proficient speaker through the trumpet and would often sustain quite a long conversation. His main work seemed to lie in keeping the circle atmosphere bright and cheery; and after perhaps a tense moment of communication, he would interpose some remark which immediately lightened the atmosphere.

He seemed also to be the one to encourage the spirit-people to use the trumpet; and we have often heard him talking to them and telling them just what to do. If a spirit could not give the message, Little Peter would invariably do so; and he took great pains to make things clear and to give the evidence in a satisfactory way.

This completes the "family" of helpers to whom we owe so much. Their untiring efforts, their patience, their loyalty, and the sincerity of their desire to maintain a clear channel of communication by which the vital message of man's spiritual destiny may be given to this stricken world, leaves us with happy memories and a debt of gratitude for their companionship. It is a debt which we can endeavour to repay only by passing on to those who have not had this privilege, the knowledge and experiences which we have gained; and by devoting ourselves to this cause of truth for the benefit of mankind.

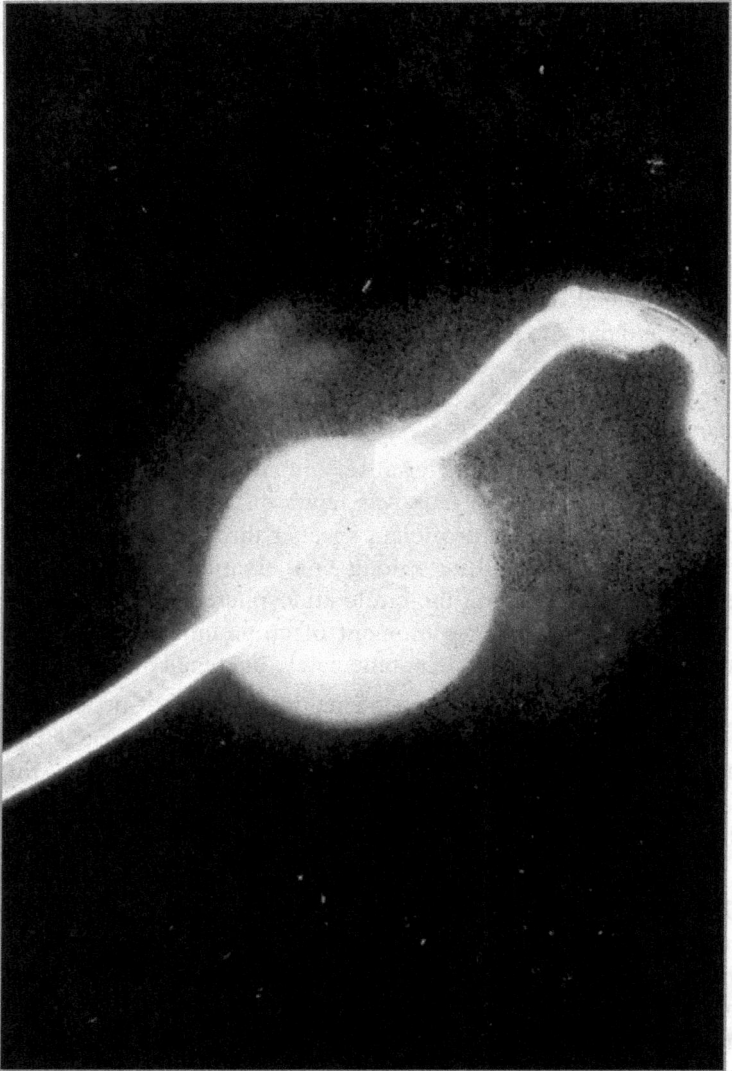

PLATE 3

Unorganized energy. Note the positive structure within the band of energy, also the central sphere of activity. (See Chaps. XI and XVII.)

Photograph by Mr. S.J. Spiller.

CHAPTER IV

SÉANCE, JULY 27, 1940

(By William E. Harrison)

PHENOMENA commenced during the playing of the first record, when four trumpets standing on the floor fell to the ground.

Two trumpets were then levitated ceiling high and were whirled about at great speed, performing circular movements, figures of eight and other evolutions. They were also used as batons to beat time to music and tapping on the floor. This continued at frequent intervals throughout the séance.

Mouth-organ and small handbell, together with two trumpets, were levitated and used together.

Levitation of all objects was particularly good and frequently reached ceiling height some ten feet from the medium.

VOICES. Small childish voice of child control known as Little Peter (who is the interrogator in the following conversation) greets us with: "Hullo, everybody, are you all happy tonight?" Then to a young lad: "Hullo, Johnny" (acknowledged by Johnny). Later: "Who bought vegetables today and left them in the shop?"

Lady says: "I did."

Peter: "Would you like a marrow?"

"Yes."

"I know where there is one, I'll try and get it."

After a little badinage with other sitters the marrow is brought through trumpet and placed in hands of W.E.H. (Marrow was about 8 inches long and 3 inches wide.)

Peter: "Who likes scent? There's a lot here. Have you got a bath?" All sitters then are freely splashed with perfume and we hear it splashing in centre of room.

Peter: "Is anyone wet through? I am sorry if you are drenched, but we couldn't help it."

Peter, later: "I want a man with glasses."

A lady answers: "Yes, he's here next to me."

Peter: "Has he been abroad?"

"Yes."

"Well, he might recognise this." A bronze image is then passed through trumpet into the sitter's hands.

Peter, to another sitter: "Would you like a salt spoon?"

"Yes."

Peter: "All right, it's a big one. I'll see if I can get it." After a few moments we hear something rattling in trumpet, which is then put in lady's hand. It is a spoon about four inches long.

Peter: "Where's the lady who plays the organ? There is someone to talk to you." '

Trumpet goes to Mrs A. and a voice (not Little Peter's) says: "God bless you. Give my love to Harry and both the boys."

This voice claimed to be the brother of Mrs A. by the name of Harold. Harold then gave a personal message, which was acknowledged by Mrs A.

Peter then gave the following messages through trumpet to sitters.

To Mrs R. "Do you know Elizabeth Mary?"

"Yes."

"Give her her mother's love—can't get through."

"Who is Emlyn?"

"Yes. I know."

"He's here. Wasn't he very fond of cheese? He says it in a funny way." (Mrs R. says it in Welsh.) "Yes, that's it. His head is better now."

Peter, to one of the sitters: "Hallo, Kirky." (acknowledged).

To Mrs Hayward: "Your mum's here, and thanks you for the flowers for her birthday." (today).

Peter: "Is there a lady here who works on the railway?"

"Yes."

"There's an old gentleman here with a big beard—says he's your grandad. He can't talk yet, he might later on."

Voice speaks to Mrs P., says he's her son Peter and gives a personal message to his family (understood).

Another voice speaks, which says: "Where's Nance?"

"Here!" Voice says, "It's Arthur," —gives message to his family, and speaks to his mother and brother (understood).

The Guide, speaking through medium, asked that light be put on and the medium given a drink, after which they would continue and endeavour to provide materialised forms. (Circle had been in progress 1 hour and 5 minutes).

On resuming, a figure builds up who is well-known to regular sitters as "Peter"—the Chief Control (not the child). His features and beard were seen by all; he speaks in a clear voice: "Be of good cheer, do not worry about things. All will be well."

Another figure (not very clear, but who appears to have a heavy, white beard) travels around the circle, but is not definitely recognised. Little Peter says it's the grandfather he spoke of earlier.

The next figure is the young man, Arthur, who spoke a little earlier. He came straight to his mother and sister and was recognised.

The last one is a guide of the medium, who showed himself to all the sitters very clearly. He gave his name as Abdul and was complete with turban; appeared to be a young, olive-skinned man—an Egyptian. He gave a greeting to all sitters.

A carnation taken from a vase on the shelf is then illuminated by slate and we watch it taken across the room and put in the hand of Mrs L.

Peter now says (through trumpet) that is all for tonight, says just a few words on need for keeping cheerful and then "Good night, everybody."

A noise of something being lifted across the room is heard, then a blessing, given through the trumpet by a voice known as "Brother Paul", brings the circle to an end after 1 hour and 40 minutes.

Upon lights going up, it was noticed a heavy fire-screen had been moved to the centre of the room and a vase of flowers placed neatly each side.

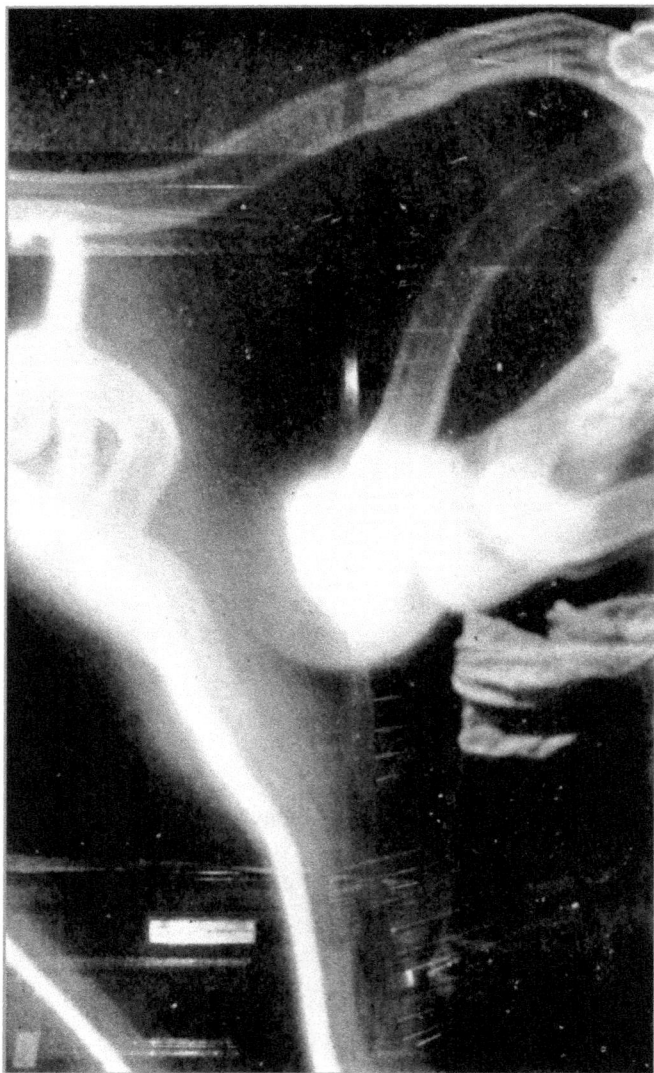

PLATE 4
Unorganized energy similar to plate 3 (see chps XI & XVII)
Photograph by Mr O. Mackinnon Charles B.Sc.

CHAPTER V

SÉANCE, JULY 20, 1940

(By the Author)

We; the undersigned, positively declare that we distinctly recognised, beyond all doubt, the materialised form of Jack Webber at a séance on July 20, 1940 (with Mr Arnold Clare as the medium). The illumination was sufficient to permit our close examination of the features which were clear, precise and unmistakable.

(Signed) W.E. Harrison, E.M. Harrison, Vera Clare, Harry Edwards, Phyllis Edwards, Mrs J.B. Webber, Gladys Layton, Stanley Croft, M.C. Jackson, G.J. McCulloch.

The foregoing statement, signed by ten people who knew Jack Webber well, provides yet further outstanding evidence of survival. All the signatories knew Jack Webber intimately and included Mrs Webber, Mr and Mrs Harry Edwards, six members of the late medium's developing circle and three other friends of the Balham Psychic Society.

The séance was held by the Balham Psychic Research Society through the mediumship of Mr Arnold Clare on Saturday, July 20, 1940.

The plaque used by Mr Clare in his mediumship work is of large area and is so brilliantly lit that it will illuminate an object four feet away; this plaque was held directly under the chins of the materialised spirit-people; and, as may be gathered, the faces could be seen distinctly.

The first form to materialise was Peter, one of the medium's Guides. A Western face, with finely chiselled features, a slightly bent nose, and a tawny beard-totally unlike the medium's face. Peter manifested strongly; and the plaque altered its position to show the face, such as in profile, in differing positions, proving the head was three dimensional. Against the illumination the form of the body and shoulders could be distinctly observed.

Jack Webber was the second form to appear. He first showed himself to the sitters on one side of the circle only (i.e. to Mrs Clare, Mr Harrison (President of the Balham Psychic Society), Mrs Layton and Mrs Webber, in order of seating). This first appearance was for only a few seconds' duration, and while each person recognised the medium, not a word was said, for each felt "almost afraid to speak"—as one sitter said. The plaque fell, and a little more time was taken for Jack to build up more strongly. As the plaque rose for the second appearance, Jack showed himself to the other side of the circle (i.e. Mrs Harrison, myself, Mrs Edwards, Mr Stanley Croft). This time the form remained for nearly two minutes; and the head came within six inches of our faces. Remember, nothing had been said as to who the visitor was. As I saw the face, I recognised Jack; I did not speak at first. I looked again, studying the features well; and only then, after I had coldly and calmly assured myself beyond all doubt that it was Jack, did I acclaim him by name. I said, "It is Jack, most definitely."

The writer noted that the illuminated surface was sufficiently bright to light up the sitters' faces as well as that of Jack; this is indicative of the strength of the light radiation, so strong that the positive statement made in the foregoing declaration can be made with absolute assurance. With this second appearance, the ectoplasmic cowling had receded back over the head, showing Jack's characteristic straight hair brushed well back. (Mr Clare's hair is shortish and rather unruly, and his eyebrows are dark and pronounced, whilst those of the visitor were very light as in his physical life.) Jack went from our side of the circle to the opposite side and spoke a few words, the tonal qualities of his voice being clearly recognisable.

Again, the plaque went down for a short time for a further strengthening of the form. Then for a third time Jack appeared, now with only a very slight vestige of ectoplasmic cowling, the head standing out clear and sharp. He travelled round to all sitters within the radius of action, showing himself within a few inches of the sitter's eyes. I suggested to a near-by sitter that he should note the positive shape of forehead, nose and chin, and in response the plaque moved upright to show the whole face and head in profile against the brilliantly lit surface.

An ectoplasmic "cable" was seen connecting back from the manifestation towards the medium.

I have seen many materialisations, but never before have I seen one so plainly. So much so, that I am prepared to swear by all that I hold sacred that it was our friend Jack who stood before us! No finer or more absolute proof of the truth of survival could be given to us than the return of Jack Webber to his own séance room, to his wife, members of his own circle and friends.

A second control of the medium, an Egyptian known as Abdul, next materialised, with a large squarish face the colour of sepia. This head was much larger than the medium's.

"Little Peter", one of the boy controls of the medium, showed himself to us, no more than three feet high; and he spoke and laughed with us.

A description of the other phenomena that occurred at this séance now follows.

At the commencement of this sitting, three large trumpets, one 30 inches high, were placed some four feet away from the medium. As the opening hymn and prayers were proceeded with, the trumpets were in movement, their illuminated bases being easily discernible.

For the following three-quarters of an hour, two and three trumpets were in simultaneous and continuous movement. They synchronised with the gramophone music or executed independent actions. They weaved intricate patterns at amazing speed; and although the circle was fairly large, there was still insufficient room for their complete evolutions. At times, the trumpets were in movement over the heads of the sitters farthest away from the medium, i.e. eight feet from the medium to the nearest end of the trumpet. They turned, reversed, joined together three in a row and moved at a speed far beyond that attainable by human manipulation: all this in total darkness without hitting a sitter.

During a conversation, conducted by "Little Peter" by means of direct voice through the trumpet, seven coins were apported; six of them very large ones made of copper, of the size of the old five-shilling pieces and weighing nearly one ounce each. All the coins were different, and over a century old.

One of the controls, who assists with the process of apporting, is known as "Simba". A sitter (Mrs Layton) saw him clairvoyantly and interposed with a description of him. She asked if she had described him truly, commenting on the scar on his head. Immediately came the reply that the description was a true one, and also the information that the scar was caused in earth life by a lion's claw. The control then said he would endeavour to show one.

Within a minute at most a lion's claw was apported, followed by three more. The claws were undressed and had pieces of skin attached to them. [It is pertinent to comment here on the production within so short a time of a stated object following a casual remark. Not only was one claw apported, but four in all.]

Lastly, a solid metal idol, four inches high and weighing a quarter of a pound, was produced and given to the author. Thus, nearly a pound of metal, with the coins and the idol, were apported on this occasion.

The procedure during the act of apporting was as follows: The trumpet would first be elevated with its broad end towards the ceiling as if it were searching for the apport, then it would swing and, at times, revolve very quickly; and in this movement the apport would be gradually heard to take form, as judged by the strength of the taps and knocks heard within the trumpet. At times apports would follow quickly one after the other. I sat in the second seat from the medium; and I am certain that no person could have moved about to the extent that would have been necessary to manipulate the trumpets and objects in a normal manner. Further, the apporting of lion claws after only a casual remark concerning them must be accepted as evidence of a most significant nature.

We next saw a length of ectoplasmic material, some three to four yards in length, descending in front of the medium's body, reaching to the floor and stretching out along it as far as the centre of the circle. Its colour was a murky white, and in appearance it was like a fine quality fabric but without any weaving or pattern—not unlike fine, very thin, whitish rubber sheeting.

With the plaque held about two feet from the floor and shining downwards, we saw the above formation coming down in front of the medium's body to the floor where it commenced to twist very tightly into rope form, the far end of which twined itself round the small end of a trumpet.

Then we saw the end of the rope nearest the medium used as a point for leverage, elevating itself rigidly on end, lifting the trumpet with it to the height of about a foot before collapsing and falling to the floor.

After a short lapse of time the plaque was on the floor about three feet away from the medium, lighted side uppermost, when full-length materialised forms approached the area of illumination. Voluminous ectoplasmic material could be seen surrounding the forms like full skirts, the whiteness of them continuing upwards as far as the light could illumine. The heads and faces were out of vision. The forms approached the light in a gliding movement, very slowly, gradually approaching the illumination until they were within an inch or two of the plaque.

Again, the plaque was placed on the floor, lighted side uppermost. First talon-like claws, about two inches long, protruded on to the lighted surface. Next, the ectoplasmic material spread over half the plaque in a single layer; almost transparent like a spider's web—no "net" or fabric marks could be seen. Then we saw an amazing thing happen. The indefinite edge of the ectoplasmic material became gently animated and moved; and small claw-like protuberances emerged, withdrew; and emerged again. Thus, we were able to see that the material possessed a degree of "life" sufficient to enable the performance of distinctive actions. The claws were dark, of full density, and their use became apparent with the next operation.

The material was cast over the whole area of the plaque; and, immediately, the far edge of the plaque would be grasped and pulled along the floor towards the medium. After drawing the plaque for a distance, the ectoplasm released its hold and slid over the plaque (the edge of the ectoplasm being indefinite). Then the plaque was again gripped and again moved forwards, backwards and sideways. These actions were repeated several times, and while they were taking place the remainder of the ectoplasm could be seen reaching backwards to the medium and stretching upwards along his body. The operations took place at the writer's feet and the illumination from the plaque was of sufficient intensity to show that no other agency was responsible for the moving of the plaque. Thus, we learn that ectoplasm is sensitive to intelligent control, both "nervous" and "muscular". The sure accuracy with which the fine ectoplasmic material was cast in a single layer just to reach the far edge of the plaque denotes perfect control of the material.

A more definite form of control of the plaque was seen when a small perfectly formed hand shrouded in ectoplasm held one edge of the plaque. The fingers were not talon or skeleton-like, but fully formed as human fingers. The medium has large hands, with pointed fingers, while the hand we saw was much smaller, with plump fingers and blunt ends. These fingers were plumper and shorter than those of the ordinary human hand.

The séance ended with the gramophone being taken around the circle; at times, levitated high in the air, playing all the time—the needle never slipped. It was wound up, and the sound-box replaced accurately at the commencement of the record. The table on which it had stood next rose in the air and passed around the circle gently, touching each sitter. This came to rest in the centre of the circle with the gramophone placed on top; the mechanism was switched off; the sound-box turned over to its rest and the case was closed and fastened.

When the light was switched on, the medium in his chair was seen to have moved forward about three feet from his corner and was close to the table. During these movements not even the slightest sound was heard within the circle that could be attributed to either the movement of the gramophone, the table, or the medium in his chair.

CHAPTER VI

SÉANCE, NOVEMBER 17, 1940
(By the Author)

REPORT of the sitting with Mr Arnold Clare on Sunday, November 17, 1940, at 3 p.m., at the Balham Psychic Research Society.

Commencing from the medium's right the sitters were: Mrs Hart, myself, Mrs Edwards, Mrs Layton, Mr Hart and Mrs Clare.

This sitting was of an experimental nature, for Mr Clare had not sat for physical work since August, and it was not known whether the mediumship had suffered through in-action. Mr Clare himself was happy in mind but a little apprehensive.

In the centre of the circle were four trumpets made of celluloid and a small one of aluminium, two large plaques liberally coated with luminous paint, a mouth-organ and two small bells. Mrs Clare sat by a portable gramophone on a table between herself and the medium. Though there were only seven persons present, the seats were spaced out widely so that the diameter of the circle was between seven and eight feet.

The light was extinguished, and the proceedings commenced with the singing of one verse of the hymn "Nearer, My God, to Thee", followed by a prayer from myself and then the Lord's Prayer.

Our fears for the mediumship (through inactivity as previously mentioned) were soon dispelled; for immediately after the light was switched off and the first two lines of the hymn sung two trumpets were seen levitated high up in the room near the ceiling, gently swaying in an undulating way in time with the rhythm of the hymn; and so continued throughout the opening proceedings.

After the Lord's Prayer had ended, the trumpets explored the circle, going from sitter to sitter and high up to the ceiling, making contact with a hanging electric pendant.

It has been mentioned that the sitters were some eight feet away from the medium at one part; yet the trumpets travelled out over their heads beyond the circle limits: the small ends of the trumpets—that is, those ends nearest the medium—being at least seven feet away from him.

Throughout the first half of the sitting the trumpet movements were very strong; at times two were weaving intricate patterns at amazing speed, so that the luminous bands around the trumpets appeared like blazes of continuous light (strong wind currents were created by this action); whilst at other times the trumpets would gently caress the faces and bodies of the sitters.

The small aluminium trumpet was used in the first outstanding incident of the sitting. The mouthpiece of this trumpet was barely one-third of an inch in diameter.

In between the changing of the gramophone records we sang a verse of a hymn, and while we were doing so we were accompanied by the thin childish voice of the spirit control, Little Peter.

I was noting how clearly and distinctly the syllables of each word were being articulated, and my mind was marvelling afresh, as I had often marvelled before, that a spirit-voice could be so perfectly produced. To my mind this conclusively demonstrated the improbability that any human voice could produce syllables so perfectly through a mouthpiece with such a small aperture.

It was as if in direct response to my thought* that the Guide Peter asked Mr Hart to take hold of the trumpet and wedge something into the small end. This Mr Hart did, by screwing into it a length of handkerchief (about five inches), the remainder of the handkerchief hanging down loosely. So tightly was this screwed into the trumpet's mouth that the latter could be swung by it.

The trumpet was then passed over the illuminated surfaces of the other trumpets on the floor, so that all sitters could clearly see what had been done. The Guide Peter informed us that Little Peter would try to speak through the trumpet with its mouthpiece closed up. I was therefore intensely alert, awaiting the effort.

---

* It has been repeatedly observed that responsive action by the Guide or Controls follows mental questioning by the sitter and similar incidents are reported by other observers.

The trumpet then rose in mid-air and Little Peter, first making an ejaculation through the trumpet, then spoke a complete sentence distinctly. To my ear the words definitely appeared to come from the open end of the trumpet—that is, the origin of the words spoken was from within the trumpet.

It is obvious from this experiment that to produce a voice speaking words from within a trumpet with one end sealed up and the other end illuminated and facing the sitters, the mechanism for producing sound waves audible to the human ear must have been situated within the interior of the trumpet itself.

A moment's reflection about this action is worthwhile. A child's voice issued from a metal cone, in mid-air, with the small end, effectively sealed, facing the medium, some four to five feet away from him. The broad end was facing the sitters and illuminated, so that any interference from that end would be immediately observed.

The first general observation is that, under the given circumstances existing at the sitting, the act so performed could not be carried out by human action without it being noticed; and therefore, the fact that such an act was performed proves its supernormality. And more important still, it proves that survival can be demonstrated by phenomena of this kind. Such evidence rests on the fact that, in the stated conditions, a child's voice spoke a sentence of understandable words with an intelligent meaning and one that could only have been produced by some mind-controlled, non-human, voice mechanism. The thin tonal quality of the voice was totally unlike the masculine notes of the medium.

To continue with the narrative.

The trumpet then came to myself, suspended in the air, and the Guide Peter asked me to withdraw the handkerchief. I placed my fingers round the handkerchief, just where it entered the trumpet, and held on. The trumpet was then drawn away, pulled free from the handkerchief.

I realised that a considerable part of the handkerchief had been inserted into the trumpet by Mr Hart, so, holding the handkerchief at the point where it came out of the trumpet, I tied a knot to indicate the length that had been inserted.

Peter then asked me to place the handkerchief over the trumpet so that it could be returned to Mr Hart, who sat opposite to me. As I did so, it slipped off. Immediately the trumpet dipped towards the floor and in an uninterrupted movement secured the handkerchief and carried it across to Mr Hart. The time between the handkerchief leaving my possession and being received by Mr Hart was not more than a second.

As the handkerchief was returned, I said I had tied a knot in it to indicate the length inserted. While speaking, Little Peter chimed in and said he also had tied a knot in the handkerchief; and this proved to be so.

Thereby within the time-space of a second, the handkerchief being in motion all the time, including its falling towards the floor and its rescue, another knot was tied. It should be remembered that the broad end of the trumpet over which the handkerchief hung was luminous and visible to our eyes all the time. Under these conditions and within a second of time, a second knot had been tied. I state categorically that it would not have been possible, under such close scrutiny and in such a fragment of time, for any pair of human hands to have tied the second knot.

At the risk of redundancy, I repeat that every sitter on this occasion had had considerable experience of physical circles—the novelty had worn off—had active minds trained to observe every action and to observe every gradation of light, critically and analytically, seeking the reason for each movement; and that it would have been absolutely impossible for any human hands to have taken hold of the handkerchief and to have tied the knot in it in the illumination present without it being seen.

This incident, small in itself, is typical of the ingenuity of the spirit operators, performing new, unrehearsed acts; and so, constantly varying séances of this kind.

When the séance was over, we examined the handkerchief and the knots. I tried to screw the same length of handkerchief into the mouthpiece of the trumpet. I had difficulty in doing so, however, and Mr Hart had to complete the operation up to the knot I had tied. This, of course, shows that the mouth of the trumpet was indeed thoroughly blocked up, further, that it was not possible under the given circumstances attending the incident, and in the time available, (the hanging end of the handkerchief being visible all the time in the luminosity present) for any human agency to have extracted the handkerchief, spoken through the trumpet and reinserted the handkerchief.

Apportation followed, a variety of coins, ten in number, in the way customary with Mr Clare's mediumship, the same aluminium trumpet being used for this operation.

First the trumpet revolved at great speed in a circular motion high up over the centre of the circle; it then darted to a position about two feet in front of, and three feet above, the head of Mrs Clare; remained there for approximately a second of time; a tinkle was then heard as a coin fell into the trumpet, making its physical presence known. The coin was then directed into the hands of a sitter or hurled with violence to a far corner of the room. The trumpet then returned to the same place and the process was repeated, another coin received, and so on. Once the trumpet came straight to my hands and gave me two coins at the same time. By this means half of the coins were apported.

Again, the trumpet whirled round at great speed. This time the area for receiving the coins was quite near the floor, and it was from this position that the rest of the coins were similarly received and distributed.

Some observations are pertinent.

(a) The manner in which the trumpet in total darkness finds unerringly and unhesitatingly the hands of the sitters, sitting spaced apart, or hurls the coins across the room without hitting any sitter. This would be an exceedingly difficult, if not impossible, task to carry out by normal action.

(b) The ten coins came in two groups from two areas, one fairly high in the room, the second near the floor.

(c) The coins must have been in a state of ordered suspension, while the trumpet was collecting and delivering the coins in ones or twos.

(d) The coins in suspension were probably in a nonphysical state, awaiting their re-translation into a physical state.

(e) The coins were mainly collected singly, though once, as mentioned, I received two at the same time.

(f) The spirit intelligences able to effect this phenomena are able to control the ordered process of re-materialisation and at the same time the distribution of a number of objects apported together in one group.

(g) The intelligences are able to control and regulate the process of changing objects from a non-physical state to a physical state, to hold them in abeyance, and release them as and when they are required.

(h) Owing to a metal trumpet being used, the sound of the coin could be distinctly and clearly heard as it fell (or was re-transformed, back into physical shape), helping to establish the fact that from the source of arrival they were collected in a methodical, intelligent manner.

To again interpose, and revert to the argument of those who, while admitting the supernormal nature of psychic phenomena, state it does not necessarily prove survival.

Surely here is evidence of a most complicated (to us) feat of intelligently controlled chemical change. If our scientists were to try to emulate it, one can well imagine the extensive laboratories and involved apparatus which would be necessary. Yet these spirit-people are able to produce the act simply, and without, as far as we are aware, the use, as we understand it, of apparatus.*

Apporting means that the form and structure of a given piece of matter, of certain shape and design, is so changed that it can be transferred instantly from place to place, no matter how far those places may be apart. That in its new formation it is superior to climatic conditions and disturbances is evidenced by the fact that if the object retained a semblance of solidity it must be affected by friction in passing through the atmosphere at tremendous speed. Also, it is able to pass through solid barriers, such as walls, with greater ease than sound penetrates, for there is no limit to the thickness or number of thicknesses an apport may pass through. It is directed to the given spot where it is to be reformed into its precise original physical condition and held there until the moment arrives when it is to be so retransformed.

All this, happening without any visible mechanism, is surely indicative of the active operation of discarnate minds possessing a knowledge of physics, of which man as yet is totally ignorant.

---

* These observations were written before we received Peter's explanation of the process of apporting. The points raised are relative to the subject and do not cut across Peter's statements.

It obviously is not a "freak" of nature. It is a planned act, carried out regularly and systematically. It can only be the result of applying definite-law-governed forces to matter by an intelligence. As man is totally ignorant of the processes involved it cannot be the product of the medium's subconscious mind, for there neither exists today, nor is there evidence that there ever has existed, any human experience from which any human mind can draw such precise knowledge. It is futile to dismiss apporting as impossible because we do not understand the way it is done. We have an analogy in our application of radio science to sound. By means of intricate apparatus man is able to take physical sound waves in their precise form of word syllables or musical notes; change their condition of being into a state of electrical energy; discharge that energy across the world, and at the opposite side receive it by an apparatus that changes it back from electrical energy into physical sound waves, whilst retaining the clarity, precision and character of the sounds. A generation of thought has been spent upon the achievement of this modern "miracle". A wealth of experiment, of trial and error has provided the many steps along which man has progressed to accomplish the now commonly performed feat of world radio.

I hesitate again to give expression to the thought, for it is so very hackneyed, yet it is true that this very performance would have been considered absolutely impossible and a dream of the wildest imagination by many scientific minds of a hundred years ago and less. Therefore, is anyone justified in condemning as "impossible" the act of apporting, say, a lion's claw from its physical condition, lying in the African jungle thousands of miles away, transferring it immediately from the jungle to a séance room in London, and there changing it back into its original form? Is anyone justified in such condemnation, any more than the scientist of old who would have discounted the possibility of world radio?

Our difficulty is, that here we are faced with an accomplished act, without our understanding by what means it is performed. Because we, as yet, cannot see the way it is done (there not being any mechanical apparatus to dissect), it would be as short-sighted and as remote from fact to deny that it is possible to do so, as it would be to deny the fact of radio transmission.

A great wealth of thought and knowledge, slowly gained, was necessary to effect radio transmission; and is it not logical to assume that much thought and experience has also been expended by discarnate minds in perfecting their knowledge of the *modus operandi* so as to apply the directive control necessary to accomplish an act of apporting? It must be the result of applied intelligence! Whose intelligence? It cannot be man's, for it is still beyond his understanding or performance, as radio transmission was beyond his understanding about 20 years ago. If it is not the mind of man which carries out the act, whose can it be? It must be an intelligence which knows more of the natural laws than we do. It must be that of a discarnate entity.

The conclusion must be obvious, that as the act of apporting is performed, so does it prove that the survival of man with enhanced opportunities for progression in all things is a reality. On this hypothesis, I suggest that a physical phenomenon of this character does prove survival and that there is no other alternative.

To resume with the report of the séance.

I noted that the trumpet movements in front of my wife were characteristic. She was sitting next to me, some eight feet away from the medium. The trumpet came to her, large end foremost, and then reversed so that the mouth-piece of the trumpet faced her, revolving, as it were, upon a swivel situated near the centre of the trumpet, an action impossible normally to perform without some mechanical appliance. It should be remembered that at this time the floor space within the circle was occupied by luminous trumpets, and that our eyes were above these, so that any form or object superimposing itself over the illuminated surfaces would have been seen.

The phenomena with Mr Clare's mediumship are usually divided into two parts: the first part, that of the activity already described and the second half with materialisations and ectoplasmic activity. This concluded the first half.

In the second half of the sitting under review, only one materialisation of a head was seen, that of the Guide Peter, whose bearded face, aquiline nose and dominant features are described elsewhere in this volume. The face was plainly illuminated by means of the plaque. The plaque then moved from the head downwards, showing the full length of his body shrouded in ectoplasmic material from his head to his feet.

The plaque was then turned over illuminated side uppermost. A white form approached it, gradually coming nearer to the plaque until it stood touching it and showing with clearness the upward stretch of the ectoplasmic material, in a rounded formation, similar to that of a gown. Although it is not possible to estimate correctly the area in square yards of the material in existence at this time, I can say, conservatively, that it was at least five feet high, and many in width (in folds). It must be remembered in the descriptions of ectoplasm, etc., in connection with Mr Clare that the plaque he uses will illumine clearly to a distance of at least four feet.

A flow of the ectoplasmic material was next cast over the plaque in a single layer. So fine was its nature that against the brilliant luminosity of the plaque it was almost transparent; only becoming more obvious as it creased or rucked-up towards its edge.

A trumpet was next pushed outside the circle between the chairs of my wife and myself, leaving the mouthpiece halfway between our chairs: it was at least eight feet distant from the medium. The plaque next rose on its side and moved to the trumpet's mouth where

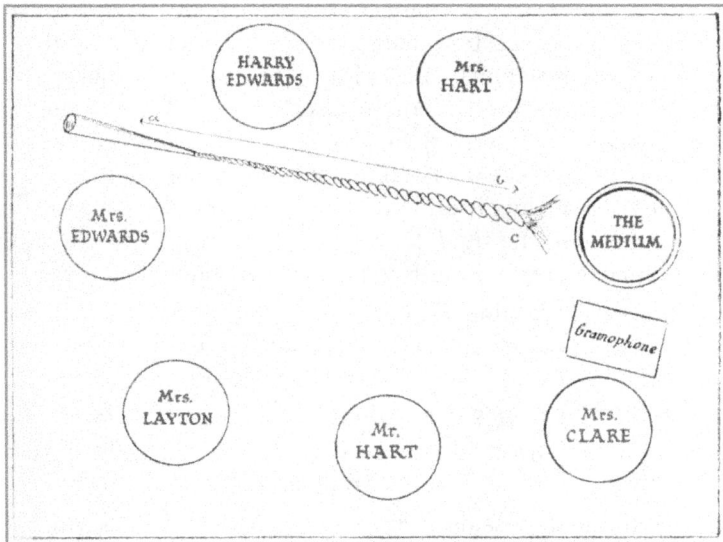

FIG. 3

Diagram showing the movement of the plaque between the phenomenon and the sitters. The line *a-b* indicates the position of the moving plaque. The fulcrum is denoted at *c*.

ectoplasmic material connected with it. The plaque then travelled back towards the medium, showing the continuous length, ever broadening as it got nearer to the medium.

Thus, we could see a continuous length of ectoplasmic material stretching from the feet of the medium to the trumpet. This material did not end at the medium's feet but rose upwards to the source of the emergence (unknown).

Now the distance between the flow of the material and my feet was only about eighteen inches—and that is a generous estimate (it will be recalled the mouth of the trumpet was alongside my chair). Here is a most noteworthy incident. The plaque moved between the ectoplasm, myself and Mrs Hart, that is within a space of eighteen inches. (See Fig 3.)

A moment's reflection demonstrates that considering we could see in the illumination the ectoplasm rising upwards to the medium, and that this same ectoplasm in front of us was clearly illuminated, it is obvious that neither the medium nor any other person could possibly have passed the plaque between us and the illuminated structure without detection. Just another little incident in which the mediumship is proved in a more eloquent manner than by that of ropes or other restrictions. In the clear light from the plaque we saw the ectoplasm twist tightly, forming a sort of cable. It was rigid. This twisting process occurred within the space of a second, as if the material was animated by thought—as if the material was consciously organising itself into a rigid rod. Then from the fulcrum point (see sketch) the rigid ectoplasmic "rod" or "cable" with the trumpet attached rose upwards to an angle of about 60 degrees.

The trumpet, weighing 7½ ozs., being held in perfect alignment with the rod. It remained so for a second or two, then the whole organisation collapsed. The trumpet fell to the floor, the ectoplasm vanished, and the plaque then fell too.

A pressure of at least 3½ lbs. is required to lift the trumpet from a fulcrum three feet away from the trumpet mouth.

It is obviously impossible to reconstruct this feat, as described, by normal methods.

Then followed the most outstanding incident of the sitting. The plaque was placed on the floor lighted side uppermost and a stretch of a single piece of the almost transparent ectoplasmic material cast over it, reaching across two-thirds of the plaque. (See sketch.)

Within and on the material appeared a dark mass, about two inches across and irregular in shape; indeed, its shape was never permanent as it was continuously in movement. To my very close observation—the plaque being at my feet —this opaque mass was not visibly connected to anything: it was like an island. This island effect is vouched for by my wife, but not by other sitters. At this point I would stress that I was intensely alert; and noting this effect I called

FIG.4.
An impression of the emergence of two claws from the island opaque mass in the centre of the almost transparent ectoplasmic material spread over the illuminated plaque.

* See Chapter XII on "Ectoplasm" for further reference to this Phenomenon

attention to it, but apparently the activity of the mass so interested the other sitters that my remark was lost in the general descriptions of it being given by them. Yet I am positive that the island effect is correct. The description of what followed is vouched for by all sitters.

First there emerged from the opaque mass two pincer-like claws, quite dark and opaque, about an inch and a quarter long. The ends of the claws were sharply pointed and curved inwards; they were mobile and moved towards and away from each other in a pincer or gripping movement.

These claws were visible for about ten seconds. (With faculties braced to observe every detail and action, one is apt to lose the sense of time, it may have been ten or twenty seconds—but I always endeavour to present a conservative estimate—there is no need to exaggerate.) (Fig. 4.)

The claws then withdrew and were absorbed into the mass.

Next emerged two formations like finger-tips of a more evolved order, followed by two more; so that there appeared four together just like the first joints of four spatulated fingers—only they were not graded in shape like the fingers of a human hand but were in line. They tried to grow out but seemed to fail in the effort and withdrew into the darkness of the island mass. (Fig.6.)

The next emergence was that of two jointed formations— just like fingers, of average length, which moved away from each other at the ends, as if they were joined at the base as in the case of the human hand. These in turn withdrew. (Fig.5.)

It should be noted that while I am describing these as separate incidents, the movements were continuous; the whole mass being active and rarely still.

Lastly, we saw the re-emergence of four finger-tips, which grew outwards and absorbed the whole of the dark mass, showing as an immature hand about the size of that of a child of eight, except that the fingers were thick, and the ends very broad. We saw the hand, during the two or three seconds that followed, grow to the proportion of a normal hand, quite opaque but covered with the web-like ectoplasm. (Fig.7.) It had four fingers and a thumb. The thumb turned to the edge of the plaque, went behind it and the hand then gripped the plaque, bending it over until it closed up, then it opened the plaque again. (This plaque was a piece of stout cardboard.) The plaque was then violently folded backwards and forwards and finally was ripped into two pieces.*

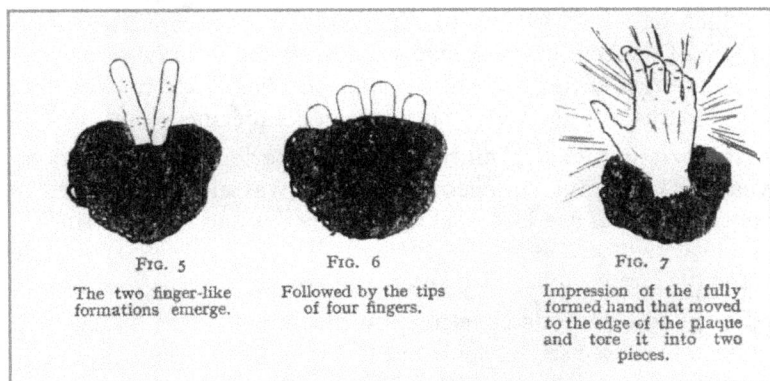

FIG. 5	FIG. 6	FIG. 7
The two finger-like formations emerge.	Followed by the tips of four fingers.	Impression of the fully formed hand that moved to the edge of the plaque and tore it into two pieces.

FIGURES 5, 6 and 7

Mr Austen, of the *Psychic News*, and I experimented with the same plaque a few days later; and it was only with difficulty that Mr Austen succeeded in tearing the plaque in a similar manner. This indicates that the hand formed, in the way I have described, possessed considerable strength.

I cannot say at this stage that the hand was not connected to the medium by an ectoplasmic rod or other means, as part of the hand had left the clear luminosity of the plaque, but never all of it. The fact remains that the hand itself was formed out of ectoplasm, and when finally formed had the power of gripping the plaque, bending it, and subsequently tearing it.

I reassert that all this took place at my feet, that I was bent over observing it as closely and intently as possible. My eyes were not more than thirty inches away from the plaque. My mind was tensely alert, and I declare that the above record is a true description of what took place. The other sitters were also observing the phenomena keenly and were audibly describing each new change and formation. I was not the only one who saw it, as the following testimonies show.

The final phase of the sitting was the draping of a single stretch of the ectoplasmic material right over the plaque. It came before the

* See Chapter XII on "Ectoplasm" for further reference to this Phenomenon

eyes of Mrs Hart and myself first. In the beginning, we could not see what we had to observe, there being what appeared to be a shadow in the top left-hand corner of the plaque. The rest of the plaque looked just "light". Then, by looking into the light, we could see that the whole surface of the plaque was covered by a single stretch of the ectoplasm. Readers will note that so transparent was its nature that at first we could not see it. There were no woven or fabric marks, it was as a film or piece of cellophane.

Appreciating the difficulty we were experiencing in observing what we were given to see, the material was either thickened or rippled so that as one looked at it obliquely one could see the ripples, like "watered silk", as Mrs Layton described it. This was passed right round the circle so that each sitter could observe it.*

The plaque, with its covering, returned to Mrs Hart and myself, and gently passed across our faces, touching them as it did so. Thus, we were able to feel the material. To my forehead, over which the material passed, it felt quite dry and like a very soft fur. Mrs Layton described it as like chiffon. Each sitter was allowed to experience this as well.

As compared with my experiences of touching and holding ectoplasm with Jack Webber, this material was quite different. It was dry and soft, and, I should judge, of slight density, whereas with Jack Webber, ectoplasm was always wettish to the touch, and of heavy density. At this point I would rather reserve any further expression of opinion, re comparisons, for the following reasons: The material we saw this afternoon was of a very fine texture indeed, which may account for the difference in density. The material had been in existence some considerable time, which may account for the dryness, and in any event, there is a great difference between consciously feeling a substance with sensitive fingertips, in which one has ample time to receive, record and analyse impressions and a fleeting touch to the not so sensitive forehead.

With this the sitting drew to a close, the gramophone, records and table were transferred to the centre of the circle, the record taken off, the mechanism stopped, the sound-box placed on its rest, the case closed and the clasp fastened, all by spirit agency.

We sang a verse or two of a closing hymn, and the medium returned to normal consciousness.

---

*See further reference to this in Chapter XII on "Ectoplasm".

REPORT ON SÉANCE, NOVEMBER 17, 1940
(*By Matthew James Hart*)

Among other phenomena such as independent voice, trumpet movements and the apporting of old and foreign coins, there were two outstanding incidents which I here describe.

Placed on the floor within the circle among other things was an aluminium trumpet having a luminous band at its wider end and which was about two and a half inches in diameter. A voice had been received through the trumpet during levitation. It was placed in front of me and I was asked by the voice to block up the small end. This small end was about ⅜ inch or slightly more in diameter, but certainly not as much as ½ inch.

I did this most effectively with a handkerchief by twisting one corner up and inserting it in the small end of the trumpet, turning trumpet and handkerchief in opposite directions until I had forced a third of the latter into the aperture, leaving the other two-thirds hanging loosely.

I held out the trumpet for return and it fell to the floor; but was soon levitated again and the loose end of the handkerchief was shown to the other sitters by drawing it across and holding it in front of the luminous bands of the other trumpets lying on the floor.

The trumpet then rose directly before Mr Edwards and he received evidence of voice despite the fact that the trumpet was blocked. As if this were not sufficient, the trumpet was now given to him so that he could feel how effectively the small end was closed. He was invited to remove the handkerchief. This he did, saying at the time he had tied a knot in it to indicate the length of the part that had been inside.

The handkerchief was taken from him and passed directly back to me (no pause at all), the voice stating "I have tied another." When the handkerchief reached me there were two knots.

A luminous plaque was on the floor, luminous side up. There were two or three taps on the floor as if made by a shoe; then there appeared on the edge of the luminous surface what at first appeared to be a lady's shoe. Whatever this was it is impossible to describe effectively as it was definitely not of the world we know. Not for two seconds together was it still or of a definite shape, but constantly changing. At one moment it seemed to be a small fist, from which emerged talons, short fingers or claws. At another, two claws only, resembling the nippers of a crab. Again it would change and appear as a child's hand. But never at any time was it of quite definite form.

Suddenly, as if to demonstrate the strength present, the plaque was held with one edge resting on the floor whilst pressure on the top edge caused it to bend into almost a semi-cylinder. After this pressure the board was vigorously brushed backwards and forwards on the floor and finally torn across and thrown down.

Note: *Mr Hart's, description of the formation of the hand is not so definite as mine. The reason for this is that Mr Hart was several feet away, on the opposite side of the circle from me, and the plaque and the formation were at my feet.—AUTHOR.*

REPORT BY MRS GLADYS LAYTON

At the request of Mr Harry Edwards, I am reporting my witnessing of two remarkable incidents at the sitting.

During the course of the séance, varied phenomena have taken place, during which a trumpet went to Mr Hart. The child Peter, one of the controls, asked him to block up the small end of the trumpet, which he did with a handkerchief, twisting it into the small aperture. This being done, about half the handkerchief was left hanging down from the small aperture, which could be seen over the lit-up surfaces present. The trumpet was then levitated and Little Peter spoke to us in a remarkably clear voice. The trumpet then went to Mr Edwards who, on Peter's direction, took hold of the handkerchief and the trumpet was pulled away from it. He was then asked to lay the handkerchief on the trumpet, which slipped off towards the floor as he did so. The trumpet, in a continuous sweeping movement, rescued the handkerchief and in the same movement gave it to Mr Hart. As this was being done, Mr Edwards said he had tied a knot in the handkerchief to mark the length of its insertion into the trumpet, and then Little Peter immediately interrupted by saying he had tied a knot as well. On inspection, this was found to be so, though only a second had passed between Mr Edwards placing the handkerchief on the trumpet and its delivery to Mr Hart. The handkerchief was within my view during the whole process.

Later on, occurred the second incident. On the brilliantly illuminated plaque, which was lying on the floor, lighted side uppermost, there appeared in a film of ectoplasm that had been cast on to the plaque, a dark mass about the size of an egg that was in continuous movement, and constantly changing its shape. There protruded from it a number of distinct formations, claws and fingers, and finally, it resolved itself into a perfectly formed hand which moved to the edge of the plaque, gripped it and bent it double several times quickly, and finally ripped the plaque into two pieces. This feat required considerable strength.

CHAPTER VII

SÉANCE, NOVEMBER 30, 1940
(Report by Colin Evans, B.A.)

I WAS invited to sit on Saturday, November 30, 1940, in a large group séance with A. T. Clare as the medium. He is secretary of the Balham Spiritualist Society, on whose platform he sometimes gives the address and clairvoyance at the Sunday services, but I was told that he does not sit professionally. I did not count the other sitters but am under the impression that they numbered about eighteen. I did not inquire nor learn whether any of the other sitters either paid any person or organisation or donated or subscribed to any Society or other fund; the manner of my own invitation prevented the question from arising in my case.

The séance lasted about two hours. It was held for the most part in darkness, but dull red light and firelight were at numerous intervals switched on for fairly long periods, during which similar phenomena occurred as in the dark (details below). No test conditions of any sort were imposed, though one test tentatively suggested by me during the séance was readily and most successfully complied with. The medium was not subjected to any restraint or check or control by sitters. The general effect produced on. my own mind was one of complete genuineness in respect to all the phenomena; but only in respect to some of the phenomena: was there such proof of genuineness as would have ruled out any possibility of doubt if a sitter had any predisposition to suspicion. The fact, however, that some of the phenomena concerning which there was fool-proof evidence, making doubt impossible, were among the rarest and most important of the phenomena, than the ones otherwise liable to be most doubted, lends a presumption of genuineness to the rest.

After extinction of lights, the séance was opened with a brief invocation and the Lord's Prayer. Three "trumpets", all made of transparent rigid celluloid with broad strips of luminous paint all round, two of them about twenty-four inches long and one about eighteen inches; two "mouthorgans" (not luminous) and a small glass pot, such as is used for some brands of fish paste, etc., examined and empty; an old-fashioned musical box, and a luminous "slate" consisting of a sheet of plywood (larger than the "slates" commonly used—I guessed its size as 14 by 10 ins., perhaps) coated on one side with luminous paint with a handle fixed to the other side, were placed in the middle of the floor. The medium sat in one corner of the room and I was seated in the diagonally opposite corner, with other sitters all round the walls. The distance between my seat and the medium's was perhaps 20 ft., with the accessories mentioned placed halfway between us, or about 10 ft. from the medium.

During the short invocation there were loud sounds of a sort of fumbling kind, with rappings and knocks against the trumpets in the middle of the floor, and two of the three trumpets were seen to be jerking slightly; they fell over; one of them was righted, rose a few inches wobblingly in the air, and fell and rolled in a direction away from the medium towards my right. At this time, a small electric fire, giving a red glow and a little dim visibility, was still alight. There was no sign of movement by the medium, either visible or audible.

One of the medium's Guides then spoke, giving a brief address. This Guide was named "Peter" and spoke perfect English with the slight but noticeable accent of a cultured foreigner. This control's accent is noteworthy for this reason: I have some knowledge of phonetics, and am convinced that the control's precise pronunciation—with its characteristic vowel qualities, and certain consonants, were such as would be beyond the mimicry of anybody who was not either a trained phonetician, an accomplished linguist or a very exceptionally able actor with special dialect training—in fact, I do not believe the last-named could do it unless he were also one of the two former; I noted particularly the non-diphthongal character of the long vowels, the particular nuance of broad e's and o's, long and short, and narrow short o's; the difference between the English so called dentals, and the genuine dentals of the control (point-tooth, not point-gum, plosives), and absence of aspiration in the phonetics sense with voiceless plosives; also the nuances of syllabic stress and of phrase-intonation. The timbre of the voice itself also was, while quite unforced, natural and very resonant, entirely different from that of the medium's own voice. The latter's speech is that of the average middle-class Londoner of secondary education.

Peter's speech was not in direct voice but by means of trance control of the medium—Peter himself drawing attention to this fact "for our information". After the electric fire had been extinguished, first one and then both of the larger trumpets were levitated almost to the ceiling—to a height of some seven feet—and floated all round the room, with perfectly controlled and unhesitating steady movement, pointing first to one sitter then to another, with motions of the two trumpets quite mutually independent, the broader ends being often 12 or 15 ft. from the medium, but always pointing away from him, so that the narrow ends, nearer him, must have been not nearer to him than 10 or 13 ft.

As Peter finished speaking, these two trumpets lowered their broad ends to the floor and, with a little fumbling, picked up the third (smaller) trumpet between them; after which all three remained suspended in the air and moved about independently of one another for a few moments.

During most of the séance, records were played softly on an electrical gramophone and amplifier in a corner of the room away from the medium's corner. The lady in charge of the gramophone tried to change a needle and reported that she had dropped the needle on the floor and could not find it in the dark. The medium's child control (also named Peter, but called "Little Peter") spoke in direct voice, his voice coming from close to the gramophone and well away from the medium's chair; and apparently found the lost needle, without the intervention of the lady in charge: then a box of gramophone needles was levitated and floated about the room, rattling. No needle was on the floor when looked for in full light after the séance.

From this point on "Little Peter" seemed to take charge of the séance, and was speaking most of the time, in direct voice, usually coming, beyond doubt, through one of the trumpets; sometimes when the broad end of a trumpet was right against my face; sometimes in mid-air or near the ceiling in the middle of room; sometimes close to other sitters; at other times apparently from high up near middle of room away from all trumpets. The voice and intonation suggested a cockney child, but (possibly through imperfection of the ectoplasmic voice-box or distortion by trumpets) sounded always a little unnatural in timbre (which I have noticed to be the case with many child guides using adult mediums).

Disconnected notes were rather unmusically played at intervals through the mouth-organs or one of them, apparently about breast-high in the middle of the room while trumpets were whirling; and in a not very successful attempt (musically) to "accompany" the singing of a song.

I was frequently tapped or touched or stroked by trumpets, with what seemed a perfect control of their movement, suggesting that the responsible agency could see me clearly despite the complete darkness then existing.

The movements by which I was touched were too rapid and assured and direct to be consistent with a groping or tentative feeling of the way; and never either just missed or hit with violence, but were such as a person seeing what he was doing would have made.

Strong and very cold winds blew at intervals for about a minute at a time, about six times during the séance. This phenomenon was much more pronounced than the wind that could have been made by movements of the trumpets which were in motion at the time.

About three-quarters of an hour after the commencement of the séance there was a very strong smell of a floral perfume, suggestive to me of an ordinary commercial toilet scent, as used by women; and a considerable quantity of liquid perfume was sprinkled in drops over my head and face, feeling like a heavy rain, while other sitters all round the room reported the same thing at the same time.

Four different sitters, all at some little distance from me, but also at some considerable distance from the medium's chair, were personally addressed by "direct voice" through one of the levitated trumpets, in voices not loud enough to be very distinct from where I sat, but all of which were apparently readily accepted by the sitters addressed as the distinct and recognisable voices of friends and relatives ("dead") well-known to them. The conversations which ensued were apparently fully evidential and satisfying to the sitters concerned. One of these sitters was a young lady who, I learned later, in conversation with her and others after the séance, was attending her first séance; and was a complete stranger to the medium.

Two of the trumpets having fallen to the floor, the third continued to float around the room; and I saw it approach a sitter and apparently tip itself up, when that sitter announced that a coin had fallen into her lap. A moment later the same trumpet, clearly visible by its bands of luminous paint, came to me, without for an instant having ceased its steady movement round the room with its wide end pointing away from the medium, and touched my hand; then tilted up and from its wide end fell something which alighted by my foot, which I stooped and picked up, finding it to be a very large heavy coin, about the size of an English five-shilling piece. On examination in the light after the séance it proved to be a Russian coin. A similar thing then happened to five other sitters, and then the trumpet floated up towards the ceiling, remaining poised about the middle of the room; and at slow intervals further coins, to the number of another sixteen, were dropped to the floor one by one, "Little Peter" counting aloud as they dropped. A few of the larger ones I was able to see as they passed the luminous band on the transparent trumpet, thus seeing that it was from within the wide end of the trumpet that they dropped; but at no time was there any sound of more than one coin rattling in the trumpet; and I satisfied myself after the séance that the larger coins could not be passed into the very narrow small end of the trumpet. One of these additional coins, a German 10-pfennig piece, was dropped into my own hand. Others proved afterwards to be English coins of bygone reigns (George III, etc.) and foreign coins of various countries, including India. A lady present mentioned that at a previous séance with the same medium she had by a similar process received a spade guinea.

Brother Peter then asked for full lights to be turned on for a few minutes prior to an attempt to produce a different "phase" of phenomena. This proved to be materialisation, as a number of materialisations followed, taking up most of the remaining time of the séance, after the lights had been again extinguished.

While the lights were up, the medium was seen to be in apparently unbroken deep trance in his chair, exactly as before the commencement of the séance and as at its conclusion.

After the break, when the room was again darkened, the luminous slate was seen to be raised very slowly from the floor, reaching a height of about eight inches, still with its luminous surface floorward and moving upward with a purely vertical movement impossible if normally lifted by human agency unless the person lifting it had been standing in the middle of the room and leaning directly over it and this movement commenced instantly the light was extinguished, without allowing time for the medium or any sitter to leave his chair with sufficient stealth to be unheard; while the use of an outstretched arm or foot or any kind of rod or tongs or other accessory for lifting it from a distance would have lifted it with a slant or tilted to one side or the other. It was much more brightly illuminated than most luminous paint-covered "slates" which I have seen used at séances, and gave a light which appeared equal in visibility—conferring power—to that of a pocket electric torch shaded with two thicknesses of tissue paper or one of newspaper. The brightly illuminated patch of floor beneath the slate when it reached a height of about eight inches, or perhaps rather more, was then gradually veiled by what looked like a fine semi-transparent textile fabric of very subtle texture gradually materialising "from nothing" until fully formed, draped over the slate. There was no rustle or sound of any material.

The slate then descended slowly to lie on the floor again, then rose suddenly and swiftly to about six feet from the floor, and took up a horizontal position, luminous surface upward, and then slightly tilted upward, till it was seen to be held immediately below the chin of a fully materialised head; whose features and head-dress were as clearly and distinctly visible as it lit by a pocket-torch held close up to it. The head-dress appeared to be some kind of white or whitish thick-textured woollen hood, rather suggesting a monk's cowl widely opened to give a clear view of the face.

A curled moustache and small but distinct "imperial" goatee beard were seen, being that of a living entity and not of a mask or inanimate structure. The features undisguisably different from the medium's; the nose fuller and more fleshy; the mouth thinner-lipped and of more sensitive shape; the eyes quite different, more deep-sunk, and the eyebrows fuller; and the forehead larger, broader and higher, and with fuller curves at the temples; and the chin and jaw larger. The remainder of the figure (apart from head and head-dress) was not visible at all. The materialisation made the circuit of the room close to the sitters, pausing opposite each sitter and (in my case, certainly—and I think in the case of the other sitters) bringing its face to within twelve inches of the sitter's eyes for careful scrutiny, with the luminous slate held immediately under chin.

By the Guide's request during the first materialisation, all sitters linked their hands. To do this, I had to put away the note-book in which I had been making notes of phenomena as they occurred, and my report of the séance from this point on is therefore from notes made from memory immediately after the séance and not from notes made while it was in progress, as in the case of the earlier part of the séance.

Sitters were allowed to release their linked hands during later materialisations. The medium, I was told, was not linking hands with sitters.

A second materialisation was produced and shown in similar manner, and was that of another Guide, with quite different features. He was wearing a large turban, with a sparkling jewel of some kind set in it. While this entity was showing his features I, without speaking aloud, formulated a clear-cut mental request to be allowed to see more of the figure than the head. As soon as I formulated this mental request, the slate was lowered so that at first it showed nothing, then, starting from near the floor, it was made to shine on and show the clear outlines of legs from ankle upward, and body up to waist, clothed in close clinging but heavy textured whitish material of some sort, and then showed what looked like a misty unoccupied gap above the waist, as if, except for whitish transparent atmospheric cloud, there was nothing tangible above the waist. Brother Peter's voice spoke through the entranced medium, the voice obviously coming from the direction of the medium's chair at some distance from the materialised form; while the materialised form was still visible about eight feet from the medium's chair. I then made another mental request, which was apparently ignored or not sensed by any human or discarnate intelligence operating; and I therefore repeated it aloud. It was that we should be shown the medium while we were shown a materialisation, so that I could repeat to sceptics the fact that a materialised form and the medium's own body had been simultaneously rendered visible in different places.

At first there was no reply. The materialised form disappeared, but the slate remained levitated. Then there followed the heavy noise of the portable electric fire being lifted from the hearth and placed on the floor nearer the middle of the room. Suddenly it came alight, having apparently been supernormally switched on without the action of any sitter. In the reddish but clear light of the electric heater and in front of the electric fire there was seen slowly materialising what appeared to me to be a baby's form in white clothes, moving slightly, and seated on the floor silhouetted darkly against the electric fire on its further side (to me) while its clothes, partially transparent, allowed the fire to be seen through them where they were draped loosely away from the body. The luminous slate was shone on the face and body for a moment on the side unlit by the electric fire. The slate then floated across the room and was carried up and down clearly showing the medium's face and figure in his chair in a corner of the room. While the medium was being thus shown by the luminous slate, the child was seen slowly de-materialising, until there was only a small amount of transparent drapery or textile of some sort fluttering in front of the electric fire; this drapery then vanished completely, appearing not to move away but to thin into non-existence. Immediately after, the plug of the electric fire was abruptly pulled out of the wall socket without human intervention. Trumpet levitation, complete with a rod-like structure, was shown in the light of the fire.

A final materialisation seen clearly by me was that of Jack Webber, the medium who passed on recently, Brother Peter had asked if any sitters knew Jack Webber; and I replied that I did; so did some other sitters. His characteristic features, full face and profile, were clearly shown and were unmistakable, the slightly receding chin and low forehead being such as would have required the amputation of solid masses from the medium's face and head in the event of impersonation by him. I knew Jack Webber very well by sight and was under no possibility of doubt as to the features I saw in the materialisation being the same as those with which I became familiar during Webber's earth life.

Little Peter then materialised, showing only his face, at a height of some three feet from the floor. The face was obviously too small to be that of any adult. It was obviously a complete face and not a middle portion of a larger face partially surrounded by any black covering; and it was obviously alive. However, its features were not clearly visible to me in detail, though I gathered that they were to other sitters.

I did not get any clear view of materialisations of personal friends or relatives that I think, I gathered, were recognised by two other sitters.

At the end of the séance, the small glass pot, slightly damp inside, was found on the floor near the wall farthest from the medium. It smelt of the perfume with which we had all been sprinkled.

PLATE 5

A 45-lb. table levitated by manipulation of gravity and etheric forces.
Note the absence of physically constructed ectoplasmic rods.
(See Chap. XIII.)

Infra-red photograph by Leon Isaacs

PART II

CHAPTER VIII

INTRODUCTION TO PART II

WHEN the discussions with Peter commenced and the idea of publishing them was first formed, I had in view a series of talks that would be confined to explaining the simple mechanics of each phase of phenomena. I soon realised that to present a cogent chain of reasoning, the explanations travelled far beyond the mild comprehension of myself and those present.

It is obvious that the limited knowledge of the sitters handicaps the Guide in his explanations; for unless we were able to comprehend his observations we could not proceed intelligently.

Had our sitters been composed of members who were authorities on physics, philosophy, radio-activity, biology, chemistry and so on, Peter would have been able to give more advanced wisdom, again up to the point of their ability to understand. Further, the questions put by such authorities would have elicited more detailed answers to the points at issue.

This position is frankly realised by the author and his friends, but to obtain such a well-versed commission was, for a number of reasons, out of the question, especially in wartime.

Firstly, the scope of the work in this section is the product of sitting on an average once a week for nine months; and it is extremely doubtful if any expert would have been willing to devote so much time to the matter.

The difficulty did not end there: for owing to Mr Clare's war service and his uncertain free hours the meetings could not be held regularly, so that no advance dates could be determined. It must also be kept in mind that Peter's explanations cannot be divided into water-tight compartments, for the whole story is a related structure; and the reader will not be able to obtain a true picture until he has read every chapter, for each part dovetails into the rest.

This presentation will, however, serve a useful purpose, firstly because it will be understood by the majority of those interested in survival; and secondly it will serve as a foundation for the extension of the knowledge by more technical minds at a later date. I am permitted to say, that should any commission of experts be formed in the future, Mr Arnold Clare would be most willing to collaborate.

I am mindful of an attempt to arrange through the good offices of Miss Mercy Phillimore, Secretary of the London Spiritualist Alliance, a representative commission to observe the Webber phenomena. It had to be abandoned as it was not possible to obtain the services of suitable commissioners under the conditions extant in these days.

In spite of the obvious great importance of this work and the benefit that would accrue to humanity from a fuller understanding of the spirit realm, science, as represented by its leaders, is generally reluctant to devote any appreciable time to its study.

Seventy years ago, Sir William Crookes cited:

> "I have both seen and heard, in a manner which would make unbelief impossible, things called spiritual, which cannot be taken by a rational being to be capable of explanation by imposture, coincidence or mistake. So far, I feel the ground firm under me; but when it comes to what is the cause of these phenomena, I find I cannot adopt any explanation which has yet been suggested."

Since that time a number of noteworthy mediumships have functioned, and in some cases well-authenticated reports have been published. As a rule, these recordings have been restricted to a recital of the bare facts—and rightly so—with no attempt to provide explanation of causes and *modus operandi*.

It would be natural to conclude, following the published weight of evidence of unexplained acts and forces, that scientific faculties would have been very keen to conduct research on the issues; but experience has shown that this is not the case. Again, I refer to Sir William Crookes who lamented:

> "I confess I am surprised and pained at the timidity or apathy shown by scientific men in reference to this subject. . . .
> I invited the co-operation of some scientific friends in a systematic investigation. But I soon found that to obtain a

scientific committee for the investigation of this class of facts was out of the question."

That attitude of seventy years ago has unfortunately mainly continued unto the present day. True, we have had the support of a number of individual scientists of repute, such as Sir Oliver Lodge; but we have not had any investigation by scientific associations, who invariably have ignored the findings of the individual investigators. These remarks do not apply to Societies for Psychical Research, whose careful and meticulous investigations have proved to be so valuable, but to scientists in general, who have formed the opinion, without investigation, that all séance-room phenomena are fraudulent. It is a position based on the premise that as spirit activity seems so opposed to the factors governing matter and the known natural laws, the Spiritualist case must be wrong. They have ignored the view that if a new fact seems to oppose what is termed a law of nature, it does not prove the asserted fact to be false, but only that we have not yet ascertained all the laws of nature and forces that are so employed, or that we have not learned them correctly.

The records in the first part will have been seen to be outstanding in character; and having assured ourselves of the truth of the facts, and also that they are confirmed by similar occurrences at different times, in different countries, through different mediumships, it would be cowardice to suppress the truth. It would also be cowardly to ignore the facts and the teachings of Peter simply because they may cause to be altered, readjusted or re-written some of the presumed established conclusions of psychic science.

It is with no apology therefore that in the second part of this book a challenging contribution is made towards the fuller understanding of the laws and forces involved.

Throughout the whole history of investigation one essential has been found absolutely necessary for the production of phenomena. Whether the medium be primitive, lettered or unlettered, the presence of a Guide has always been required to direct through the medium's voice or by other means the conduct of the work.

This presence has proved to be one of the major obstacles the scientific mind has to face and accept. The weight of evidence and communication has made the acceptance of the reality of the Spirit

Guide more easy in these days; but it presented a difficult problem in the early days; for while they found it difficult to countenance the presence, they had to endure it, with scepticism. The savants of those days took the naive and sublime view that the Spiritualist theory should be discarded during the experiments but when the manifestations were accompanied by intelligence, they needed the Spiritualist hypothesis but only as a working hypothesis. In other words, the investigator must in order to get results at all, adapt himself to the presence of the spirit operator under whom all mediums in the trance state work.

One of Arnold Clare's Guides, Peter, is mainly responsible for the phenomena and teachings here described, and it is noteworthy that he has been able to deal fluently with a vast range of subjects. He would speak so fast that it became difficult for the experienced stenographer to take the words down, and he had to slow up his delivery. It has been an achievement that would give pause to any exponent of the art of oratory.

His observations disclose a realm of vast activity, containing potentials the magnitude of which cannot yet be even dimly comprehended. They disclose not only the methods whereby the so-called dead can for a brief time rehabilitate themselves in physical garb, but also deal with elementary and primitive forms of life and their functions.

The references dealing with the "little people" throw some light upon a comparatively new conception of a state of being; and the detail with which this is narrated provides abundant food for speculation. If one admits the reality of life at all in the spirit world and that life is thereby progressive, it can only be one of degree; and as we in this life have witnessed the evolution of living things from the Jellyfish upwards to man, so it is not unreasonable to assume that there are also gradations of life in spirit.

It is easy for a critic to dismiss the matter as absurd: that course has been the refuge of foolish sceptics in the past who denied with equal vehemence that the earth was spherical or that a heavier than air machine would ever fly.

More pertinent is this challenge. Here we give you the recorded fact and the explanation of its accomplishment given by the chief operator. One cannot deny the former, for it is the truth, no matter how strange it may appear; and if the fact of its performance is strange, why refuse categorically the explanations because they too must of necessity seem strange.

What alternative reasoned hypothesis can the disclaimer put forward to account for the phenomena?

It would have been far easier for Peter to have contented himself with repeating theories we had formed previously, or to cloak the performance of apportation in ambiguity. Why need he have introduced such a revolutionary explanation of the force of gravity or cut across our preconceived theories of the functions of "voice-boxes"?

Every inquirer should be bound by a law of honour to face fearlessly every problem and every hypothesis presented to him, and it is with this object that the explanations are submitted.

We are, as Peter says, "paddling on the foreshore" of a realm of infinite activity; and as such, the explanations are in their early stages. We have first to grasp an idea—its development being a heritage of the days to come.

.　　.　　.　　.　　.

An effort has been made to summarise previous knowledge and experience so that they may be related to the explanations. In presenting such summaries, difficulty has been experienced in choosing from the accumulated mass of evidence the most relevant and important items. I have stressed the fact that there has been close similarity between all the various reports of each phase of phenomena, and therefore the summaries and quotations given have been chosen as being generally representative of the whole. They include extracts from incidents in the mediumships of Margery Crandon, Rudi Schnieder, Miss Goligher, Valiantine, Count Rossi, Home, Slade, Eusapia Paladino, Jack Webber and others. With the exception of Jack Webber, I have had to rely upon printed records, but with J.W. I write from an intimate association; therefore, if the references to this medium are frequent it is because I prefer to speak of what I know rather than about what I have read.

As one studies the history of physical mediumship; it becomes clear that with each succeeding mediumship progress is made in the character and quality of the phenomena; this progress is illustrated in the photographic records. So it is with Arnold Clare, who today is able to have manifested through his mediumship phenomena of the highest order.

In the past many phrases have been used by the Guides (Peter uses new ones) to name certain structures or processes. We have such phrases as Walter's "talking apparatus"; D'Angello's "magnetic fluid" and "vital power"; Professor Castellani's "X force", "radio-active potencies" and "the psychic force that holds the molecules of the astral body together"; Muldoon's "positive and magnetic principle" and so on. Sir William Barrett, in summing up some of these references, "attributes the phenomena to some extension in space of the nervous force of the medium, just as the power of a magnet or of an electric current extends beyond itself and influences and moves certain distant bodies which lie within the field of the magnetic or electric force."

By themselves these phrases and inferences mean little, and indeed, may be misleading, causing theories to be built up upon abstract references by the Guides, who, when asked for an explanation, simply provided the best phrases likely to be within the comprehension of the receiving sitter. But now, in view of Peter's explanations, these seemingly ambiguous terms take on a new significance; they come to life and we can begin to perceive intelligently and more accurately the intention behind the references. They build up a composite picture providing a related tenable hypothesis covering the whole field of manifestation.

Peter's statements may create some controversy among those who subscribe to certain theories elaborated from man's interpretation of the circumstantial evidence of the séance room. Further, the nature and work of "nature spirits" may not be to the taste of those who have regarded all physical phenomena as of a purely spiritual character; and they may be shocked to read that certain works they may have witnessed were the result of labours of sub-human entities.

It is felt essential, however, no matter how adversely the explanations may affect some readers, to publish faithfully the explanations as given. By doing so, expression may be given to one new proven thought, or probable line of reasoning capable of being proven subsequently. If one part can be shown to be wrong, then it may all be wrong; but if one part is proven and the remainder stands up to reason as a coherent whole, then the entire structure is worthy of our most earnest consideration.

CHAPTER IX

THE ETHERIC REALM

IT has been somewhat puzzling to determine the exact order in which Peter's revelations should be given so that the sequence of chapters will build up a constructive story step by step.

What has made it even more difficult is that no part is complete in itself, each chapter having a direct bearing upon the others.

It would have been preferred for this opening chapter to have been last owing to its complex nature. Yet it must come first for it deals with a subject that is the basis of all spirit activity and it is essential for the reader to have in his mind the foundation upon which each explanation depends.

It is therefore necessary to provide first of all a general statement as to what is known by science to be the meaning of the realm etheric and the constitution of matter.

Peter's statements in this chapter were the last to be received. It will be found that they contain references to some of his previous statements (appearing in subsequent chapters). This may render the reader's appreciation of this chapter a little difficult and in consequence may not be able to grasp its meaning and implications on the first reading. It is suggested that this chapter be read through to obtain a general idea of the subject, continuing with the rest of the book returning to re-read this chapter again afterwards.

Until recently matter[1] was known to be composed of molecules and atoms, just little lumps of matter, coalesced together into large or small lumps. The invention of the X-rays disclosed subsequently that atoms are made up of electrons and protons whirling round within an etheric content. Perhaps the best description is that given in the words of Sir Oliver Lodge in his book *Ether and Reality*[2] as follows:

1. Reminder from Publisher: This book was written in 1942
2. *Ether and Reality* was originally published 1925.

"We can now summarise briefly what we know. The two opposite charged particles, the negative and the positive, are called respectively an electron and a proton. They are both exceedingly minute. They are far smaller than atoms, incomparably smaller, the smallest things known; even if there were a hundred or a thousand of them in the atom, they would not be in the least crowded, there would be plenty of empty space. Different atoms are now known to be composed of a different number of electrons; and by their different number and grouping they constitute the different chemical elements. The atoms of all the chemical elements are built of electrons and protons and of nothing else.

On this view the existence of an electron can be fairly understood. Can the existence of a proton be understood too? No: there we are in a difficulty.

The proton is more massive than can be easily accounted for: and why it is more massive we can only guess: indeed, at present we can hardly guess, or at least the guesses are not very satisfactory. That remains at present an outstanding puzzle: the question is one that has hardly yet been faced. One guess is that the electron is hollow like a bubble, that it has an electric field which by itself would cause the bubble to expand, but that it is kept in equilibrium and of a certain size by etheric pressure. On this view there is no substance in its interior: in itself such an electron is not massive at all; its apparent mass is due to its electric field and nothing else. Whereas the interior of a proton, instead of being hollow, may be full-filled with an extra ether: all that which was removed from the electron being crammed into the proton, so as to account for its great massiveness or what we may call its weight. A proton is more than a thousand times as heavy as an electron, about 1840 times by direct measurements; and what is called 'the atomic weight', for the weight of an atom depends almost entirely on the weight of the protons it contains. The hydrogen atom contains one only, the helium atom contains four, the lithium atom seven, the oxygen atom sixteen and so on—in accordance with the list of atomic weights long empirically known in chemistry, the heaviest being uranium, which contains 238. The atomic weights are certain enough; the number of protons in a specified atom is fairly certain also. But what is not known is why the proton has such weight, and why the weight of an electron is so much less. In every other respect the two charges seem equal and opposite: electrically they are equal and opposite . . .

We are safe in saying that the weight of matter depends on the protons, that is the positive units, which go to form the nucleus of the atom, while the chemical properties of the atom depend on the electrons which circulate around the nucleus. These planetary electrons are active and energetic and produce conspicuous results; they characterise the atom by its spectrum; they confer on it its chemical properties; but they add to its weight hardly at all. . ."

So we see that matter is not solid at all, it is a vast number of revolving electrons around a nucleus. Thus, we are able to perceive clearly that all matter is in a state of vibration; and the manipulation of vibrations or frequencies is the method the spirit operators employ for certain phenomena in the séance room.

The electrons and protons move at great speed within the framework of the atom, and are so small that they may be compared in Peter's words to footballs whirling around inside Westminster Abbey; the space within the atom in which the electrons and protons move being occupied by ether. This ether thus takes on the characteristic of the particular atom, so becoming, in Peter's words, "bound ether".

Certain conclusions carry us further. As electricity is a vibration of ether, and the atom and its components are electrical energy, so is all matter ether in a particularised condition.

Matter, therefore, is a combination of positive and negative electrical charges moving in an ordered manner associated one with the other by the ether which is thereby the basic substance of the whole universe.

We know that ether fills all space and is the medium by which light and heat reaches us. It has been computed that etheric waves move at nearly 200,000 miles a second. Although we have been unable to measure or weigh ether, we know that it must occupy what we call space because heat, light, electric and sound waves travel through it at ascertained rates, particularly does this apply to radio waves, proving there must be a medium through which the waves can regularly travel.

Its pressure, as Peter says, is immense, ponderable, and penetrates all things. Its pressure may be so great that no adequate conception can be given in finite understandable terms; it may be millions of tons to the square foot.

It is difficult for the mind of man to conceive ether as it is, as we are in it, like deep-water fish in the depths of the ocean: we are part of it, as it is the all-pervading interpenetrating power. Without it we could not see, as there would be no medium to carry light to our eyes; we should be utterly cold, as there would be no means of conveying warmth throughout our world.

Peter tells us that the manipulation of gross ether is the raw material of the spirit people as wood, iron and clay are ours, so that ether must be a connecting link between the realm physical, the realm of energy and the realm of spirit.

In our world our senses only permit us to perceive a very limited range of etheric vibration. That extra vibrations exist we know by the limited range of light waves that our eyes permit us to see, or the limited range of sounds that are audible to our ears.

We know of the presence of the ultra-violet, infra-red, unknown and X-rays, which our eyes cannot receive. We know there are extensions of sound vibrations at both ends of the scale which our ears cannot record. Thus human reception is extremely limited as compared with the known range of experiences that might be ours were we to possess extra perceptory senses.

The fuller life open to spirit-people can be more clearly visualised if we use the argument that, as our soul body and mind leave the prison cell of the physical body, an extended etheric sensory perception naturally follows. This argument is supported by our knowledge of the spectrum which tells us that outside our very limited perception there is a vast field of ordered frequencies with potentialities permitting another form of tuned-in existence to receive and use those potentialities.

This modern knowledge presents a picture that would have been an inconceivable fantasy to the scientist of a century ago. May it not be that this glimpse we are seeing of the realm etheric provides a definite postulate for much that the spirit-guides could only hint at obscurely in the past.

Peter refers many times to 'bound ether', that is, ether associated with a given condition. When it loses that boundness or character, decay sets in. Here again is a firm argument. Compare a piece of tough oak with another piece that is in the process of decay. Some change has taken place, in which the piece of live tough substance has been transformed into a condition of crumbling dust. Some quality has left the original oak. Its character, its personality has gone; and there is no organisation within it. This change is consistent with Peter's explanation. For if we bear in mind our knowledge of the construction of matter and the importance of the vehicle of ether for its being and motivation, we arrive at the thesis that, as the forces within the atom disseminate, the ether loses its character or boundness; and so the vibrant organised mass comprising the piece of oak loses its character and its organisation. The individualised ether in the fullness of time changes from the condition of bound ether into free ether; and so this piece of oak loses its character and decays.

Another simile may assist towards visualising the realm etheric. We are told that all matter (including our dense bodies) is subject to the ponderable inter-penetration of ether. The living sponge at the bottom of the sea provides a good illustration. There is the pressure of the water, equal in intensity all around it; and penetrating throughout its whole being. Thus, we have to view our bricks and mortar, our chairs and tables, our dense bodies, as sponges in the etheric sea. This may be hard for many to conceive or accept, and yet it is in perfect line with our knowledge and Peter's observations.

As all matter is a state of vibration formed from etheric potentials, and each matter component possesses its own individual vibration, yet still allowing co-operation and association with other components, so there can be no rigid dividing line separating one piece of matter from another, solid from fluid, fluid from gas, or physical substance from substances built by spirit action, such as ectoplasm.

We are continually discovering both slower and quicker vibrations or frequencies than those previously known. We are learning how by different amalgamations of electrons, protons and their associated forms, we are able to obtain substances with new potentials. What is there then to debar the probability that there is no borderline between that of matter as we know it, and dense or gross ether. If we admit this probability, we draw a step nearer to realising how discarnate intelligences are able to manipulate dense ether for various kinds of manifestations, i.e. ectoplasm, materialisations, voice instruments, rods of strength, and so on.

Just as man is able, through his knowledge of atomic structures, to form new agencies, so are the spirit-people, with their greater wisdom and their closer affinity to the realm etheric, able to build up, for a period, a materialised form or an etheric structure to carry out the purpose of the moment.

As energy is the foundation of matter, and as man is able by directing that energy to accomplish his set purpose, so does it become tenable that spirit-people can direct similar energy or other qualities of that energy to the etheric potential; and so create substances or instruments to accomplish their purpose. When they withdraw the energy, in a similar manner to man cutting off an electric current, it is understandable that the created substance or instrument will disintegrate back into the ether from whence it came. This readily explains Peter's references to the dissolution of ectoplasmic material.

Worlds are still being formed in the solar system; and as we know, they are also immersed in an etheric surround—otherwise we should not be able to see them—the assumption is tenable that they are subject to similar etheric activity and influence.

It is perhaps permissible to remark here that as we know each solar system to be the ordered, revolution of bodies around a nucleus (the sun in our case) we thereby have a vastly enlarged example of atomic movement. Since the same principle of ordered movement applies to the components of an atom as to the components of a solar system, it is surely pertinent that ether and its potentials are the "father and mother" of both.

As the reader keeps the sense of this in mind, so will he be able to understand more readily Peter's explanations, which permit the curtain to be lifted a little and allow a glimpse into that which has been for so long an impenetrable mystery, cloaked in obscurity by the vague term "astral" or "cosmic" chemistry.

Peter's observations followed this question:

Question[3]: "You have spoken a great deal about ether and it would be most helpful if you can tell us more about it.[4] We recognise the vast

---

3. Unless otherwise stated, all the questions to the Guide were from the author.

4. The discussions on this topic were some of the last to be held.

scope of the subject, but perhaps it would clear the air if you could give some definition of the classifications of what is bound ether and gross ether."

Peter: "Except for one or two points, it is a mighty big task. In referring to 'bound either' and 'dense ether' I think those terms are synonymous—they can be interchanged.

"If we were referring to Bound Ether in relation to the medium's form, we should be referring to that part which is the etheric body. It is what one might term differentiated ether. It has character because it is in a different state of motion or vibration from that of the free ether. Bound ether can be considered as like the air you put into a bottle, it is confined there whilst the free ether would be comparable with the atmosphere outside. It has no character of its own apart from its essential make-up except in such cases as where it is related to certain areas, such as hilly districts, heavily tenanted quarters and the places which are beautiful or foul, in which case the air and ether would become affected.

"Bound ether maintains the life of its material counter-part so long as that life serves a useful purpose; and decay sets in when the ether becomes loosened. It reduces its vibration and as it slackens it gradually becomes absorbed into the free ether, very much like the slow removal of the stopper from our bottle of air. As this bound ether disintegrates so does the physical counterpart crumble. Now can you see the purpose of it?

"That is bound ether—it is ether which has character—the character of the object with which it is associated. It is the egg to the pudding—the binding, do you see?

"Ether, as a whole, fills the whole of space. If it were possible to fill it, that is in the sense that you would use the term. Space is limitless, as you know, but I must use terms which are readily understandable by you. It is not quite the same ether as you know on earth, because the earth itself bears an ether with character. To you, as to all other things upon earth, it is without character, in the same way as the negative polarity of your electricity is of the same polarity as that of the earth.

"Ether being characterless can be impressed by the minds of man. It will take on, almost permanently, conditions of its environment; because remember ether is ponderable in that it does not shift or move.

You can compare it with a jelly. If you tap it on one side, the vibration is felt at the other—the whole wobbles. You cannot measure ether at the moment. Scientists have tried to measure ether drift, the drift of the sea of ether past the earth; they were on the right road, in a way, when they sought the highest points, but they did not go high enough. They would have to ascend to at least a height of eighty miles above the earth's surface, and then it would perhaps be impossible to measure with their present-day instruments. The earth carries its own ether, but it soon becomes isolated from the sea of ether. That is a good term— "the sea of ether". It fills all space. It interpenetrates everything. It is denser than material for it has no holes or spaces in it. It has no chemical composition. It is more solid than the earth—in reference to its own environment and not yours. You know how you walk through water. As you walk through it up to your waist you push it aside. Well, you do almost the same in ether; but you do not create a space behind you.

Water and you cannot occupy the same space at the same time, but ether can and does. But you see what I mean. It is equally as solid and real as are your bricks and stones."

Question: "A glass of water is permeated by ether. We conclude the ether content within the glass of water differs from that without?"

Peter: "Yes, of course. That is why I have referred to it as bound ether."

Question: "It has weight?"

Peter: "Its weight is so great that you cannot measure it, because all your standards and measurements are taken within the etheric mass. You see, it is so vast, and it so fills all space that you do not and cannot comprehend it.

"We cannot get outside of it to weigh it. Ether has a frequency, and when a change is made within the ether, material bodies are formed. What takes place is a change of frequency in the immediate environment of the material body in such a way that it is different from its apparent source.

"It is operated on by the intelligent mind in a case of usage of the natural processes by the higher developed mind. A man operates upon it by his thoughts; and the level of those thoughts is determined by the quality in which they are radiated. And so you have, as it were, etheric thought strata—the strata or layers of different combinations or rates

of vibrations. If you cut through the surface of the earth, you would
see a sort of graining, marking the different periods during the earth's
formation. It would be precisely the same if you could take a large
knife and slice through the lower stratas of ether, that is those strata
associated and bound by the earth's area of influence.

"You can tune in to these strata according to your own mental
processes. They are, as it were, mental records wherein are stored the
thoughts of the ages. They are the very source of knowledge—
memory, experience, to which the whole of man's and nature's
evolutionary processes have subscribed.

"If you think of water and its natural characteristics, you have
something of the idea of ether. You see! But not quite the same thing.
It fills everywhere it flows, although, of course, there are wider
differences. Consider it as being constantly in a state of motion without
the whole of itself moving; the movement within the whole being
aided, fluctuating, as it were, according to the pulls it receives from
the thought-force finding its level or strata according to its intention.
The thought gravitates to that stratum most in harmony with it for good
or for ill."

Question: "With regard to ether and health! I believe that we can do
a great deal for ourselves by consciously tapping etheric vitality. Can
you give us any idea of that?"

Peter: "Yes, of course you can. That is right: but first of all, you
have to convince yourself that such a thing is possible. You must
remember always the trinity of man's make-up, the triune constituted
by his physical body, his soul body and his spirit. I have already told
you of the soul body which carries on certain processes of mind
control and operates in relation to all things concerning the natural
realm, within which realm comes the realm of ether.

"If there is complete understanding between the mind which is of
the soul, in this instance—and the brain, one is able (referring to the
soul) to demand the necessary health and power, which is in effect a
sympathetic vibration; and so incorporate it into oneself and ultimately
into the body. For remember this, that before a mould manifests
physically it exists etherically, i.e. within the soul. God loves the man
who, when fortune goes against him, keeps his own fortress unharmed,
i.e. he retains all his physical potentialities. God has not forsaken that
man. A human physical failing is a disharmony within the soul or a

lack of its wisdom. It seems a far cry from ether, but it is not. It is not even next door—it shares the same room."

Question: "You have said that health and illness are first built in the soul body. Can you explain to us how it is that, say, a healthy physical body obtains a complaint such as headache or nerve trouble?"

Peter: "It is so simple, yet I cannot say yes or no. You will probably think I am, what you might term, 'going a long way round'. If you can fix in your mind the idea that the soul existed before the body (you will not dispute that) there you have the answer to your question. The soul is by no means perfect, in so far as its desire for life is concerned; and it likes to enjoy the lusts of the flesh whatever they may be. If you get headaches, they may be due to several things. One might be due to over-indulgence, which is a form of unwisdom or, if it is more deep-seated, it is a deficiency within the constructive powers of the soul to complete the building into the physical of a durable nervous sensorium in regard to that particular part. Now you want to know what this relationship has to healing.

"First of all, you have to have faith in the healing power. You have to be conscious of the existence of that power. You see, all of that which contributes to life is linked so closely together, that when you start to talk of one thing, you are not far distant before you have crossed the bar into the next realm. It is difficult unless you can envisage the whole thing completely."

Question: "That implies that harmonies and disharmonies, health and illness, are built up first in the soul body, therefore the soul dominates the physical body?"

Peter: "There you have it perfectly."

Question: "I am puzzling how those conditions can be built within the soul body in the first place?"

Peter: "We go back to our first words, to what I have told you about breathing—rhythmic breathing—not only in relation to the balance of air but primarily to the supply of bound ether associated with that air for the maintenance of the etheric body through which the soul works. You can by thought-control direct the temperature of the body; but, in the main, because of your form of living, the body is more susceptible to temperature changes than it would be if you lived more naturally. I told you, you were paddling on the foreshore that separates your known from the unknown. You say the earth is real and concrete. It is concrete but not real. Only those things that are permanent are real. It is we who stand upon the shore of reality facing you; and you are facing reality, but the distances are so vast that you cannot take it in in one glance. But we are talking about ether—the common denominator that separates the visible from the invisible (invisible to you), separating the perceptible from the imperceptible."

Question: "Is ether the vehicle of the spirit world and essential for the existence of spirit people?"

Peter: "No, not in the sense in which we have been speaking of it. It is the realm or the material of the soul. It is what I have called the material with which the soul works. It is its clay and stone."

Question: "You say that in the manipulation of gross ether you are in your element. If gross ether is your clay or stone, are you not akin to it, or related to it?"

Peter: "Would you relate yourself to a clay building? Would you consider yourself a part of the bricks of this house or the coal that you burn in your fire? The same applies; and, do not forget, the word 'gross' is used, which gives a different significance. Many beautiful paintings that you see upon walls are of similar material to the clay within your bricks. It is the application that makes all the difference. I have used the word 'ether' generally for all things when referring to the various substances through which we work and which we use, although there are perhaps other names you would give it; but my answers would then have become too involved. Where I have specified, I have said the 'gross' ether or the 'bound' ether, whereas perhaps other people would use other names. Dense ether is a gradation of the gross but similar."

Question: "Referring to psychic rods—and their etheric conductors! Can you tell us how the voltage you spoke of is applied to them?"

Peter: "Well, it is the same principle as those employed by you, with this difference: that it has the same qualities but it is of such a frequency that you cannot record it. You have upon earth what is known as low-frequency and high-frequency current. Low-frequency travels through the mass of the conductor but the high-frequencies travel only upon the surface. As the frequency increases, it is taken further from the centre of the material towards the surface—which I believe is termed the 'skin effect'. If you were to link yourself with high-frequency (not a high voltage) you would find it would burn but seldom kill because of its 'skin' effect, showing a tendency to travel rather more within the etheric part of the conductor than in the material. It is an easier passage for it; so therefore, if you could increase the range of its frequency intentionally it would become further removed from the conductor. You almost have it in the case of what you term 'radiated frequency'. Through the coils they use for its inductive qualities, the frequencies travel almost clear of the physical conductor. And so you go on; in the case of radiotelegraphy you have its radiation across distances via the ether. The disturbance at the terminal, or what you have termed the antennae—aerial—agitates the ether throughout. We carry it beyond the stage that you have reached by bringing it within the scope of those voltages spoken of in connection with the psychic conductors, or what you have termed 'rods'. Do you see, and cannot you see that with the advance of your knowledge of radio activity you are coming to closer contact with understanding the principle of etheric energy?"

Question: "May I refer to the talk on ether which we had last time? There are one or two points which perhaps you would elucidate a little more. You spoke about the zones of ether that carry thought and experience. The first question is: Do the spirit-people draw from and contribute to those same zones?"

Peter: "On the one hand, they draw from, and, on the other hand, they influence those zones which are available to the mind of man. Their own intelligence, however, is drawn from zones or strata far higher and beyond the receptivity of their minds. For instance, in the case of making revelations to the earth—you call it new inventions—they are placed within handy reach of the mind so attuned to receive them. What use man makes of them thereafter is man's responsibility."

Question: "The wisdom that you have. Is there a sort of stratum or zone of wisdom for record purposes that you can draw from? Is it the same as that you have just mentioned?"

Peter: "It is the same but, of course, there is a residuary intelligence—that which we can draw upon from our own strength, but anything beyond that we must have recourse to those zones of supply. Remember they are limited. We cannot reach out for everything any more than you can, but only according to our illumination. You must consider the realm which we are discussing as being ever present, there is no past and no future—just experience."

Question: "Do the zones only contain the experiences of the immediate present and of the past?"

Peter: "They contain in the records everything from the commencement of evolution insofar as the material and physical realms are concerned. Simply, before there was matter, life existed within the ether; and those records are the same now as then, and always will be. The other zones are progressive—they are constantly being added to from the experiences of the past, so that when the mould is full and the physical pattern complete, you have the end of that evolutionary cycle. Can you see?"

Question: "Could you ever reach the end of a cycle of that nature?"

Peter: "Yes, of course. You do not think so because that is not within the ken of the children of today. Your geologists, however, will tell you that during certain periods of the earth's history, there has been some unexplainable catastrophe which has occurred with great suddenness. 52,000 years is approximately the period of one of these cycles."

Question: "And these catastrophes—are they arranged or do they evolve?"

Peter: "They are arranged by nature. There is intelligence behind nature. I have been instructing you in that. I have spoken of an over-soul which is not individualised. That is the difference between man and animals in its wider and larger aspect. With man you have an individualised or polarised spirit intelligence. The use of these two words no doubt will help all your readers to understand my meaning. The egotist will understand 'individualised' and the scientist will understand 'polarised'.

"Man being an individualised or polarised spirit, each is different from his neighbour, but in all nature and especially in the case of animals, you have not that difference. If you study one only of a particular type, say a lion or a tiger, you study the species. They have no individuality. They have what is known as the over-soul which copies them as a species, but not as individuals. You say, 'I have a cat or a dog which definitely has an individuality!' My answer to that is 'yes' because of their close association with the human being. Who can say that at some time in the future that cat or dog you fondle so much will not earn the right to become your brother and that it will stand on two legs rather than four? It is not beyond the realms of possibility, but I am not going to express any opinion now."

Question: "With reference to bound ether. Can you associate that with the physical construction of atoms, or can you explain the relationship of ether to the atom and its component parts? Does that association create the boundness of ether?"

Peter: "It is easy to ask the question but difficult to discuss something which for you does not exist. It is the nearest approach to the real thing that I can see, but there may be others more qualified than I to give an analysis of what an atom looks like. Imagine a dewy morning with many gossamer threads: hanging at the end of each thread there is a little scintillating globule of water, and if you examine one closely you will find that it is constantly moving. Can you picture that? That is what atoms look like reaching out into infinity! Have you seen a waterspout? Well, that is like the atom in action within ether. It is a whirl of energy; and it is its speed or its vibration or its frequency of motion that gives it its peculiarity. It has a positively charged centre, 'proton' (that is your word for it). Now you have a positively charged body. Very well—that is not happy by itself, it is unbalanced; so it attracts to itself negative charges or what you call electrons. Very apt names, I would agree. As soon as it has collected about it sufficient to neutralise and to render it satisfied, it has no further concern, no interest in anything without itself. Do you see? During this process it is still whirling round, and according to the nature of its centre so are governed the numbers of electrons necessary to render it static. Almost immediately following that, there is set up within itself a state of stress within its ether. This is due to torque which characterises the ether or etheric medium through which these natural forces can operate. That ether becomes individualised because of the strain. It has a zone or sphere, or influence around it which makes it similar to our globule of water.

"In a few words you have seen the creation of the atom as directed by some superior mind in the beginning, and it was not until that action took place that you had anything living physically. That was the work of God in the first day of creation. The first 'day' was of a length or period of 52,000 years; and the six days it took to create the earth was actually six times that time. A truer story was never written if only we had the right mind to read it."

Question: "What was the implication of the gossamer thread?"

Peter: "They stretch into infinity. Now you take in imagination a bunch of those threads with globules I mentioned attached; and whirl them around your head in such a way that, in a manner of speaking, they are equally spaced. You would have them revolving, with you as the pivot at the centre. The invisible connection between that power and the atom is intelligence, which is concentrated at the centre. It is, if you like, a polarised radiation similar to that radiated by man— individual man."

Question: "Regarding decay, you told us that ether loses its characteristics. Is the initial movement towards decay from the ether or from the forces within the atom?"

Peter: "It is due to your being within the sphere of influence of the larger atom which is the earth and of the forces pushing towards its centre. There is definitely a pressure. And this pressure is great. All the same there is bound to be a reaction otherwise you would have a destruction of time, in fact the earth would not exist. You must remember that a given action always calls forth an opposite, or reaction; but although the opposite reaction is oft-times observed in other things, there is reaction."

Question (Mr Hart): "Do material and ether occupy the same space at the same time? An article develops, or has with it, its own characteristic ether which remains bound to the object and keeps it intact. According to our science, no two materials can occupy the same space at the same time; but I now find that material and energy or force can occupy the same space all the same time, Therefore, do ether and material occupy the same space at the same time?"

Peter: "Yes, definitely."

Question (Mr Hart): "Science, I think, is beginning to realise that the true life is spirit. You are living the true life? . . . "

Peter: "No, I am not. I am still living a life just as speculative as yours; but we are one jump ahead of you. We have gathered, too, facts which are a part of reality and which show you, as a comparison, the enormity of the findings of the great journey that yet lies before us. We have a greater awareness of the reality; and we have a better understanding of the unity of life. That is why we are here to bring it home to you."

104

Question (Mr Hart): "Life is spirit; and life on earth is merely the existence of spirit in material. You, as spirit, exist without material. That is the difficult part for us to understand. Is our existence in material merely for experience, to improve our life, to progress upon our path-way?"

Peter: "As blinkers are to a horse, so with a physical body is your understanding upon earth. It can only see a little bit ahead. It has to be blinded to all else otherwise it becomes fearful. But the horse wishes to shed its blinkers; and because you would know, you feel that also. It is the feeling that any normal being has, the craving to know what is outside those 'blinkers': the trouble is the finding of the key which will open the way. Yet the finding of the key is so simple that it is profound. You have the right idea, and we will pursue it further."

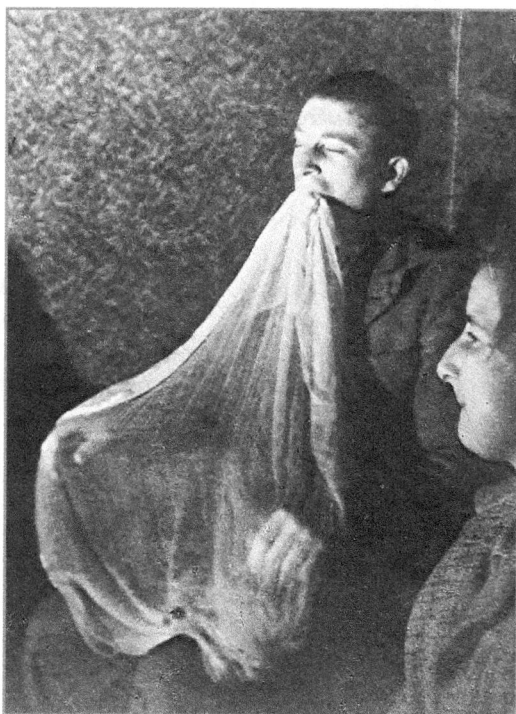

PLATE 6
Ectoplasmic material, Grade 2. (See Chap. XII.)
Infra-red photograph by J. McCulloch .

CHAPTER X

THE DEVELOPMENT OF PHYSICAL MEDIUMSHIP

ANY approach towards understanding the "mechanics" of psychic phenomena demands a study of mediumship and its development.

The science of mediumship in all its forms presents so wide a subject that no attempt is made here to deal with it generally or extensively, but rather to confine investigation to that branch, of mediumship known as "physical".

Broadly speaking, mediumship can be divided into two sections; firstly, for want of a better word, "mental" mediumship and, secondly, physical mediumship. While mental mediumship can be dissociated from physical mediumship the latter embraces both.

Physical mediumship presents definite acts, which must be performed through the operation of law-governed forces. Such acts are today described as supernormal because as yet man does not possess the knowledge of the manner of their performance.

Physical mediumship may be termed that which evolves ordered movement of matter, the production of sounds and voices, the creation of ectoplasmic structures and the materialisation of spirit-people in physical form, as well as other activities.

A great deal of theory has already been advanced relative to mediumship, but I am hesitant to add further ideas without substantiating proof to support them. In the past the difficulty has been that we have been presented with completed acts of supernormal character without our having any proven knowledge to assist us to understand the mechanics involved. It is as if a primitive man were shown a television radio receiving set in operation and then with his limited vocabulary and mental outlook tried to learn, in a few steps, the processes involved in producing the result. One can well imagine the difficulty a radio exponent would experience in attempting such explanation.

We are in much the same position as the primitive man in our efforts to appreciate the science of psychic activity. With the passing of time and the study of authenticated records, we have been able to determine certain provable facts by observation and comparison. The new theses advanced by Peter are in line with these facts, though the explanation of the manner of their production may be different from previously conceived hypotheses.

In the past, we have been too free in constructing our theory upon general and ambiguous statements by the operating spirit intelligences. We must not blame the Guides because of their ambiguity, for it may well be that faced with our questionings they were in the same position as the radio exponent just referred to, who might tell his primitive man that the pictures and sounds from radio television were—"pictures and sounds travelling on the winds" as being the nearest understandable formula the limited mental equipment of the questioner could appreciate. Therefore, it is probable that the Guides have in the past taken the line of least resistance and satisfied us, for the time being, by abstract references to "voice-boxes", "psychic rods" and the like.

We are today in much the same position, but we have advanced a little; and even a lay mind can comprehend the explanations Peter has given. Some of his statements affecting the mechanics of supernormal action are not as yet provable by man, but they do possess the merit of being probable and logical— other statements are definitely provable. It is suggested that when the probable but as yet unprovable statements are related to those that are provable, there is a chain of connected reasoned ideas which explain in an elementary way much that has been a complete mystery. Our ability to comprehend Peter's explanations has been made easier through the recent advance of human knowledge affecting radio activity, which provides parallels of thought facilitating our comprehension.

The view is taken that when with different mediums comparable results occur, and spaced apart in time and place, similar in structure or effect, then there is reason to deduce that such results are common qualities of such mediumship. For example, with Jack Webber I was able to provide photographic evidence of a number of phases of physical phenomena. By themselves they are unique and of interest; but when similar photographic results are obtained through a number of other mediums (if only one or two to the present time)—then it is reasonable to accept that evidence as being a common quality of such mediumship: and thus, what might be regarded as "freakish" becomes normal reasoned performances.

The proof of a statement or the probability of a statement being true may not be at once obvious from the matter immediately pertinent to the statement, as the proof, or probable proof, is only discernible by comparison with the evidence relating to another aspect of the subject. For example, it would not be easy to comprehend the theory advanced for the development of physical mediumship without understanding the powers, functions and limitations of the Guide in control of the medium; or why a representation made to the Guide may not be permissible without knowing the functions of the controls, i.e. the potentials of bound ether, the grades of ectoplasm, etc. Therefore, the reader is requested to take the whole theory advanced as a coherent structure; and not to isolate any one view from the whole text.

As a preliminary to the recordings and explanations that follow, advice from Arnold Clare's Guide for aiding development of physical mediumship is given, in the hope that it may benefit those seeking such development; and also as a contribution to the study of mediumship, which, after all, is the stepping-off point to the study of phenomena.

Broadly speaking, there are two conditions of trance: "partial trance" and "complete trance". To the lay mind that has not experienced any state of trance, it is difficult to define precisely in words what "partial trance" signifies.

It is one of those conditions that has to be experienced to be comprehended. Suffice it to say, that in partial trance the medium is conscious of what is taking place; a degree of normality is present, though the psychic activity taking place is supernormal. Examples: A medium speaking in partial trance may be giving a free flow of oratory and of ideas relative to a subject of which the medium knows little or nothing, and yet be conscious of the words that he or she is uttering. Physical mediums (as with Miss Goligher, occasionally with Jack Webber, Marjorie Crandon and others) may be aware of the very act of the movement of objects. Indeed, they can actually see the movement taking place, and are able, too, to converse with voices produced via a trumpet suspended in the air in front of them. The condition of partial trance may be said to vary from one per cent to ninety-nine per cent.

Complete trance is far more easily explained, for then the medium has no conscious knowledge of anything at all, not even thought—in other words, the medium is in a state of unconsciousness.

As indicated above, physical mediumship is possible with either complete or partial trance-voice mediums like Valiantine and Mrs Perriman were, to all intents and purposes, normal while their mediumship was functioning.

A developing medium therefore should not be discouraged if he does not attain the condition of complete trance. It is on record that a photograph was obtained with ectoplasm covering the head and face of Jack Webber while he was fully conscious of what was taking place. Nevertheless, for physical work, a condition of complete trance is generally necessary, especially in the early stages of the development.

Peter commented on this:

Peter: "It is very uncommon for voice or other forms of physical phenomena to be manifested except in a condition of absolute trance. When such does occur, the mediumship is a freak mediumship."

Peter gave further advice which now follows on a method he advocated for the development of physical mediumship. It should be observed that this information, and indeed all the information concerning the various matters on which he spoke, was obtained as the result of numerous sittings and discussions. It has therefore been collated and presented with as little interference with his words as possible. Some redundancy cannot be avoided as often a new thought has been presented in a repetition of the same subject.

Preliminary to a sitting, Peter has advised.

Peter: "The medium should look forward to each sitting of the developing circle with anticipation and eagerness. It is most important that the day on which the sitting takes place should be one of complete preparation, anticipation and happy thoughts, clean linen and things like that. This, it will be found, is simple to learn in a very short time.

"It is better that meat should be taken sparingly. You should not sit too soon after eating. Whilst at least three hours should elapse between a meal and sitting, you should never sit hungry. Very light refreshment may be taken if it is necessary in between. We do not impose any restrictions, but we advise that less meat be eaten. The wise thing is that there should be no 'Do nots' or 'Dos' because if there were there would be danger of one swinging too much to one side or the other.

"The wise man's or woman's economy should be so trained to accept any call in reason made upon it. The meat you eat is not important, it is the method of your eating it, and why you eat it. It would be wise to deny it at first, but there is no need to feel upset because you do eat it. At least, limit it on the day of the sitting."[1]

A summary of other suggestions by Peter is as follows:

Peter: "Before sitting in the developing circle the medium should sit quietly for a while in the séance room and engage in rhythmic breathing exercises. This exercise should be conducted with the medium's mind and body completely relaxed.

"The air should be inhaled and exhaled through the nostrils only and not through the mouth. The breathing should be natural, excessive inhalation is a deterrent; but it is important that the exhalation should be complete. Stress is laid on this point: every effort should be made to expel as much breath from the lungs as possible.

"In addition to this exercise just prior to the sitting, it would be beneficial for the medium to engage in this exercise daily whenever opportunity presents itself. He should then relax his body completely and the mind should be detached from normal thought occupation."

On a subsequent occasion, after the above had been read out to Peter, he added:

Peter: "That is right. Perhaps it would be better for me to say something more about that, because by intelligent co-operation so much more value is to be obtained.

"When you breathe in always through the nostrils, you are not only inhaling the air but also the ether stream—the free ether. Now that ether is characterless, it has no character of itself; but as it passes through the sieve, as it were—the 'sieve' I said—it receives its character impressed upon it by the mentality of the breather. This is important. As the nostrils are the filters for the atmosphere necessary for the well-being of the body, so are they the filters for the ether rejecting all things that are inimical to the individual, whilst passing on those things that are good. But it works both ways, for it rejects also those things which cannot be appreciated by the individual—that is, things spiritual.

---

1. In actual practice physical mediums do avoid meals for a time prior to sitting, except perhaps for a cup of tea. They are invariably good trenchermen and meat-eaters.

"Therefore, in this practice with inhalation and exhalation the mind should be gently focused upon the 'all greatness' of the spirit. It has the effect of creating those conditions which, individually, we have to create ourselves.

"The way of achievement by this method, intelligently applied, ensures permanency and good health, which, you will notice, many mediums lack."

Peter was asked to give further information as to what is received and what is rejected as the ether stream is inhaled.

Peter: "The best way to answer is this. The ether stream which is taken into the system through breathing is characterless in itself. When it has been breathed in through the normal act of inhalation, it is impressed by the thought and character of the individual. That is understood. Therefore, by rendering that etheric content more potent, more vital, through control of thought, in breathing, you can transform that stream of ether into a veritable dynamic force. We have already spoken of the etheric body and the soul body—they both depend upon the ether inhaled with ordinary breathing for their vitality and sustenance. The more it is impressed with noble thoughts consciously directed, the more will the sub-conscious mind be brought into line with things spiritual. Therefore, instead of having a part of your 'household', as it were, against you, you make of the soul a strong ally—the three of you (physical, spiritual and soul bodies) working all together, as a whole. For it must be remembered that the soul is the repository of all the experiences to do with the natural world and that world only. Therefore, its desires are primitive; it is selfish. It is controlled by two strict laws, that of attraction and that of repulsion—which is oft-times the progenitor of hatred. That is one part.

"By breathing rhythmically, the physical body profits from the air you breathe because it is taken in steadily; and therefore, the heart motion is more regular with the steady supply of oxygen. The ether which is inhaled with it does not go into the lungs. It is retained by a sieve. The sieve is contained at the root of the nose, and it is from there it is dispersed. There it receives the impression of the thought intention—so far as psychic work is concerned. That is most important. Not only is it important in the way of physical health, but it also gives a greater etheric vitality. I think this answers the other part of the question.

"When you breathe, it is to breathe with intention and to say, 'with each breath I breathe the spirit of life', 'Each breath makes me free', 'Each breath makes me stronger spiritually and physically'. It is not altogether what you would term auto-suggestion, although it is true there is an element of that; but the idea is to impress the breath with your character, your idea of the moment. You can use it for weal or woe."

Peter has been speaking of the "three of you", the Physical, Spiritual and Soul bodies. These should not be confused with the etheric or astral bodies. Peter has given the following definitions of the etheric and soul bodies—it should be observed that his conception of the soul body is at variance with the orthodox conception of the soul.

Peter: "Etheric body. The etheric body is only seen surrounding the physical body as an iridescent silver extension. It is the reservoir for the physical body—its store-house.

"Soul body. The soul body is that part which belongs essentially to nature. It is primitive. By nature I mean the natural world, as associated with all the vast experiences, from the mineral up to the vegetable and finally animal kingdoms, to be associated with man. It has all the experiences garnered in from those sources, therefore it has of itself no spiritual character. It is the driving force of the body in relationship to the animal realm, and 'man' is the only enemy, that man has as an individual. He is the one who drives you on through desire only. He is the repository of memory."

On commenting that the above explanation differed from the orthodox interpretations of the Soul, Peter added:

Peter: "That is where man has stumbled along, The spirit cannot be seen except where it animates the soul body with which it has been associated for so long. The soul body is the exact replica of the physical, but the spirit is not contained in form. The spirit is free. You cannot see the spirit; for, if you were able to see the spirit visually, you would see the end of all things; but when I say I can see you in a physical sense, I see your soul body.

"Astral body. The astral body proper is the soul body—that which you see clairvoyantly. It is the spirit which animates it, as the astral animates the physical. Actually, the astral body is the exact replica of the physical in every detail whereas the etheric body is not."

Question: "Is ether a separate component from atmosphere? Can you give us any formula applicable to ether?"

Peter: "The chair in which you sit will remain a chair for so long as the ether associated with the material of which it is made does not disintegrate or disseminate. The ether is associated and takes a form of individuality from that with which it is associated. You have several sorts of air do not forget. You have air in one part which is pure; you have another which is less pure; and in other districts where there are mountains you have it rarefied. All are totally different—but yet of the same substance. It is the same with ether. Ether cannot be described any better than as a huge jelly substance—if a change takes place on one side of it, that change is transferred throughout the whole. The same applies with individual ethers: i.e. those others associated with different matters and substances. With the air, you have ether in its highest form; it is finer as it bears all the potentialities of life. It does not become impressed with the character, however, either for good or for evil until it reaches a certain point in man's economy: i.e. the sieve of which I spoke, situated at the base of the nose. I use the term 'sieve' because that is self-explanatory. As air is necessary for the maintenance of the physical body, so is ether necessary for the maintenance of the soul body; and as air makes it necessary for the physical body to work to contain the soul body, so does ether maintain the soul body as a fitting vehicle for the spirit. You will understand that I am trying to explain infinite things with finite language."

A question was asked: if the rapid and quick breathing, at times noticed with development, was an aid or not.

Peter replied:

Peter: "That is wrong. That is harmful to the medium who has to be artificially stimulated by the controls. We are not the controls [see section dealing with the function of the Guide] but then, you see, it has to be done by them to achieve contacts for the work on which they are engaged. It should not be a part of the development. It is a part which is artificial, and it is harmful to the medium. It is better for him to practice rhythmic breathing; which would be a definite aid to himself.

"The method I have given to you is most valuable; and almost, I should say, essential. As you practice it, you contact sources of wisdom where we can talk: we cannot approach where the breathing is speeded up. There is too much noise in that case, and we must have quiet within the medium. Development is quick if you do it that way"

It will help the reader to understand Peter's intentions if the section dealing with the functions of the Guide and the Controls are considered in relation to the above and also to the observations that follow.

There are two forms of control: (a) the control from without and (b) the control from within. The control from without being the control by thought "plugged in" to the medium's etheric condition. The control from within being the possession of the medium's body and faculties by a control. Peter instanced that "John", another of Arnold Clare's directing spirit operators or Guides, could change with him instantly and with ease. On being asked how this was effected he said:

Peter: "It is following on the present question. The idea of the system of which I have tried to tell you, is that we do not take control of the physical body of the medium in the way that direct control can be ours. The control is not of the body. It is a control as from a distance—that is to say, we do not control the physical economy of the medium but do so simply by a method of 'plugging in'. The trance state is induced by the medium. For a change over, all I have to do is remove my thought concentration and John to exert his."

Peter then gave the following analogy. His words should be borne in mind when considering it—that the trance state is induced by the medium thereby issuing an invitation for the entry of the Guide.

Peter: "For example: I come into your house, I have freedom of movement, but to your private room I have no access. It is out of my range of freedom. It is, as it should be between good friends, that I recognize it as your sanctuary and would not enter therein because it is a place which is private to you. But if I wish to speak to you, I knock on the door, or ring you on your house telephone."

A question was asked as to whether it is advisable to hold the breath for a short period. Peter replied, that whilst that practice was good for normal breathing exercises, it was not advisable for the exercise of psychic development, and added:

Peter: "Supposing you were waiting here to make contact with me, you would not hold your breath then. But whilst it is good out of the developing chair in the normal practice, let me impress this upon you.

For development do not over inhale for that is dangerous to you. Just sufficient to fill the lungs."

Question: "Do you advise any number of sitters for the developing circle."

Peter: "The fewer the better."

Question: "Is the trance state aided by our spirit controls or Guides?"

Peter: "That is true. That is why in some cases it varies. Many are rather temporary and unsatisfactory. The movements of the medium are awkward—there is much contortion—there is much noise and there is not an easily rapid transfer of thought and movement between the medium, now entranced, and the controller. I have said many times 'We are masters of originality'. We can find out alternative ways to produce the same result. Well, in the case where the trance of a medium is assisted and aided by the control, it is because the medium knows no better and the control, oft-times, has no patience. I tell you this in all seriousness—there should not be allowed into the sanctum of anyone, persons of another world; and the wise one will not allow it. You are a kingdom unto yourself, the autocracy of which should not be shared by another, no matter how dear or close that one may be."

Following this observation, Peter was asked:

Question: "Most developing mediums hope for a state of absolute trance; should he attain it how can he distinguish who shall take possession or determine the degree or quality of possession?"

Peter: "You must accept the control or not accept it. The fault is not with the one with high ideals. It is a case of seeking wise leadership or not: it is often a case of getting results quickly without learning first through the wisdom of others."

This answer not being too clear, Peter was asked further.

Question: "Assume that I am sitting for the state of complete trance—I am willing to surrender myself for work by the control—I should welcome it—but how am I to retain that individuality when I am sitting for complete trance? How am I to distinguish whether a control is beneficial or not if my consciousness has lapsed?"

Peter: "We sit here with the control that you allow. You would not be able to judge, but those with you would judge. There should be no difficulty in recognising the nature of the control. You would know if the movements are awkward and there is lack of correct control. In the right way there is complete co-ordination; movement is natural and normal."

Question: "Then the responsibility rests with those sitting with the developing medium to differentiate whether the control is desirable or otherwise?"

Peter: "Yes. For instance, you see, every method of sitting in a developing circle is apropos to 'hidden mist'. Those who most desire it may miss it, although they have all the equipment; and the one you least expect to receive it, does receive it, though he may not be mentally equipped to provide a useful instrument."

Question: "Does not a trance state allow the entry of someone else?"

Peter: "That is a point which is going to cause a great deal of discussion; for you must remember that development up to the present stage is built upon a tradition (of development) dating from the early days when things were a little more crude. Well, the mind of the developing medium has witnessed this before and he oft-times goes through the same contortions, because his self-consciousness has become impressed. The point is this—in development—a medium reaches out for someone to take control. This is not the best way to sit. There should be no endeavour to reach out for control of the body: there should be a 'sitting in silence' for the feel of a personality, which is not due to direct control, but the infusing into his own mind of an impelling thought such as those which are now reaching you.

"I do not deny that the control or the system that has been used for development of psychic faculties does produce some good effects, but in one realm we are speaking of things psychic, and, in another, of things spiritual. Those that do benefit are robust people who can stand the control and be quite all right: but where there is one who does profit by the association there are many more who do not; so you must judge for yourself. I am simply passing my opinion; and if they still feel prepared to take the responsibility and bring forward these controls, there is nothing against it. Someone will profit. ·

"I would like to clear up for you why rapid breathing throws the physical organism out of gear. Everybody has known this phenomenon; and each has a form of rhythm of his own even if it is not perfect. So long as that is maintained the complete individual continues to work together in close harmony. When, however, the control begins to make his way or intrude within the individual's domain, he has gradually to speed up the breathing which can only be done by stimulation. Thus, more easily is he able to take complete control by throwing that rhythm out. What is done, in fact, is to distort the focus between the physical, etheric and soul body. If these three focus differently, then the control can better take complete command. That is the only way I can explain it. The very fact of the control's gradual withdrawal means a gradual return of the medium's full consciousness; although, of course, there is a temporary phase in which there might be an increase in the rate of breathing. I tell you this—that if you were conducting a physical circle, through your knowing this you could teach the controls and show them the other way; you would be in a position to advise them not to be too much in a hurry; and if you were persistent in it, you would even help them to do better."

Question: "Then does the mental equipment of the medium limit the power of the controller to express himself?"

Peter: "It does in the case of the form of control we have had under discussion—the rough method (control from within). The limit is set. By the other method it is not so much limited; but the well-equipped medium naturally is a better instrument for us; he also leaves his mind elastic, to know 'why' and desires to seek further. Those with a limited mentality have set themselves a limit which they cannot pass." (Here Peter is referring to the class of medium who has no desire to understand the functioning of the mediumship.)

Question: "Can you overcome the medium's sub-conscious mind, and his own ideas, theories, etc., when you control?"

Peter: "The method of development I recommend is the only way by which we can do it (control from without). You see we are outside the medium and we have not enveloped him. Therefore, you will often find that where the subconsciousness of the medium and the desire of the control clash, it may be indicated by a pause in the speech, or a mix-up of words. You may have noticed just now I wished to use the word 'method' and I said 'measure':[2] that is an indication, but we correct it because we are outside the influence of the medium. If the sub-conscious rises, then it cuts us off."

---

2. This incident happened, though it is not apparent in the text.

Question: "With reference to accelerated breathing, you said 'It is done by the controls to achieve contact'. We understand that you control the conditions that permit of phenomena—that is, control from without; but do we understand that the controls who work independently have to contact the medium from within?"

Peter: "Yes, in the common case. In that case the control enters entirely into the medium's aura. Or perhaps I should put it this way; he is not in complete control but becomes the medium and the medium becomes the control. He takes over completely the control of the physical organism—that is by direct control, control from within. It is necessary, to allow of the entry of that control, that the breathing of the physical body must be speeded up so as to attain complete disruption, to throw the physical organism out of natural harmony, to create disturbance—and so to enable an intruder to break in. That is why breathing is thrown out of gear. If you were nearer to me, you would find that there is hardly any breath at all. The breathing is slow, and if you had the medium under observation, you would find, oft-times, that no signs of movement are observable." (This has been repeatedly noticed, the lack of the signs of breathing.)

The following subsidiary questions and answers relating to the foregoing were made at a later date.

Question: "Are there any special attributes that a person should possess to be a suitable subject for physical mediumship?"

Peter: "Well, I think it will be better to stick to types of individual. At the same time it should be remembered that in speaking of types, there are always the exceptions.

"The types that lend themselves best of all for materialisation will be found among those of placid, calm mentality with the physical characteristic of being full bodied; more especially where there is an appearance of moisture in the body.

"Then you have those most suited for voice production. They are of the nervous temperament usually quick in speech and action, not over large in their proportion. I mean the little man, rather slender.

"For apports you have the one who is slow of speech, not very well read and is usually fond of the open life, particularly of gardens and their cultivation.

"As far as levitation is concerned, here you find the types who are usually well built, not necessarily in the sense of being tall, but in relation to their strength, and their muscular reflex: these are usually very limited intellectually. Where you get the different aspects of physical mediumship displayed through one individual, you will find a combination of all those characteristics rolled into one. One little point I would like to add. For physical mediumship and its development, it is the person with the moist palm to his hand that you should choose to sit as medium; and one with hair upon his head. There are no bald-headed physical mediums; for as their hair disappears so does their power for mediumship disappear. Loss of hair is a degeneration of the nervous part of the system and that is the part which we cannot do without."

Question: "Is mediumship more favourable to one sex?"

Peter: "Favourable to both sexes."

Question: "You say the inhaled ether is received at the sieve and there dispersed. To where is it dispersed?"

Peter: "It is definitely not material to the subject so long as the developing medium carries out the action. I will tell you quite frankly the best type of physical mediumship and its extension and range depends upon the conservation of the sexual forces. The centre from which it is controlled is the base of the spine. The ethers which you inhale when you breathe pass alternately down either the left or the right side of the spine; and according to the mental impress these ethers receive, so is the character of that carried to the base of the spine. But it has nothing to do with researches into mediumship for the moment. That is for private conversation."

Question: "When a clairvoyant 'sees', is it necessary for that part of the brain which interprets normal vision to be in action in order to receive spirit pictures?"

Peter: "Well, do you mean the part of the brain that registers the body's observations? This is stimulated but not used. That part is stimulated by the clairvoyant vision, so that the objective mind can construct a picture which is more or less a perfect production as observed by the clairvoyant vision. That centre must of necessity be used before a verbal description of the scene can be described. It is stimulated from another source."

Question: "If the reception of normal vision is dependent upon the applicable nervous system operating between the eye and the brain, is the same nervous system responsible for receiving spirit vision?"

Peter: "That is a funny question. The same senses are stimulated. You understand the system of television that you use today. You are looking at a scene brought to you from a distance and reflected upon the fluorescent screen. There you have reflected precisely the same scene, though it may be many miles from the actual place of occurrence. You see that with your eyes, and to you it is almost the same as being at the actual point of observation. That is very similar to psychic vision only that you too have a screen that operates through the same medium, ether, and stimulates the same nerve. It does not operate the same in each individual. There are some, you see, who may think they see objectively, and others by impression, but the process is the same."

Question: "I am quoting your words 'we borrow a little of the nearest sitters' aura and sort of blend it in'. We often notice that certain people feel conscious of being used in a physical circle—a sense of depletion. Do you find certain persons are better subjects than others for such assistance, and not necessarily the nearest?"

Peter: "I do not like the word 'depletion'. What I meant by the 'nearest sitter' was where the tension was thinnest the one nearest to the point where there is a thinness."

Question: "During work with your medium, John assumes control of the medium whilst materialisations are produced. Does this mean that John becomes the Guide? Is it correct, then, to term yourself as a control for your work in connection with materialisation?"

Peter: "No, I am not responsible for materialisation. There is some haziness between what is meant by Control and Guide. A Guide is essentially so because of his qualifications. I am using earth language, those qualifications embrace a certain knowledge which gives authority to teach and instruct; the desire to be influenced by old earth conditions having been entirely lost and the role of Guide chosen because of the attainment to full knowledge of what that service means. That is the main difference between Control and Guide. The Control is always a control; and refers always to those who take control of the medium's organism by direct method. For instance, in our class of work the controls only work within the auric field and manifest only in the direct voice or behind the scenes controlling the phenomena. Paul, John, Abdul, Peter, myself, we are what is termed the 'band of Guides'. The controls are Simba, Little Peter and one or two lesser-known ones who may not concern us."

Question: "When a control is operating from within, he becomes the medium, as it were, for the time being. How then is the Guide operating from without able to use the medium's body for speech?"

Peter: "He cannot."

Question: "When phenomena is in action, you get the Guide speaking through the medium in order to give directions. Is that so?"

Peter: "I cannot see how the control could be in control of the medium and yet the Guide speak through the lips of the medium. That is impossible or next to impossible. You must not overlook the fact that the Control may simulate the Guide, or, for instance, the Guide might prompt the Control; but the two cannot be mixed up together. If you had two incoming signals on the receiver of your wireless, what an awful noise it would be."

Question: "As a Guide is able to speak through a medium in partial trance, is it possible for physical work to be manifested with the medium's mind subconsciously present? Could such a medium direct experimentation?"

Peter: "No, his sub-conscious mind could, but not consciously."

Question: "Is it possible for a medium to produce phenomena in partial trance?"

Peter: "Yes, but it is freakish."

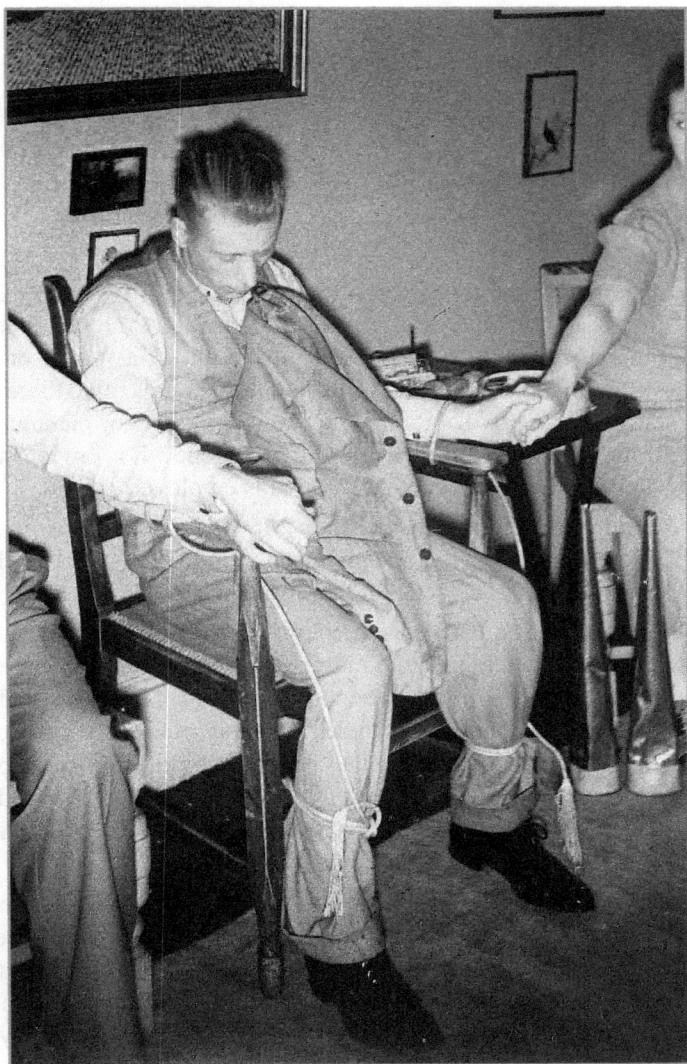

PLATE 7

The medium is roped to the chair. His hands are held by two sitters. His coat, previously stitched-up from lapel to skirt, is drawn through lthe medium's body, illustrating the process of dematerialization and the passage of matter through matter. (See Chap. XIV.)

Infra-red photograph by Leon Isaacs.

CHAPTER XI

THE FUNCTION OF THE GUIDES AND CONTROLS

IN dealing with the functions of the Guides and of the Controls, it is well to recall that any act of organisation demands the presence of an organising mind. The purposeful movement of a finger, or the lifting of an object from one place to another, requires mind direction to accomplish the act. Therefore when any deliberate or planned act is performed and carried out by non-human agency, it is obvious that the agency of a non-human or spirit mind is employed.

The reports of phenomena through Mr Clare's mediumship are sufficiently decisive for the certain declaration to be made, that they were supernormal in character and performance.

A theory has been advanced that, admitting the medium is in a state of unconscious trance, the acts may still be performed through the knowledge contained in his subconscious mind. Not one shred of evidence exists to support this theory. The sub-conscious mind of a man can only retain knowledge that is gained from past experience; and no evidence exists that man, in any age, either through knowledge, or through other mediumships, has been able to perform such acts as have been authentically reported here.

The levitation of a solid object into the air, without any form of humanly constructed apparatus, requires the application of a force to counteract the force of gravity. When the object is of a material that is non-receptive to any of our known forces such as magnetism or electricity, it appears that some force other than these two is employed.

Further, after the act of lifting the orderly controlled movement of that object denotes: a control that is not automatic but intelligent. When the object moves at once as desired at the audible request of a sitter in any stated direction, up or down: to left or right, fast or slow, further evidence is obtained that the directing intelligence is responsive to the sitter's directions.

This intelligence must possess not only an intimate knowledge of the natural laws as known to man, but also law-governed forces unknown to man. In addition, this intelligence must possess the further knowledge of how to combine and co-ordinate these forces with those we know.

Still further evidence is provided of the greater power possessed by the spirit intelligence, by the knowledge: it must have of the human anatomy and understanding of the human mind. This must be obvious to the reader who stops to consider what is implied by the creation and the potentialities pf ectoplasmic activity.

Thus one conclusion is immediately apparent, and that is, that when, through human mediumship phenomena are manifested, there must be present a directing intelligence of great wisdom.

With all mediums there is another common factor; and that is the "personality" who makes himself known through speech, via the medium or by means of the "independent voice". This personality is in command of the medium and the proceedings at a séance. We have Walter with Margery, Black Cloud with Jack Webber, Peter and John with Arnold Clare; and so on with every medium.

It is noticed that two personalities have been cited with Mr Clare. This is not unusual; with Jack Webber, Black Cloud would on occasion leave the medium for one of the other Guides to take charge.[1]

The Guide during a sitting is an autocrat, governing the proceedings with a "rod of iron". He is the sole arbiter of what may be allowed to proceed or not. As a rule, such Guides are most anxious and willing to co-operate with the sitters when their requests are reasonable.

These Guides are not vague abstract personalities, they are known by names, tell you of themselves, their nationality, the work they were engaged upon when on the earth; and at times have provided evidence to prove their earthly existences.

It is not of great importance, however, whether the controlling genius possessed a white or a red skin during his earth life. The salient fact is that these personalities must be in a condition of active existence. To prove that, they carry out their work amongst us.

---

1. For the purpose of clearness, the term Guide is used in this book to denote the personality in charge of the medium and the proceedings at the time; the other spirit operators present being termed Controls.

124

There is another aspect that may well be recorded. When one has been privileged to work consistently with a medium, and has come into frequent touch with the Guide, he becomes much more than a "personality" or the "voice" through the medium. One learns to know him, and he becomes a close personal friend, almost as "one of the family"; and very "human". He enters into the family lives of the sitters, is solicitous and loving and is revered as counsellor, guide, and loved friend.

Peter has told us that the Guide has the responsibility of creating the "conditions" in which the controls can present, the phenomena. The Guide in control does not produce an act of levitation, apportation, or any other of the acts performed. It is as if he were in charge of the power and the power switch. When the Guide has built up the necessary conditions at the séance, it is the individual controls who carry out the jobs of work.

Before dealing with the *modus operandi* described by Peter, of how the right "conditions" are created, some evidence is given to support the statement above.

On the hundred and more occasions when I sat with Jack Webber, I was able to observe the variation of the quality of the phenomena, the facility or difficulty of their production according to the nature of the sitters, the general atmosphere; and the health or disposition of the medium.

When the general conditions at a séance were co-operative and easy, the phenomena would flow freely from act to act without pause. The movements would be strong and sustained and, at times, so strong that the Guide would express himself through the medium asking for caution.

The closing act of the sitting was often the levitation of the medium into the air, bound to his chair, where he travelled around and above the heads of the sitters, finally alighting on the far side of the circle or, at times, on the outside of the circle. The Controls responsible for this act were often impatient, and did not want to wait, so that on occasion one heard the Guide admonishing the Control, especially when the medium had been slightly levitated in the middle of the séance. At times, when after admonition the Control persisted in levitating the medium, the Guide would ask imperatively for the light to be put on—thus breaking down the conditions in which the Control could act. On other occasions, when sitters were non-co-operative, or some new restriction had been imposed on the medium, or the medium had himself been upset, there appeared difficulty in producing phenomena; movement or activity would be short, snappy and with long time-pauses between each movement. Then would be heard the voice of the Guide speaking through the medium saying, "Do your best now", "Do this" or "Do that", clearly indicating that it was outside his own province to perform the act.

Peter describes the way in which he creates the right condition for action as "extending the auric field of the medium", and his words on this point are of interest.

Peter: "The phenomena take place within the extension of the medium's aura. This is done by means of bowsing-bending-reflecting." (Here Peter seems to have given us a new word "bowsing" to convey a meaning, for which our vocabulary has no word.) "It is not the sort of bending as is pictured when you bend a piece of metal, but a bending under a strain like the cover of an umbrella. Can you imagine a flame being bent over for no apparent cause, as if deflected by a steady directive wind. It is most important to get the idea. It is, as it were, bent over by an invisible power.

"If, in the circumstances, the circle is not properly arranged, the aura of the medium cannot be 'bowsed' or extended sufficiently to include all the people. If the edge becomes thin, due to certain conditions associated with the sitters, we borrow a little of the nearest sitters' aura and blend it in.

"There you have the tent or umbrella, under stress enveloping the whole circle. This tent or umbrella covers a certain area inside of which are the sitters.

"The etheric conditions within are not exactly the same as the conditions without.

"Within that area the Controls can work their will, to a certain extent, that is.

"If there are any leaks in the umbrella within, the conditions are not so good for the production of phenomena.

"We have an atmosphere of freedom in which we can operate without limit; that is without the limitation that would be imposed outside the tent. It is within the pressure existing inside the tent where the Controls are able to perform their will."

A drawn impression of this gives the author's idea of what is intended. The medium has seen this and, through him, the Guide has said it certainly does give an impression of what takes place.

A summary of a previous talk with Peter was then read to him as follows:

"The Guide in control creates the conditions necessary for phenomena to be manifested.

"These conditions are an extension of the auric field of the medium. Help may be obtained from sitters for this purpose.

"The Auric field is composed of (a) the aura pertinent to the physical body, which extends to about three inches around the physical form, misty silver in colour; and (b) the auric atmosphere that is limitless in extent: a storehouse of electric energy which belongs to the soul body and is subject to pull from each condition.

"To create séance conditions, the auric field is controlled and concentrated into the area within which phenomena are to be created, like an umbrella or tent.

"Psychic breezes are caused when the auric properties of sitters are employed."

Peter replied:

Peter: "Not quite right. I do not like the phrase, 'Aura which extends three inches.' Let me tell you once again.

"Around the normal healthy human being there is an extension, an etheric extension. You said pertinent—that is a good word. It means 'close to'. This etheric extension is the reservoir of physical strength. It has no character of its own, but is simply a storehouse of etheric energy used for the complete and successful working of the physical body.

"It is not wise for me to give measurements in regard to this, it varies so widely in extent."

"Close to the physical body it has the property of scintillating colours. This is due to the mental changes or flux of the individual. The aura proper has its own basic colour. All other colours are added by mental stimulants. I mean, of course, anger, sorrow and things like that. It has for its basic colours, orange, purple and slate grey. These are always impressed first. That is the aura or atmosphere; and that is the part which is capable of extension."

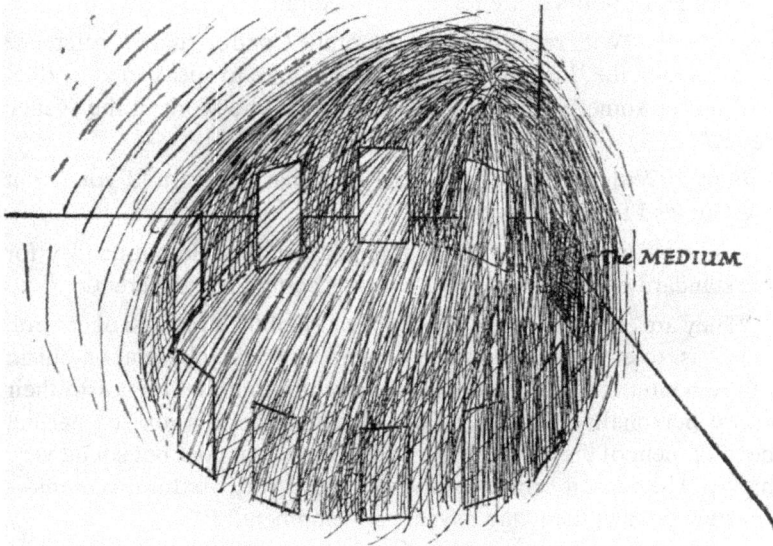

FIG. 8

An impression of the bowsing of the auric field—the creation of conditions
to permit phenomenal action. The rectangles represent sitters.

Peter was asked if he could say whether the forces used could be
compared with any of the forces of which we are aware. He replied:

Peter: "The nearest force we know comparable to that used in
producing action is a magnetic force, but this force is of a different
quality and stronger in character. A compass point can be diverted
from its position by directive power. This magnetic force is superior
to your known force. It is allied to electrical energy. This power force
has a potency different from that of the forces known to you: for
example, wood is a good conductor of the superior force, whereas it
is impervious to your known electrical and magnetic forces. Tin is a
good conductor, aluminium is not so good; but the difference is slight
and would not impede action.

"You will notice that while I am talking, the respiration of the
medium is almost non-existent. You will find this is so only during
speech, and that it is not because he can hold his breath but because
of the relaxation of the body.

Hence no ill-effects are felt by the medium."

Question: "With regard to the work of the Controls and the reference you made to the 'little people', would you like to speak to us on that and tell us something more of the 'people' who work in the séance room?

Peter: "With pleasure, I can deal with that. I have told you about the Guides I think—(yes).

"Controls are called by that name because they do not qualify for the standard of Guides and their work is completely different.

"They are called Controls chiefly because of their method of control, which is, to enter into complete possession of the physical organism of the medium, i.e. they impart directly through that organism their entire personality. This is a fault, because there is not the perfect development of the medium spiritually. Now that does not sound very happy. The reason brings us back to those very vexful questions— spiritual development and psychic development.

"In the case of controlled mediumship (I use that term for want of a better) you have a display of purely psychic phenomena with very little of the spiritual. The Controls themselves are quite good but they are little removed from the limits imposed upon man in the flesh. Their range of vision is very much restricted; and can act only within the realms adjacent to earth. It is the natural phenomenon of man since the dawn of history; and you might call it quite simply primitive religion—very primitive. They can perform what would be termed miracles, but it stops at that. It goes no further; and in this scale of operation you have at once all the elements that comprise ancient magic, both black and white, the difference being the intention and the will of the medium and those who comprise the group.

"Now that is control and its function.

"I have referred on several occasions to the little people (for want of a better term). These little people are known best by the name 'nature spirits' or, collectively, as 'elementals'. They are very similar to the human race, but possess certain features which are accentuated, that is to say their bodies, if you could see them, are slightly out of proportion with features which are characteristically the same no matter what particular force they represent. Temperamentally they are light-hearted. They lack completely moral character, as you know. They are neither essentially bad nor good. They are ever ready to obey the direction of the human mind where there is close kinship between the mind of the man or woman and themselves.

"They are able to manipulate the natural ethers with the utmost ease, producing natural things such as stone, flowers and all things like that.

"In the scale of evolution, they stand between the animal realm and man himself. The one goal they desire to attain is the human form complete. In the séance room, as far as physical phenomena are concerned, their services are very necessary; in fact no work could be achieved without their aid in producing solid objects brought from a distance. In many other forms of phenomena, their services are utilized; but always under the direction of the Control, who is very closely allied to themselves, yet superior in mentality. (In the case of this medium [Arnold Clare], the one used is called Simba.) They love to disport themselves by simple antics such as causing things to move; and invariably their presence is betrayed by the aimless moving of objects within the vicinity of the medium, that is, more or less, movements without a definite purpose.

"They, too, are responsible for the maintenance of séance conditions; and their services are quickly withdrawn if any offence is given by anyone present unless the control has instituted some form of discipline. They are subject to discipline, but that is only in relation to their normal work which ranges from the geological realm up to all the activities of nature, including flowers and insects; they are even associated with the air that you breathe, and the water that you drink.

"That is why I have said séance-room work is a natural religion, a primitive religion of mankind. That is why we are anxious to lift it more from the realm of the soul and the natural side of man, so that it may be directed purely by the spiritual, of which man, more and more, is becoming aware. That is our mission and our work to do.

"You will remember, too, that I have said on one occasion that phenomena would go on in the presence of the medium without intervention from a discarnate entity, but it will lack the purpose and be entirely sporadic because of the familiarity and the link between the medium and these little people."

Question: "That explains the movements we sometimes see in the presence of a medium, when he is normal."

Peter: "That is right.

"The same 'little people' can be pressed into service even for certain types of healing; but their services are not often used—only for psychic healing; and then for the ailments affecting chiefly the bony structure and deformities.

"To sum it all up, you might say they are the soul of nature. As man himself has many complex parts, so has the soul of nature many parts working together to accomplish something far too immense for the ordinary mind to grasp. They are not left to wander aimlessly in space but are directed by superior intelligences who press them into service according to their capabilities, with only one purpose in view, development and progress along the road of the whole realm of nature, to keep it in step and in tune with the whole life and scheme of creation whilst working ever towards the perfect plan ordained by God."

Question: "We have often been told that there are other workers such as spirit chemists in the séance room. Are they there in addition?"

Peter: "Not through any direct interest in the production of the work or of the séance, but as witnesses learning the laws. They are there in order that they may impart their experiences to man if he is sufficiently attuned to their own minds to be receptive."

Question: "We are also told that healers associated with a medium are there to protect him or look after him."

Peter: "No, not essentially there to protect him any more than they would function in that capacity in any other form of work. No, they are there because of their knowledge of the cosmic rays which are so essential to the healing of the mind and body of a sufferer. The benefit of these rays is very similar to that gained from your radio therapy. You see they make use of certain wave lengths or frequencies, which are a coarser form of the finer cosmic rays. You see the association."

Interrogation: "We have pictured a number of personalities each doing his different job!"

Peter: "If you demand an answer from a Control you get it, but they may not have sufficient understanding to answer it correctly although they think it is the truth as they see it. I would not deny that such personalities are present, but they are there only as observers."

Question: "You said the method of control depended upon the fact that the medium had not attained spiritual perfection to any extent. Is it possible for the medium to attain it?"

Peter: "How do the Controls work in the case of one who has not attained spiritual perfection? In this case, the Controls are still associated with the medium but work without his spiritual aura. They are similar to the 'little people' in that they follow the direction of the Guides. They are happier working thus—they are freer. In the case of one who works spiritually, he must have always the ideal in front of him; for once he loses faith in himself the contact is snapped."

Question: "With the medium who is psychic only, the phenomena is still produced?"

Peter: "That is quite correct, and usually more robust too. There is nothing to learn from it."

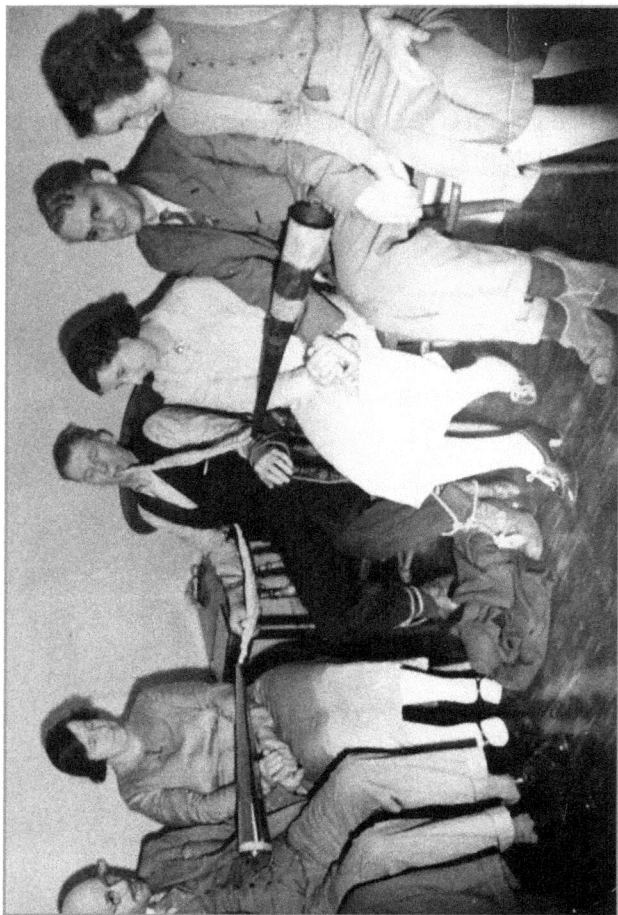

PLATE 8

Two grade 2 ectoplasmic formations organised for voice and forceful levitation purposes. The formations have considerably depreciated from their actual working condition to withstand the stress of impure infra-red rays used for the photographic exposure (See Chaps XII & XIII)

Infra-red photograph taken by Leon Isaacs

CHAPTER XII

ECTOPLASM

OBSERVATION of physical phenomena, with many mediums, at different periods and in all parts of the world, shows that a substance is produced either from or adjacent to the medium's body, which is the "raw material" of manifestations, telekinetic action, etc.

Various terms have been used to describe this substance: teleplasm, ectoplasm, ideoplasm, etc. We use the word ectoplasm since it has been sanctioned by custom in this country.

It has been established beyond all doubt that ectoplasm is the basis for the building-up of materialisations, for levitation by force and for the structural mechanism in direct voice. Indeed in some form or other, visible or invisible, it is the raw material of the spirit-folk for all their work in the séance room.

As, gradually, we are able to understand more about this "elusive" substance, so shall we be able to comprehend the manner of the performance of spirit mechanics. But owing to its great sensitivity and its most intimate relationship to the nervous system of the medium (if not the life force itself) it can rarely be handled or very closely studied by investigators. Indeed, apart from certain residues, which may or may not have been true ectoplasmic residue (see Peter's observations on this point), never yet has any savant been able to retain a quantity of the substance. There are records where investigators, imbued with scientific unscrupulousness, or in sheer ignorance, have attempted to take a handful of the substance with the idea of retaining it for analysis. On each occasion, although the substance was clasped within their hands, it dispersed immediately. Unfortunately, it is the medium who is harmed by such unwarrantably crude interference. Indeed, any unorthodox action by an investigator committed without the knowledge or permission of the Guide in control, invariably causes the medium serious harm, without any advance in knowledge, or credit to, the investigator.

Consideration of the descriptions of the ectoplasmic matter reported with Mr Clare's mediumship in the first part of this book and the reports that follow concerning other mediumships, lead to the conclusion that here is a substance possessing the potentials of life itself; and as such, of the most delicate nature.

The substance of the living brain may be handled wisely, but no one but a fool would take liberties with it. Similarly, while at times we may be permitted to handle or observe this substance, under direction, it is only the fool who would crudely interfere with it.

The number of mediums who have been able to produce through their mediumship, ectoplasm that may be viewed in some degree of light, or to permit of it being photographed, is exceedingly few; though it is now hoped that photographic records may be increased by the use of the infra-red ray applied to psychic photography.

A close study of the major works of the past dealing with this particular phenomenon discloses that our knowledge concerning it is very limited indeed; and apart from visual records and records of touch, we have not been able to approach the answer to such questions as "How is it produced? From whence does it come? To where does it disperse? What is its composition? The purpose and manner of its usage?"

For the first time, Peter has given us a detailed exposition that provides tenable answers to these leading questions, which may well provide the foundation upon which our future knowledge will be based. Naturally we seek proofs of each statement made and so perhaps at this juncture the best service that can be rendered is to take the observations of previous investigations with those of the mediumship under review; and to see how those observations can be associated with Peter's theses.

In the author's considered opinion there is no previously recorded fact that is at variance with the explanations given.

It is not practical to include in this work summaries of all the leading investigations, so that some of the most recent investigations will have to suffice. Indeed, there is a striking similarity between the records of all the published testimonies.

In the volumes published by the U.S.A., S.P.R. on the Margery mediumship, there are many chapters devoted to the meticulous recording of ectoplasmic phenomena. They are far too extensive to reproduce here, but it will serve to give a general view of the Margery phenomena by reprinting the generalisations of the Research Officer of the U.S.A., S.P.R., as follows:

" ... Nevertheless, from the viewpoint of sensorial experience, the word teleplasm is quite essential, and will be used without further apology. It appears that the definite physical qualities which this substance exhibits in the performance of its many phenomena depend on a greater or a lesser density, or viewed from the other angle, a greater or a lesser tenuity. Thus, when a small basket rolls on a shelf in front of the Psychic and the observer passes his clasped arms through the entire zone between the Psychic and the basket, we believe that the teleplasmic rod from the Psychic's body is either so tenuous that the arm of the observer passes through it without breaking it, or that the rod by some means comes from a fourth direction. When the scales are made to balance a four-to-one load in red or white light, we have evidence of the presence of a form of teleplasm invisible to the eye and intangible to the finger, not seen when photographed by a glass lens, not visible when photographed by a fused quartz lens. Here is apparently a psychic structure, invisible and intangible, but nevertheless emitting or reflecting an ultra-violet light. Again, when under perfect conditions of control, but in the dark, sitters receive touches by a teleplasmic terminal, we have this material in a form tangible but presumably invisible. Finally, we observe teleplasm at the maximum density seen in this mediumship, when in good red light we see, feel, handle, weigh and take the temperature of the teleplasmic mass on the table in front of us. When the substance has this density our senses not only record it, but the glass camera lens, as well as the quartz lens, confirms what we see . . .

The mass which comes from the trunk, and sometimes from the ears of the Psychic, is a light brownish grey colour, as seen in the red light. There is a distinct variety, however, coming from the right ear which is a dead white in colour, like wax, or slightly yellow; the colour of noodles. Both these forms are entirely opaque.

The temperature has been taken twice by having the mass laid on a chemist's thermometer. At one time it was 40degrees Fahrenheit and the other time 42 degrees. The room temperature at the time was 70 degrees.

The mass is cold to the observer's hand and has a clammy feeling. After the contact is broken the sitter would declare that his hand must be wet but that is sensation only. William Blake described it as 'wet with the water that wets not'. The mass is more or less like new rubber in consistency and resiliency, but the rubber feeling is more than the mere action and reaction of squeezing rubber. The mass often squirms and appears to have life itself. This liveness is further confirmed by the fact that if the sitter squeezes the mass however gently, and quite in the dark, the Psychic will groan as if hurt. At times the mass almost seems to be made up of individual fibres of live longitudinal cords about one-sixth of an inch in diameter. This is especially the case with the cords joining it to the Psychic's organism.

If one of the crude hands is palpated freely, we find what appear to be normal bones; in the right relation but rarely enough of them. Thus, the fingers seldom present more than two phalanges: the terminal one being then missing. Finger-nails may or may not be present. At one time one finger showed as if it were a fusion of two fingers with the distal phalanges split and bearing two finger-nails. All the metacarpals may be missing with the carpals present. The forearm may contain one bone or two, as in the normal. There is generally no muscular enlargement of the upper part of the forearm. It appears to be only skin over the bone.

The grey masses that form the crude hands are attached to the body by something closely resembling an umbilical cord. This cord is one half to one-and-one-half inches in diameter. It appears as if twisted, as an umbilical cord frequently is. There is no pulse in it. . . The white masses of teleplasm overlying the Psychic's face have cords of somewhat different character, issuing from the ear and the nose. . .

. . . This living mass may then extend downwards in a kind of white sheet until it reaches the table or even the floor. When it gets this size, there forms, as if for better exhibition, a long proboscis having its base on the nose, divided more or less like the four legs of the Eiffel Tower. The long staff of this grows forward parallel to the floor and over this the teleplasmic sheet hangs like a tent over a ridge pole. The largest one we have seen was about 24 x 84 inches. This sheet, which Walter calls his 'shining garment', appears sometimes as a smooth uniform mass, or like coarse or fine lace. Walter declares, and close examination confirms, that the lace, however, is lace in appearance only."

The Research Officer's observations dealing with the structure of the teleplasmic voice-box will be found in the chapter dealing with "Voice Mechanism"; but as the latter part of his observations relating to the dispersal of the substance are pertinent they are appended as follows:

"The disappearance of the mass may be observed. It seems to go back to the orifice from whence it comes. The last moment of disappearance we have been allowed to see twice. The mass shrinks in volume, but not continuously. The last view shows considerable mass, then all at once there is nothing. It is comparable to the cloud of white water-vapour seen coming out of a factory exhaust pipe. At first a large; white, opaque, substantial-looking cloud or mass—then all at once there is nothing . . .

The terminals have been seen and felt and most of them photographed in many forms. The mass may be amorphous, perhaps roughly like a small French loaf or like a dirigible balloon in shape. In the second period of red light it may be shown that this mass has taken on the form of a crude hand with five fingers or sometimes with two of the five fingers fused together. Sometimes the hand is observed to have a terminal with four fingers and thumb, with all the extremities long, perhaps seven inches, coming to a sharp point, the region of the palm shrunken; the whole hand being a caricature of a hand, or the hand of a nightmare figure. The hand, however, may show itself in every detail of improving perfection up to what appears to be a complete hand."

The last observation is of interest when compared to the building up of a hand as reported with Mr Clare (see report, p.68-9) and with particular reference to Peter's comments on the subject.

A privilege and a duty of observers is to confirm the findings of others and to compare results. Such comparisons over the last fifty years display a marked progression with the character of the ectoplasmic formations; and generally speaking, each succeeding mediumship provides a more refined and advanced type of phenomena. It will, of course, be understood that in making comparisons, no disparagement is intended. With Margery, the ectoplasmic formations were prolific, but, from their description and photographs, appear cruder than those since observed and photographed with Jack Webber and seen with Arnold Clare. It may be that the use of the infra-red ray photography permitted a finer grade of ectoplasm being photographed with J.W. than the glare of the magnesium flash permitted with Margery.

Peter tells us that no condition of ectoplasm is static; and it is interesting to observe that the disappearance of the formation with Margery is the reverse of that noted with J.W. With the latter the formation of the substance commenced with the seeming emission of the cloud-like vapour. Yet whether the vapour consistency is at the beginning or end of the phenomena, the similarity of description is marked; and it is quite reasonable that such a characteristic could equally well mark either the beginning or termination of the activity.

In considering all these reports, it is well to keep in mind that the ectoplasmic formations may be of various grades of refinement or development; it may be a crude mass or a highly organised mechanism. The texture of the substance also varies greatly according to the opportuneness and harmony of the conditions prevailing at the time in the séance room.

It will be noted that the conclusions of the U.S.A. S.P.R. officer quoted in the early part of his observations, refer to the varying qualities of the structure as probably being due to a greater or lesser degree of tenuity or density. It may well be that in view of Peter's statements a more tenable explanation lies in the varying grades of ectoplasm used and the corresponding degree of organisation within it.

Nevertheless, there are beyond any doubt characteristics in the production, formation, colour and feel of ectoplasm with each mediumship. The foregoing descriptions of ectoplasm with Margery received before 1930, and those recorded by Baron von Schrenk-Notzing and other savants of his time, are very like those recorded with J.W. and Arnold Clare; and as we bear in mind Peter's grading of the various kinds of structures, we can obtain a truer perspective of these phenomena. While Peter has broadly graded ectoplasmic formations into three categories, it is obvious that there can be no rigid division; and that one grade merges into another, as all possess the potentialities of each. It is a gradual evolution from the crudest form to the most refined and highly organised kind.

Some extracts from *The Mediumship of Jack Webber* follow:

"In dark séances, the process of emitting, ectoplasm is often illustrated by means of luminous plaques or in red light.

The process is as follows: The medium's body is bent forward whilst in the ropes, so that his head is over his feet. From the mouth there commences to emerge a substance that looks to the eye like heavy vapour. As it emerges, it 'unrolls' and pours down in front of the medium's body to the floor. At the same time, it continues to pour out from the mouth like a cascade, until there is a considerable volume on the floor spreading several feet each way. The emergence is rapid and the process of emission only occupies a few seconds. There is no noise from the medium's throat during this time.

Rapidly, in two or three seconds only, the vapourish mass condenses or becomes concentrated, until there hangs from the mouth a length of material-like substance.

The texture of this material varies according to the conditions prevailing at the sitting and the condition of the medium himself. When conditions are good the texture is fine and close. When the conditions are not so good, the material is coarser and rents may be seen in the fabric.

This material has often been handled under the Guide's instructions, by the author and other sitters. It is moist, though not very wet and possesses a peculiar odour. On a number of occasions the author has been invited to unravel the material and open it out. To do this, however, extreme care has to be taken. The width of the material when opened out is wider than the outstretched arms of one person. Whilst unravelling the ectoplasm at one sitting, the author was unable to stretch it out to its full extent; and the assistance of the next sitter was allowed by the Guide. The full extent must have been two yards or more.

The return of the ectoplasm is instantaneous. The author has had gentle hold of the material one moment; and within the second that followed, the material has been whisked away with

> a sound like the twang of a piece of elastic and it has disappeared.
>
> Several descriptions of this material have been given by sitters as 'closely woven silk of rich quality', 'like wet toy balloon rubber', 'a wide piece of thin seaweed'.
>
> This formation has no pattern such as 'net'. It is like a skin rather than a woven fabric. This drapery is most gossamer-like and is so light that its texture is as a spider's web. Yet its density is great and the weight heavy to the hand."

The incident next related tells how two photographs were secured under unusual circumstances, demonstrating the rapidity with which the formations disappear.

> "The author was in charge of the photographic apparatus and white light and all was ready to take a photograph should the opportunity come. The sitting was proceeding, and throat noises were heard coming from the medium, when the unusual instruction was received 'photo and light'.
>
> A photograph being anticipated by the character of the throat action, the infra-red was immediately flashed by pressing the switch, the right hand came across and closed the shutter in front of the plate, returning to the white light switch. Both these switches were of the press kind, so no delay was caused. The three movements were therefore rapid and the only interval between the photographic exposure and the white light was the time to close the plate shutter. Two seconds is a generous time allowance.
>
> Plate No. 9 [1] was the first to be taken and it will be realised that the absorption back into the medium of the ectoplasmic formation was therefore instantaneous.
>
> A few minutes after the plate had been changed . . . a similar instruction was received 'photo and light'. On this occasion Plate No. 10 was secured. The author was ready for this instruction and the period between the infra-red flash and the white light was not more than one second . . . ."

There is a variation between the time taken for the disappearance of the ectoplasm in the Webber and Margery descriptions. Peter's

---

1. The Plate numbers refer to those in this book.

PLATE 9

Ectoplasmic formation of Grades 1 and 2. This formation dispersed witihin a fraction of time following the photographic exposure.

Infra-red photograph by Harry Edwards

PLATE 10

Ectoplasmic formation of Grades 1 and 2, which also dispersed witihin a fraction of a second. (See opposite)

Infra-red photograph by Harry Edwards

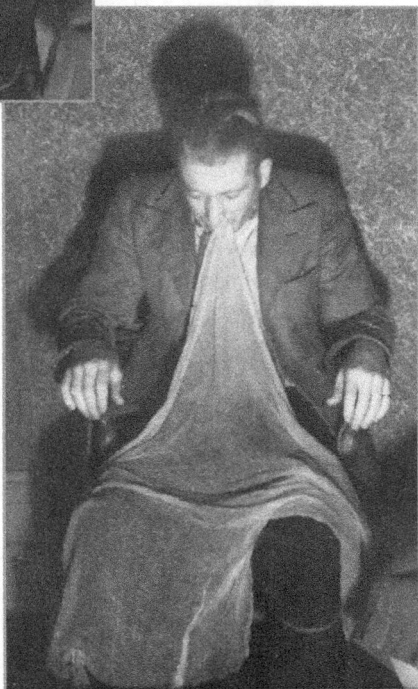

explanations give the reason for this. It is in the different grades of structure present on each occasion. With Margery it appears to have been of the cruder kind and had to be returned (wholly or in part) to the body. With J.W. the formation was probably a combination, part from the body and part from the ether (it may have been that the whole came from the ether), so that its dissemination was immediate through its instantaneous return to the etheric particles from which it had been constructed.

It may be noted in my reporting of the J.W. incident I wrote "voluminous material passing back into the medium". This illustrates how easy it is to fall into error and form a wrong conclusion by resting on observation only and forming assumptions therefrom; and if Peter's observations are accepted, how knowledge is slowly gained and we are forced to correct ourselves. So far, all research in the past has come to the conclusion that all grades of ectoplasm return back to the medium's physical body. Peter says this is not so.

According to Peter, ectoplasm of a refined type is not reabsorbed by the Psychic's physical organism but disintegrates back into 'the ether from whence it comes.' This process of dissemination is both logical and practical, for when one considers the wide expanses of physically constructed ectoplasm, as shown both by description and by photographs, to assume that this volume of physical matter re-enters the throat or other orifices or sources of emergence, is far more improbable than the reasoning of Peter.

We know how materialised forms disseminate into "space" through observation of the manner of their disappearance; and therefore the dissemination of certain forms of ectoplasm follows the same process.

The two photographs referred to above demonstrate beyond question, that on the occasion they were secured the voluminous expanses of ectoplasm in a physical state disappeared within a second. This means that the intelligence in control had to negotiate the disintegration of the mass within the very limited period of time between the infra-red flash that recorded the phenomenon and the putting on of the white light, thereby implying instantaneous action. How well this evidence supports Peter's newly disclosed process.

Here is evidence that the scientific mind has to account for and accept. In the past scientists confronted with a phenomenon they could not account for by their previous knowledge have either discounted the act or have taken refuge in building up an argument to account for the act by fraud. Within the last two years an eminent researcher, whose name is regarded in certain national quarters as being a leading authority on physical phenomena, endeavoured to explain the process by regurgitation. That is the medium, prior to sitting, swallowed many yards of cheesecloth, regurgitated it during the séance, displayed it for fraudulent purpose, and then swallowed it again, the process being repeated, as the medium required. This is typical of the wilfully crass ignorance the Spiritualist movement has to encounter; and the incredible thing is, that some people prefer to accept such an absurdity rather than a simple and tenable explanation supported by abundant testimony and photographic proofs.

Here is another example of "explanation" by one who will not accept the evidence of his own eyes and senses. Dr. Dunlap, the noted American Professor of Experimental Psychology, after seeing the preliminary photographic evidence of the existence and nature of psychic rods with Margery, was able to be present at sittings and to "see" for himself, yet dismissed the phenomena as being produced by the use of "the intestine of some animal, showing the stumps of some blood vessels and stuffed with some substance like cotton, through which ran several wires."

So long as men of science are satisfied to discount the wonderful work of their "spirit co-workers", so long will the true appreciation and understanding of this realm of activity be prejudiced by obstinate and brutal ignorance.

A further illustration of Peter's reference to the different grades of ectoplasm is provided by the comparative photographs of ectoplasmic energy with Margery and J.W. With the former, the substance shown is of a cruder kind, Grade 1; whilst with the latter the refined character of the formation is obvious. The cruder or "fungoid" type of substance is also seen in the photographs of substances emerging from the nose and ears of J.W.

Further useful comparative study is provided by the following extracts from Geley's works and investigations, dealing with the appearance and action of ectoplasmic formations:

> "The volume of substance extruded is variable, sometimes abundant, sometimes scanty, with all intermediate grades. In a few instances it covers the medium like a mantle.

The substance may be white, grey or black, the first being more frequent, possibly as more easily observed. Occasionally all three colours are visible at the same time. The visibility of the substance is variable; it occasionally is stronger or weaker. To the touch also it varies according to the form it takes at the moment, seeming soft and inelastic when widely spread, hard, knotty and fibrous when it forms cords. Sometimes it feels like a spider's web, but in the thread-like form it seems both stiff and elastic.

The substance is mobile. Sometimes it develops slowly, ascends and descends over the medium's shoulders, breast or knees with a creeping movement; sometimes its motion is very quick, appearing and disappearing in a flash. It is highly sensitive; and this sensibility is communicated to the medium, who feels painfully any touch upon the substance. If the touch is rough or prolonged it produces a sensation in the medium comparable to a touch on raw flesh.

It is sensitive even to rays of light. A bright and unexpected light perturbs the medium, but this effect of light is also variable; in certain cases, daylight is endured. The magnesium flash causes the medium to start violently, but the substance can stand it. This allows of instantaneous photography . . . .

It has a constant and immediate tendency to organise itself; and does not long remain in its primitive state. Often this organisation is so rapid that its first amorphous state is scarcely seen at all; at other times the amorphous substance and more or less complete forms embedded in the mass can be seen at the same time; for instance, a finger on the fringe, or even heads and faces wrapped in the substance."

In Baron von Schrenk-Notzing' s book, *Materialisations*, there are over three hundred pages and over two hundred photographs appertaining to the phenomena of ectoplasmic formations and materialisations, which provide additional detailed corroborative evidence supporting that already included in this book. In no case is the evidence at variance with any of the aforementioned excerpts.

The reader will have been able to observe from the reports of the various mediumships quoted, that there is no outstanding departure in formation, emergence, disappearance and other characteristics including the organised creation of claws, hands, etc.

The works mentioned by no means exhaust the range of published investigations: there are many, particularly continental, in which similar supporting evidence is provided. It is felt that no useful purpose would be served by reproducing here further excerpts, as the result would only be to reiterate the same symptoms, the same characteristics, the same methods of activity.

A useful purpose may be served, however, by summarising the similarities briefly before entering on Peter's explanations; and it will be seen that in no case are they at variance with the records of many mediumships, of many nationalities, in various parts of the world, that have functioned during different periods of time.

The similarities are:

(1) The varying grades of refinement.

(2) The first appearance being of the crude type.

(3) The sensitivity of the substance and its reaction to the medium.

(4) The ability to organise.

(5) The mobility of the substance.

(6) The feel of the substance to the touch.

(7) The characteristic of "heavy vapour" during its development.

{8) The "wetness", suppleness, elasticity, brittleness, etc.

(9) The rapidity of disintegration.

(10) The presence of cords connecting to the medium.

(11) The unstable conditions of the substance.

(12) The formation of such members as fingers, hands, faces, from the substance. (Specially note the reports of the Clare manifestations).

(13) Similarity in colour.

(14) Similarity in sources of emergence.

(15) The sheet-like structure of the formations.

(16) Its coldness.

So, bearing in mind the foregoing, we now proceed to Peter's explanations and the relating of the evidence to the thesis.

Peter introduced the subject by saying:

Peter: "This is a very difficult subject to tell you about. Perhaps it will clarify the general position if I tell you for the first time that ectoplasmic substance exists in three forms. There is Grade 1, which is a crude form, and which looks and feels like an inert mass of spongy substance. It is of close texture and seldom is seen in any particular form or shape. It could be best described as a fungus both in appearance and to the touch. That is the nearest description I can give."

Question: "What is its purpose?"

Peter: "It has no purpose. It comes directly from the physical body. Remember that."

Question: "Is it an organic tissue growth?"

Peter: "That is difficult to answer directly. It is organic yet not so, in that it does not reside as part of the physical organism. It is not a part of the physical body. It is produced by a method of 'astral chemistry'."

Question: "Does it contain any other elements than those of which the physical body is composed—such as salt, lime, etc.?"

Peter: "It is very curious. It contains nothing like salt, or anything of the normal mineral world at all. It is a very primitive substance; and if we were to consider it as a fungoid growth, it would convey more clearly what it is. It is best described as a fungus as in the vegetable kingdom. It is the lowest and the most primitive form of growth. Now this is important: this grade of ectoplasmic substance is withdrawn again into the medium's physical body by its dispersal.

"It will help you to understand this by considering Grade 2. This being a refinement of Grade 1 in that it is organised and can be utilised as additional members (under given conditions) comparable with those of the physical body. This substance can be transformed into rods and psychic instruments possessing great strength. In appearance it is apparently opaque. It has solidity, yet, in an instant, it can become disorganised and is inert—without life. (See Plate 13. p156)

"Its formation is slightly different from that of Grade 1, in that from suitable centres of the medium there is projected what can best be termed "rays" with qualities similar to that of your own wireless radio. It is of such a frequency that it forms particles about itself, not from the medium but from the ether round about, so that it becomes three dimensional.

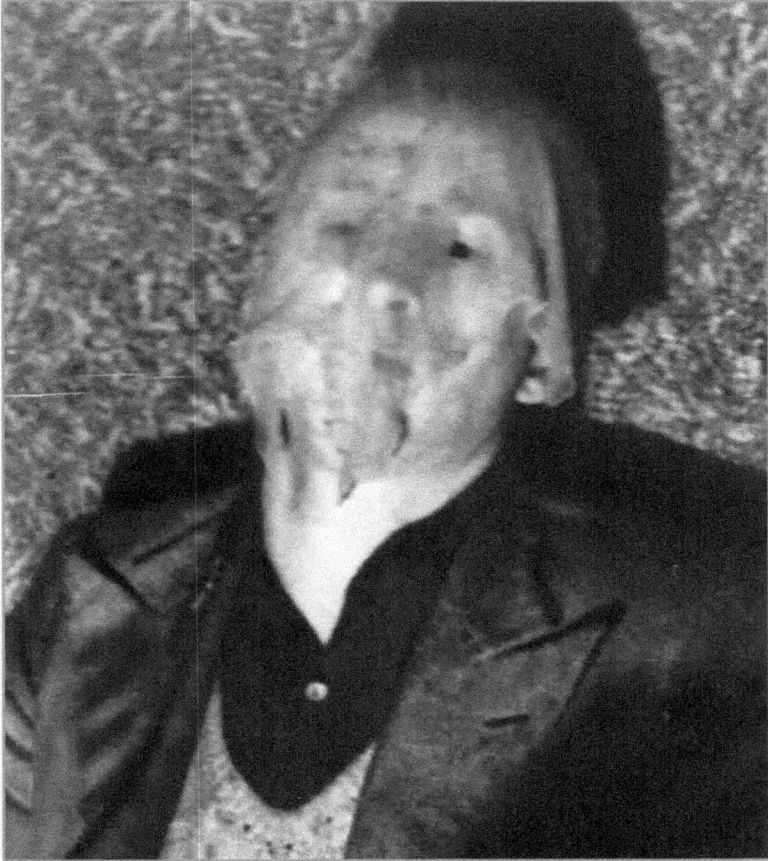

PLATE 11

Ectoplasmic formation, Grades 1 and 2, photographed over the face
of the unentranced medium in red light.

Infra-red photograph by Harry Edwards.

"There may be under certain conditions (that is when circle
conditions are not good) elements extracted from the medium, but that
is rather the exception than the rule.

"The mobility of the ectoplasm is controlled by the extension of the
medium's nervous system.

"Remember this always, it is difficult to give a word picture which
conveys, however good the description, anything like a true picture

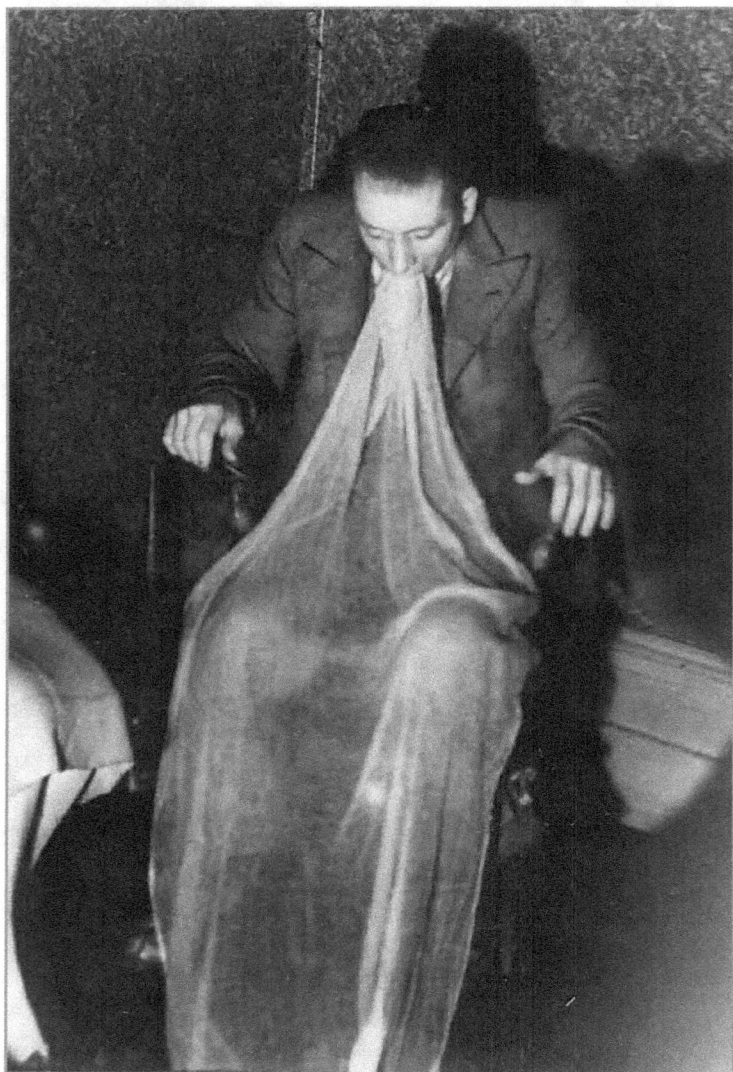

PLATE 12

Considerable volume of Grade 2 ectoplasmic material. Estimated to be over 4 yards long. This disperses in a fraction of time. (See above.)

Infra-red photograph by Harry Edwards.

of what it is. I will tell you this though, that one day man will be able to form this substance himself by the utilisation of those same rays."

Question: "These rays. Can you tell us more about them?"

Peter: "Thunderbolts are formed in space by the combination, by accident of course, of certain electrical forces that fuse atoms of matter and weld them together into one whole, creating something out of an apparent void. Well, that is very similar to the process that goes on. Instead of getting metal or a combination of mineral forms you get a substance which is physical yet not physical. It has physical properties, yet to say it is flesh, or to say it is air, or to say it is composed of three parts of this and one part of that would not be correct."

Question: "The second grade is therefore a refinement of the first?"

Peter: "In the first grade it is not animated. It cannot be directed as in the second instance. It is a primitive substance because the medium is not suitable, or undeveloped."

Question: "It is recalled that on occasion, with other mediums, sitters have been allowed to touch the crude form and, seemingly, it reacted adversely on the medium. Why is this?"

Peter: "It is like a jelly-fish and would have a natural reaction, but not because you touch the jelly-fish but because it is made from particles from the human body. The rays are not able to extract the elements of the free ether but have to do it from the ether in an act of conversion through the physical body; and it must therefore be like a raw spot on a tooth."

Question: "Regarding the strength of the rods, created from Grade 2, we know that this is very considerable. Can you tell us the source of the strength—from whence the power of the strength is derived?"

Peter: "Yes, I can tell you, but the thing is to try to convey it to you correctly. The strength of the levers or rods is not that of the muscles of a physical body. It is not the same form of strength as brute force. The rods are rendered so rigid that if it were permissible to strike them, they would emit almost a metallic-like ring through their own strength." (See Chapter XIII on "Levitation.")

(The author has felt these rods, when they have contacted him by passing across his body, and they have felt of irresistible strength like "rods of iron".)

Peter: "Now, the application of this strength is partly by an intricate system of leverage and balance, and partly by transmitting along the course of the rod a terrific voltage, but not a voltage that can be recorded by any measuring instruments that you possess. If this power was the same as your electricity, the enormous pressure used would cause the conductor or rod to glow. I do not say that the psychic rods do not glow, but not many are able to see it. It is the indirect system of leverage plus this energy that achieves the effect of great strength."

Interjection: "I have seen the terminals of such structures glow with a blue light." (See *The Mediumship of Jack Webber.*)

Peter: "That is quite possible, but that is not always present.

"Let us now come to Grade 3. Here we have quite a different quality altogether. This does not proceed from or return to the medium. It has characteristics common to the other two grades but is created by frequencies of a higher order."

Question: "What do you imply by the word frequencies?"

Peter: "Frequencies, harmony; it is all a matter of rhythm, pulsation, the frequency of the beat or harmony. It is the same instrument but a different piece of music. This allows of a greater degree of variation in that its range of operation, i.e. distance from the medium or the central point, is limited only by the radius of the circle; and in favourable conditions—very favourable conditions—can proceed beyond.

"This form of ectoplasm is web-like in construction and would be seen as like masses of cloud or steam, yet not spreading like that. It is used mostly in forming the outlines of the materialised figures (what you call draping). Yet again it possesses something of the qualities of Grades 1 and 2, but in their finer forms.

"The secret of its mobility is the 'ray' emanating from the medium. It is not focused, concentrated focus, as in the case of Grade 2, but is more diffused. It can be of varied character; it has something of the nature of the rods and something of its own peculiar characteristic of fineness. Whereas you can vary the focus of this latter grade, you cannot that of Grade 2.

"You have noticed the focus of a cinematograph and the beam emitted therefrom. You have seen also the specks of dust playing in and out of that beam. Imagine now the beam being invested with the power and the intelligence to collect those particles and to hold and mould them. If you can visualise that, you will have a pretty good idea of the formation of psychic rods and of ectoplasm in general. Switch off the beam and the whole disintegrates.

"This ray is the focal point which collects about itself by the agency of the intelligence of the directive power or mind, through the medium, those particles gathered from the free ether.

"Now I think we have covered this form very well. The whole basis of it is the understanding of radio activity, a thing now becoming known on earth. Not only has it the power to radiate and transmit, but also to collect and coalesce atoms, free atoms, from space. We can get combinations of atoms which are unknown to you, but which have the qualities of matter; and yet not be of any known matter that you know. Why ... if we were to form rods of iron, what a job we would have to disperse them again; but I cannot pursue it any further tonight."

Two further evenings were devoted to this topic in question and answer and are as follows. Many more questions rise to one's mind, but it is hoped that the essentials covered give a broad view of all that Peter could tell us.

Question: "In a previous discussion you mentioned that ectoplasm was cell-like; and while, in your last talk, you mentioned nervous action you did not mention capillary action. Would you like to include this in the present description?"

Peter: "Capillary action. Well, in a way that would tend to lead to confusion if you assume it has a similar system to yours. Have I referred to capillary action previously?"

Questioner: "Yes—although it is not in the records here."

Peter: "You see, capillary action is not always present, neither is the system it involves. It depends entirely upon the conditions and requirements at the time, and if we are going to build a form that has actual life in itself rather than a statue of the being who wishes to present itself, then this system would be present. That is where the form becomes living, having warmth and all that; but it entails a great deal of organisation and exposes the medium to greater risks of injury. That is only natural.

"Now to give an indication of the meaning of capillary action, but yet one that is not altogether true. It is partially so yet not wholly the truth to say that it is meticulous with the capillary system of the medium. The link between the two is atomisation. The blood is borrowed from the medium and atomised. There is no direct action. It is extracted by a certain method of atomisation; and functions within the form, where it is kept moving by the etheric beats of the heart. You must understand that apart from the physical body there must also be an etheric body. I will talk to you one day about where and how the spirit works in regard to its contacts with the spiritual body. I will just give you a lead. It is directly through the blood stream." (See Chapter XIX.)

Question: "Following this statement, is it correct to state that ectoplasm does not carry a system of blood circulation, by means of arteries and veins, as in the physical body?"

Peter: "It does not carry all this as a part of its system of arteries and veins."

Question: "Does the transfer of blood by atomisation infer an actual physical quantity of blood?"

Peter: "That is right. But its circulation does not depend upon the heart-beats of the materialised form."

Question: "Further, does the transfer of blood by atomisation infer that an actual physical quantity of blood is taken from the medium's blood system and transfused into the materialisation in a warm physical form? If so, how is a physical fluid activated by the etheric heart-beats of the medium; or is it incorrect to state that the materialised form has a circulatory system?"

Peter: "It is incorrect to say that the materialised form has a circulatory system. The circulation of the blood is maintained by the etheric heart-beats of the medium. There is a sympathetic link. That is why it is often considered that the materialised form is a part of the medium. Whilst that may be true in a sense, it is not true in actual fact. It will have perhaps a composed respiratory action, but it is always sympathetic. You must remember that the substance of which it is made is partly physical and partly etheric; and who can say where the one begins and the other ends?"

Question: "When a materialised form speaks, does it use its own physically constructed larynx?"

Peter: "No. The same principle is embodied within the materialised form as that about which we have already spoken. You know the one. The etheric amplifier. (See Chapter XV.) Well, that is a part of the materialised form. You see, to have a larynx and everything in connection with it would make it necessary for it to have a complete system of lungs and all the rest of it. Well, ask yourself, would that be necessary?"

Interjection: "Yet when a materialised form speaks it speaks as though it had."

Peter: "Yes, and perhaps you would get a certain warmth from the mouth as of breath. Well, that is done in the same way as the circulation. I tell you that in the case of materialisation, in so far as the figure may be perfect, the rest, such as rhythmic breathing, and perhaps even warmth of temperature, may not be possible of accomplishment. The most difficult accomplishment would be the voice which should express the personality of the figure shown. In that case it would be possible to convey the vibrations or the chords of the medium's throat and reproduce the voice by sound from the materialised form's mouth. There can be no hard and fast rule. That again depends on the completeness of the work."

Question: "Is the finer quality (Grade 3) linked by an ectoplasmic cord or structure to the medium?"

Peter: "No, it is an invisible etheric link—invisible nearly always. It depends upon where the substance begins to manifest; sometimes close against the medium and sometimes at a distance, with no possible apparent contact. Where it appears to be close to the medium, there is always that space of invisibility if it be but about half an inch. The best conditions pertaining are those where the distance between the ectoplasmic formation and the medium is greatest."

Question: "Regarding the feel of the ectoplasmic substance, we have had reference to a 'wetness that wets not'. Can you explain this?"

Peter: "It is 'viscous', but I will tell you the best parallel you can get—it is comparable to the fish called the eel, but one which is not freshly caught and has lain for some days. It is wet to the touch and yet no dampness is apparent. Again, however, this does not always apply. You can have it brittle so that it will crackle like parchment, or you can have it damp and cold; and again, you can have it dry and supple. It depends upon the condition, chiefly dietetic, of the medium. That is, the way in which the medium lives or has lived for the few days before the sitting. Much depends upon that."

Question: "When you get the 'sheet' effect, is this Grade 2? That always feels wet."

Peter: "Not commonly so. The best condition for it is when it is in its supple, dry state."

Question: "I remember that on the occasion when you touched our faces with it, it was also dry to the touch and patternless."

Peter: "You will find as a rule that there is no definite pattern. You must have something definite, but to say it has a definite pattern would not be true."

Question: "When ectoplasm was over the plaque it was so transparent we could hardly see it until it became as if rippled. Was that rippling caused artificially?"

Peter: "It was a distortion of the etheric ray around which it is formed. When a light of too great a density is exposed within the room, the rippling becomes so great that it disperses the ectoplasm."

Interjection: "At one time it appeared as almost invisible."

Peter: "Then we were applying unequal pressure."

Question: "As a preliminary to the formation of a finer grade, possibly Grade 2, there has been witnessed what appears to be an emergence of heavy whitish vapour from the medium's mouth or other source of emergence. It has been also noted that a physical sheet of ectoplasmic substance, before disappearing, has changed into vapour. I wonder if you could tell us if this vapour comes from, and returns to, the body?"

Peter: "To say it does not come from the body is not true, to say it has no direct contact would also be untrue. It would be very similar to water trickling out of a hose without pressure and then suddenly having pressure put behind to force it into a fixed shape—the shape of the nozzle. In the case of the vapour it is a loosely formed ectoplasm that has not yet attained physical qualities. It is in its commonest form."

Question: "With your medium I observed solid claw-like growths emerge from the edge of an almost transparent ectoplasmic sheet. These gripped and moved the plaque in a controlled manner. Can you enlighten us as to the thought origin that builds the claws, etc?"

Peter: "You remember some time ago I told you that most of the formations you have witnessed within the séance room were a display of primitive life. Well, it is not far for you to go in imagination from that stage to the forming of primitive grippers. That is what it is. Now from whence comes the motivating part? It comes from the same source as that which forms the grippers. It could not produce, in the circumstances, anything better. That force is directed by the mentality of those 'entities' which are commonly termed among you as 'elementals'. Their intelligence does not go beyond that. Therefore, in primitive things they use primitive methods, and that is why it is so necessary that the Guides responsible for the medium and for the sitters should have, not only full qualifications, but also should be, with your permission, invested with the authority to govern the power. The strength that is produced with lightning-like rapidity in one quick crescendo of energy is released equally like lightning. It is the culmination of a great effort wherein the innate desire of these elementals to destroy is given for a brief time free range.

"I cannot tell you in slow motion how it is achieved, but the force released for a brief period of time is tremendous, and if not controlled could slay a horse. These grippers, I tell you, could be deadly things. We utilise the different qualifications of these little people to the furtherance of our work, gradually raising them up because they have always one object and one main idea in view—that is, incarnation as human beings whom they copy so much. I could tell you of a race of them in being today: they are not related by blood ties, but they have, in this respect, a similarity of feature, height, build, and also similarities in other directions. But if you, unknowing, saw one you would see them all, and on earth today there are, at least, between 500 and 1000 of these personalities. They are what you have termed idiots. They have no mentality and they are not violent. Their characteristics are close-set eyes, flat foreheads and an altogether small head with rather thick lips that are set like a bull-dog's. The under-lip protrudes and the whole shape takes a very acute upward bend. The nose is small, with two round holes for the nostrils. The face and nose lack character. You can call them freaks, but they are normal in their features—they are not unlike animals. But their character stamps them all—they are a type which is produced from the same mould. Life is not so placid and calm; and I think if you knew more you would give us more consideration as to what should be and what should not be. In their right spheres everything works for good, but man is the head of all animal ambition; though some like to take short cuts.

"Man in the creative sense is the apex of the whole evolution of sub-mundane life: that is to the whole of the animal and vegetable

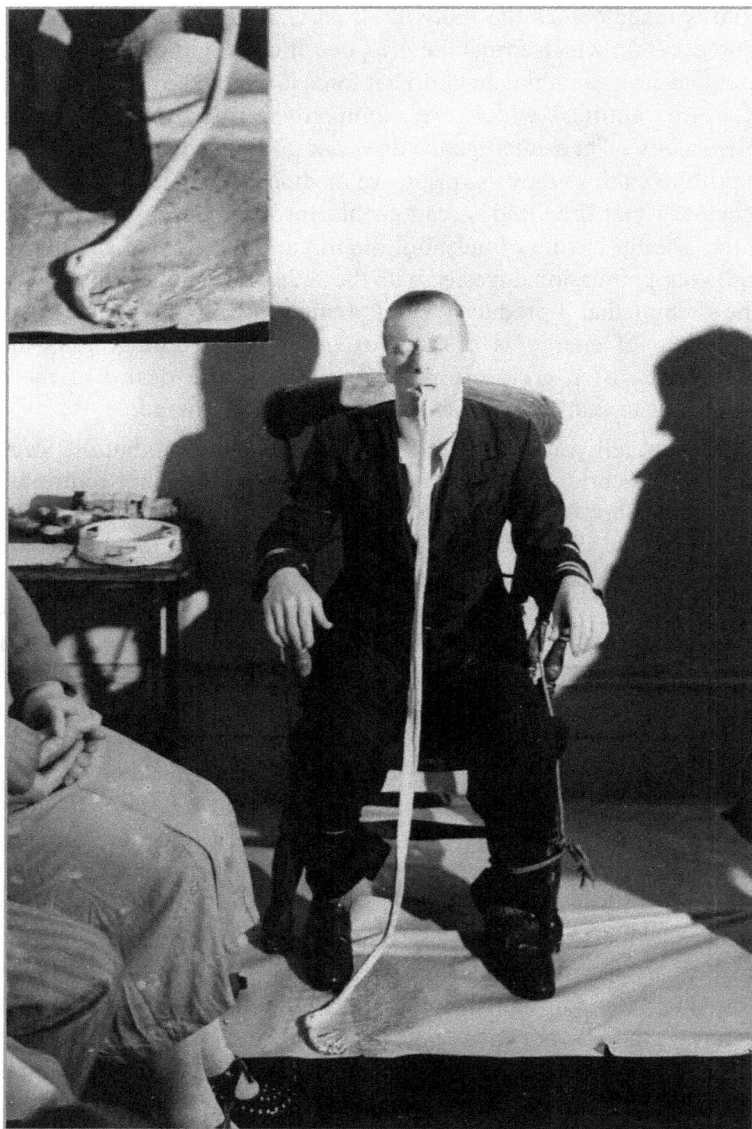

PLATE 13
Grade 2 ectoplasmic formation showing tendency of extremity
to organize. (See Chap. XII.)
Infra-red photograph by "Daily Mirror" staff photographer

kingdoms. And there is over all the sub-mundane life a brooding spirit which is not individualised. Its intelligence is colossal, in its own sphere and in its own creation: it controls its physical counterparts as a whole and not as individuals. That intelligence is striving always to keep up its creation in the scheme of evolutionary development; and if once there is a chance for these elementals to push forward and gain access to the human realm, they can never be turned out. Hence my remark and warning—perhaps you will give us greater consideration in those things that are to be and not to be. You will see now the trend of our talk."

Question: "At a later sitting, after having seen some more primitive-like forms, I observed a perfect hand, formed from an island opaque mass in the centre of a piece of almost transparent ectoplasmic material draped over the illuminated plaque; and I noted its perfection as to digital phalanges."

Peter: "But you observed something else—you observed its gradual growth."

Question continued: "Yes, I did: but in your statement on materialisations you referred to the materialising entity drawing unto itself particles from the ether. Am I right in assuming that there is a similarity of process between the materialisation of a whole entity and a portion of an entity? Was the hand part of a discarnate entity or was it an evolved 'thought' hand or was it from the earlier primitive growths and produced by the elementals?"

Peter: "It was a product of the elementals. It was a triumph for them. That progress, as you saw it, took perhaps in measure of time a thousand years to evolve from the primitive gripper to a hand with its digits. It was a triumph for them and there was much rejoicing when they had done it."

Statement: "That demonstration is a complete answer to the opinion of those who do not agree with us that life exists beyond our present physical existence. That demonstration was most illuminating to us."

Peter: "Yes. We are apt to consider our life as of the moment and not to any extent of what is past and what is to come. That is the whole question."

Question: "Ectoplasm created from etheric particles possesses physical properties of density, weight, moisture, cohesion. We can understand that matter changes its formation from solid to fluid or to gas, but in so doing it retains the elements of which it is composed. Is it possible for you to give us some idea of the constituents of ectoplasm? Are they known to man by name? For example, if water is analysed its components would be oxygen and hydrogen."

Peter: "Well, there again where you have not the constancy of ectoplasmic formation you cannot have the constancy of formulae. There are, I believe, thirty-two known atoms and from these thirty-two every substance that you know upon earth is formed by various combinations. Now you understand that. Well, it is no answer to your question to say that it is two parts water. The atoms are composed of things we know. I suppose you could call it material, yet it is not material in the sense that, if it is disturbed, it is likely to be dispersed. We can vary it so rapidly that it becomes a cloud-like steam. This accelerates decomposition; and if we were able to withdraw the bound ether associated with any article such as a table, it would collapse instead of decaying. It is the bound ether which makes it retain its character. Actually, therefore, ectoplasm is a neutral substance which is created because it best suits the purpose."

Question: "Is it right, then, to conclude that ectoplasm is constructed from the known atoms?"

Peter: "From a combination of some of them but not of the whole. What decides the particular material substance is the rate of motion and combination of atoms. You see, if we slow up that process we can make it partly physical and partly non-physical; and we can finish that by saying that ectoplasm is the 'mists of the borders' that link the physical to the realm non-physical. It is the meeting of the two. It is a physical substance with a non-physical existence."

Statement: "Some years ago an analysis was made of some ectoplasmic substance and it was said to be largely albumen."

Peter: "That is true; but never forget in all these things that it may have been produced for that action; and rather than its being a true formation it may have been specially formed. If you ask these 'little people' for something they will give it, but that is not to say it is genuine."

Question: "You spoke of the voltage sent through psychic rods used for strength. Is there a generating source for this voltage?"

Peter: "You cannot generate it, but only direct it. That direction is natural. That is, it comes within the same influence of control as the production of actual phenomena. It is a natural force. It is a force which is adapted for a particular purpose in the same way as your own electricity but is of a finer kind. It is a force which is there all the time. You simply cause it to move in a given direction along an easier path. In the first instance you will agree that magnetism is a natural phenomenon; therefore, it is from a combination of the magnetic forces that you get electrical energy. You magnetise and you create a field of magnetism in which you evolve another field which causes much electrical friction. You simply congregate it in one spot and cause it to move along the path. Electricity does not run along the conductors. They pass it on. You go round the circuit. You have in an electric generating plant a complete picture of the medium and psychic rods. You get work done the other end according to your wisdom."

Question: "We come to the 'ray' which you spoke about. Can you tell me if there is any affinity between the human body and the rays and/or between the human mind and the rays?"

Peter: "It is always apart from the human mind, i.e. the mind of man himself. Affinity—there is a connection with the rays. It is through the medium's soul body that the rays are directed and that is where we hold the key to switch off at the moment of any danger if conditions are not right. The medium is the focal point, always he is the generator; but he is not fitted with 'safety fuses' so we have to stand by the switch. I tell you, in the study of anything of this nature, electricity and its laws are running closely parallel with those of the laws we are trying to propound: the only difference being that you are not yet skilled in creating etheric conductors and have therefore to use the physical ones because that is the only material with which you can work. In creating the physical part, however, there is present the etheric part by virtue of the very nature of the materials you use; hence you get the creation of the etheric field which is not within the object (or conductor) but in the ether surrounding it. You will one day be able to control these rays. Man will, not be allowed to use them until he is qualified. You cannot remain in your present state of mind for always, otherwise not only are you lost but we also."

CHAPTER XIII

LEVITATION

THE movement of objects by means other than that of human agency is termed "levitation".

This phenomena, by virtue of its definite act, has been the subject of considerable research, notably by Professor Crawford through the mediumship of Miss Goligher.

Professor Crawford's conclusions illustrate how an advance in knowledge can be attained when there is the right combination of understanding investigator and willing medium and co-operative spirit operators.

Levitation is one of the elementary and primitive forms of action with physical mediums. It varies from wild and haphazard movement, to controlled, ordered and delicately adjusted volition. Movement of this nature is generally the first sign of the ability of the operators to demonstrate through their medium.

Professor Crawford was able to obtain photographs of the mechanism employed in lifting weighty objects; and established among other conclusions that the movement was controlled by an apparatus termed "psychic rods", constructed through the medium's psychic faculties. He also proved by patient and exhaustive research that in accordance with the general principles of leverage these rods were used in order to move an object of greater weight than that permitted by the power of a single rod emanating from the medium.

Further experiments with the medium seated on a scale proved that the weight levitated was returned through the medium's body. When leverage was employed with the rod resting on a pivot, the weight returned through the medium corresponded with the exact pressure required to move an object of a given weight by that means.

Probably owing to the nature of the experiments and the use of white light for photography, the character of the levitation noted by Professor

Crawford was restricted to the primitive or "brute force" agency as described by Peter.

With Jack Webber outstanding evidence has been recorded of the various grades of levitating power. Of the primitive kind, physical formations of great strength were observed emanating from his solar plexus. They resembled the trunks of young trees, being some six inches broad near the body and tapering off to the point of contact with the object. Heavy mahogany tables requiring two people to lift them have been moved out of a "wedged-in" position to the far side of the séance room by this same method.

Through the same mediumship the infra-red photographs of tables in levitation were secured. One of these, as shown by Plate No. 5, pictures a heavy circular table of 45 lbs. weight in suspension; this table requires a two-handed effort to lift it, and a "husky" man to do it. The other, Plate No. 14 (overleaf), shows a lighter table in movement before Mr Bernard Gray of the *Sunday Pictorial*. No psychic apparatus is visible with either of these photographs. On other occasions the author has testified to seeing massively constructed apparatus in association with primitive levitation.

Before proceeding further with this phenomenon, it is necessary to keep in mind the revelations of Peter, who divides the forces used for levitation into two main categories:

(a) Movement of objects by the "ponderous and brutal" means, that is by physically constructed psychic rods.

(b) Movement by regulating weights and gravity.

These are further sub-divided, as will be shown later, but for the moment these two broad divisions will enable the reader to comprehend the different grades of phenomena and avoid confusion by associating one with the other.

The records of the movements, and the character of the action of levitated articles through Mr Clare's mediumship, possess the same characteristics as those reported at other times and places with other mediums. The characteristics of levitation are so similar that the experienced observer at once recognises the true movement.

With trumpet levitation the movement is incredibly fast; the trumpets weaving intricate patterns, so that their illuminated bands of paint appear as fixed lines of light. When two or more trumpets are engaged in such movement they intertwine; so that if, for example,

PLATE 14
Lighter table levitated by similar process to table in Plate 5.
(See page 82)
Infra-red Photograph by Leon Isaacs.

simple figures of eight movements are in being, they cut across each other. The trumpets may be moving at great speed high up to the ceiling, with one near the ceiling and the other near the floor, in vertical action close to a wall, whilst at the same time a third may be perfectly still in the air in the centre of the activity without even a quiver of movement. The author has seen four trumpets in simultaneous levitation. To witness this elementary phenomenon alone is more than sufficient to prove the presence of forces and control beyond man's knowledge.

It should be remembered that this phenomenon, as just described, takes place in the dark. To the critic who laments that darkness is a subterfuge of the séance room, here is an act incredibly more difficult in the dark than in the light. At times there may be as many as twenty people seated close together in the form of a circle, yet never is any person struck by a trumpet; nor is such a thing as an electric pendant suspended from the ceiling down into the centre of the trumpet activity ever hit. Never has a picture on the wall, or a glass door or a bookcase or sideboard been harmed while the phenomenon is normal. Only once to the author's knowledge was a suspended electric light fitting smashed in the hundreds of sittings held in strange homes through J.W.'s mediumship, and he used long heavy metal trumpets.

This mishap only occurred through the collapse of the "conditions" due to an interference.

With Arnold Clare the circle has to be widespread in order to give room for the most expansive movement. There is no operation from the immediate neighbourhood of the medium, but movement occurs as far afield as the extended circle permits; and even then the trumpets travel outwards over the heads of the sitters farthest from the medium.

In this connection the most remarkable of the author's experiences was that which illustrated the perfect control of movement within a dark circle. It used to occur frequently at Webber's developing circle and involved a test of nerves for the sitters. Here a metal trumpet would travel in an arc-light movement, so fast that the luminosity was just a blaze of light; and a loud swishing noise would be created by the passage of the trumpet through the air. The edge of the trumpet would come within the barest fraction of an inch of the sitter's nose. I frequently experienced this. Whilst holding myself perfectly still, the trumpet-edge would almost touch the skin but never quite—a sixteenth of an inch more and the tip of my nose must have been torn off. In a flash the trumpet would sweep over to another sitter on the opposite side of the circle and repeat the same operation or gently caress the face, to return instantly to swish up and down just in front of my nose. (To prevent any misapprehension on the part of the reader, it may be stated that those responsible for the action described only carried it out after knowing that the sitter was able to stand it. It would not be attempted with any stranger or person unused to séance-room work.)

The most delicate trumpet control, as the records testify, is also witnessed with Mr Clare.

Another form of levitation is that of the medium himself, in his chair. This phenomenon has been recorded on a number of occasions with various mediums. With J.W. there are reports in the book on his mediumship, and all that need be cited here is that he has been seen in both red and white light levitated in the air: in large halls he would touch hanging pendants fifteen to twenty feet high under the roof. Mr Clare is also levitated in his chair at the close of séances.

Thus we can arrive at the conclusion that the movement of levitated objects is sure, definite, rigidly and delicately controlled, and that such movement must be the result of thought direction with the operators positively aware of the physical features within the area of action.

We have already said that levitation is graded into different categories, and Peter's explanation of the primitive method is dealt with first, as being far less challenging than the other.

Peter said:

"Levitating objects by means of rods is what one, using brute force in ignorance, would call the operation. I do not say this in a disparaging way, but it is clumsy and consumes great power and energy, oft-times to the detriment of the medium. You must understand the use of rods is very awkward in the extreme and they are also subject to limitations: for as they become attenuated they lose many of their characteristics and strength.

"Therefore, if we wish to lift something heavy we have to push against the pressure, or pull away from the pull; but in pushing against the pressure a great strain is caused upon the medium as the moisture contained in the medium's body is absorbed at a terrific rate. That is bad, because it tends to thicken the blood." (Peter's reference to "pushing against the pressure" will be appreciated after reading his explanation of the "refined" method that follows.) "This method, too, lends itself to a repetition of the same phenomena through the means of subconscious and physical action by the medium himself, which may put him in bad odour, should such movements be observed.

"For the conduct of phenomena using psychic mechanics, the conditions must be excellent. For not only are the psychic rods an integral part of the phenomena for the moment but of the medium as well. By that I mean there is a subconscious reflex action on the part of the medium physically, because the rods contain the lower impulse that would be, in a case of normality, manipulating his limbs for the same movements. Therefore, when he sits for the production of phenomena and conditions are not quite right, he is not in a state to discriminate. The impulse is passed through his nervous organism to produce reactions, and if he is not restrained the phenomena will still occur, although it is just as genuine."

This point of Peter's is illuminating when we pass our minds back to certain supposed "exposures" of mediums.

The findings of Professor Crawford as mentioned at the beginning of this chapter were mentioned to Peter and he was asked whether he agreed with the findings. Peter replied:

Peter: "That is almost so, but you must also remember that the weight of a medium will also fluctuate through the consumption of the fluid content of the body. That is a direct cause. It is a form of hydraulics. True, it is borrowed and we return it; perhaps not quite all, but most of it—but this work is not good for the medium."

It was established several times, using the same scales before and after a séance, that J.W. lost up to 8lbs. in weight during a sitting. By taking his weight at various times following the sitting, it was found that his weight became normal about sixteen hours afterwards. Mediums whose physical powers are so used in séance work should remember this, and so give themselves adequate time for recovery before sitting again.

Peter was asked: "When an object of weight is lifted, where is the basis of resistance?"

Peter: "Well, you cannot fix that; it would vary; but what are we going to move?"

Questioner: "Say a light object—such as a trumpet."

Peter: "The basis of resistance would then be, if it were close to the medium, from his knee or shoulder. It would be rigid. If it were at a greater distance, the most convenient point; and from there to the medium (acting as a 'power cable') it would be relaxed, limp."

Question: "Would one get the cruder method for levitating objects when the control of the medium is from 'within'?"

Peter: "You mean in the case of direct control of the physical organism by an invading entity?"

Questioner: "Yes."

Peter: "We have spoken of the production of phenomena and their control, that is the creation of an environment whereby the phenomena can be directed by thought (if you wish) and wherein we use a movement of brute force with rods. In this case, control from within and directive control provides almost a parallel.

"Directive control is where the instrument reaches out in thought and raises his own tonal quality to the degree where his aspirations meet and fuse with the directive thought of the Guide or Inspirer. There we have two forces seeking each other, the one lending himself to the thought domination of the other. That is in the case of directive control.

"In regard to physical control you have almost a reversal. Instead of being controlled by thought, you are entirely controlled physically, so much so that all the thought actions of the invading entity become, for the time, part of the physical organism of the instrument. The deeper the invading entity becomes immersed within the denser ether surrounding the earth, the more he loses the vision of the spheres beyond."

This answer emphasises the point made by Peter elsewhere, that it is not good for a medium or potential medium to encourage this form of control.

An illustration of such physical control is given in the case of Jack Webber. J.W. was about 5 ft. 8 ins. in height, and yet on such an occasion when invested by an entity of greater stature, he would become physically much taller, bigger and stronger. Whilst under this control he would call our attention to the change, and would ask for one of the sitters, Mr Croft, a Metropolitan policeman, 6 ft. tall, and well-built, to stand in front of him and note the expansion. (This took place in red light.) J.W. would then expand and grow taller until he was of equal stature with Mr Croft. On one such occasion he took the author (5 ft. 8 ins. tall and 10 stone in weight) by the shoulders and swung him round as if he were a bag of straw.

We now come to Peter's explanations of the more refined processes of levitation, and they contain some most challenging observations.

Before proceeding with them it may be well to recall certain definite recorded acts of levitation which, as will be seen, come within this category.

There are the Margery records, which show that sitters were not only permitted to encircle with clasped hands a levitated object, but to pass their clasped arms right over and around the object, thus proving there was no physical connection responsible. for the levitation. There are the photographs of the tables, previously mentioned, where no physical mechanism can be seen; and from the author's point of view, in red light, he has witnessed, with other sitters, trumpets floating or sailing around within the circle perfectly clearly without any visible connection. This movement was described by a sceptic as like pike swimming and darting about in a pool.

The movement of the plaque is reported in one of Mr Clare's circles, where at the time it passed between illuminated ectoplasm and between the legs of myself and other sitters. Had there been any physical control, however attenutated, it must have been observed.

It is here noted that where physical rods are employed they are always straight and rigid. (See Peter's reference to these rods in the chapter on "Ectoplasm".)

Peter commenced by saying:

Peter: "You are already aware of the limited space wherein the directive intelligences can work, that is, within the sphere of action circumscribed by the auric field or 'tent'. Within that space the force of gravity is not so greatly impressed. Gravity is in a state of suspension, so that to levitate any article, no matter what the weight may be, we neutralise the already weakened pressure or gravity.

"To get a clear conception of this, one must picture the force of gravity, not as a pulling power but as a pushing power; not as a drawing towards the centre of the earth but of a push towards the centre.

"Gravity in its operation is due entirely to etheric pressure and nothing else.

"You will see that when it comes to manipulation of gross ether we are in our element, the same as you are with your wood and stone.

"Gravity operates towards the centre of the earth. This appears to you to be so because your feet are implanted on the earth and objects move towards the earth's centre. The pressure is exerted from all directions equally, so it must get across the centre. You take the centre because you stand on the sphere and the pressure is so equal in all directions, etherically, that it tends as far as you can judge to be a pulling force directed from the centre.

"You see, you are not concerned, directly, with what are the 'laws' of gravity—it is not the law you are perceiving—it is the force.

"The pressure of the ether penetrates all things; therefore the force of gravity operates no matter where it is.

"The magnet depends upon etheric vibrations for its manifestations. The etheric content in which you are immersed is the primitive room of all life-cosmic, solar and all forms of animated life."

Question: "You said that gravity is the result of etheric pressure. Can you explain this more fully?"

Peter: "It will help you if I tell you this. All matter is permeated by the ether! . . . How is this?

"Because it is of such immense and ponderable pressure that it pushes its way through everything, so much so that whereas you consider stone and bricks as solid, actually they are full of great holes due to the pressure placed upon them etherically. The spaces within and between the particles of matter are so great that in comparison and with no exaggeration the distance between each is equivalent to that existing between a football suspended in the centre of Westminster Abbey and the walls and floor and roof. It is; after all, the element within which the ordinary magnetic power operates. If you were to place a magnet within an etheric vacuum it would not operate any more than a flame in a closed jar."

Question: "Concerning other pressures, such as the atmospheric pressure, how is this related to either the etheric pressure or the force of gravity?"

Peter: "You mean the atmosphere, referring to air. Well, air ceases to exist a few miles up, and gravity ceases to operate (as far as you are concerned) because sooner or later you must reach an area where the atmosphere enters into a neutral zone. To us, atmospheric pressure is incomprehensible."

Question: "Referring to the answer just given—you have said that atmospheric pressure is incomprehensible to you. Why is this, for we know the atmosphere has weight and therefore exerts pressure?"

Peter: "Yes, of course, it has weight like everything else. That is only because it is necessary for your wellbeing that you should be able to assess things, and atmospheric pressure is a thing which is only concerned with yourselves. It has no existence apart from yourselves. Its depth is only a few miles of your measure, and beyond that it does not exist in any form whatsoever. It therefore has no bearing on the larger problems with which we are dealing."

Question: "There is also the question of attraction between matter and matter, the greater the mass the greater the attraction. How do you relate your statement to the possibility that the core of the earth, being of mineral content, may be the centre of attraction towards the centre of the earth?"

Peter: "It seems as if the mind of man must always have a core, like an apple. Why do they say it is the centre of the earth that attracts?

"Because of the great mass of the earth's mineral centre, and the consequent pulling force towards the centre.

"Well, supposing you take two large masses of matter, polarise them to the same polarity and see what happens. Actually the one would push the other away and not attract it. Well, is it not possible that the same thing may apply in the case of gravity? Could not the mineral contents of the earth and those in space be polarised to such a fine degree of balance that each body within the solar system maintains its position perfectly? It is the evenness of pull between the heavenly bodies and the pivot, the sun, which is responsible for keeping the earth in its place; as well as the other bodies.

"This is accomplished through that little-known element, ether, a substance which can be made to bear a character according to its environs and the purpose it has to serve.

"We were talking about the two masses having the same polarity and making them reject each other. What actually takes place within the solar system is that the composition of each body is such that each repels or attracts the other to such fine limits that they are indissolubly bound within their particular orbit. In such a way, too, that all things relative to that body must normally remain a prisoner. Now listen to me. If you study that, you can study any mineral. You can study the large solar system that has its central pivot and around which revolve in their precise orbit electrons, so-called, that determine what atom it is. It is independent, in itself, of any outside control. It shows that it has a central intelligence of its own. So far as it is concerned, nothing exists outside of itself. Now can you see? It is a world of its own. It is the cheese and not the maggot. It is the motive.

"You speak of the law of gravity. It is not the 'law'. It is the 'effects' man studies, and they call the effects the law. Man is only concerned with effects and says it works because he knows what effect the so-called law has.

"Attraction of matter to matter is something apart from etheric pressure. It has a relationship, but at the same time you have a state of unbalance because if you were to put an object between two of similar weight the centre one would remain stationary.

"You have bodies drawing out and you have certain stationary bodies, more or less on the outside fringe, pulling the other way. Well, of course that proves they could as easily be pushed as pulled. You have the core of the earth which pulls, but what is space when you are considering such forces?

"There is no feasible evidence of the law of gravity you just study effects."

Question: "Can you tell us, when an object is levitated and is subjected to controlled directional movement, by what means this is done?"

Peter: "When you are sailing a boat you manipulate the sail to travel in the required direction. In the case of directing the movement of articles, we change not the sail but the direction of the 'breeze'. We direct the 'breeze' so as to move the trumpet in the desired direction, or alternately we create an inequality of 'breezes', which is the same thing."

Question: "When the trumpet moves and twirls very rapidly, is this movement produced in the same way?"

Peter: "It is produced by the same method, but what we do, instead of directing a gentle 'breeze', is to create an etheric whirlwind which has a fixed centre and spreads out fanwise; this carries with it the trumpet, which is caught up within the whirl. The trumpet has lost the physical qualities of weight, and therefore it is, in actual fact, non-existent physically, in so far as this characteristic is concerned."

Question: "Is the control of the whirl by directive thought?"

Peter: "The explanation of that at this point is liable to be rather confusing. You see we do not produce all this. We have to go deeper still and speak about such things as "elementals"."

This was the first time Peter mentioned "elementals", "the little people", "pre-humans" who have been previously described in this book. It is repeated that to comprehend them, as well as other incidental matters, one must review the thesis as a whole and not isolate one part of the explanation from another. Each aspect of the process of producing phenomena is related to the other.

It is frequently observed with trumpet phenomena that these possess individuality, indicating that a particular personality was responsible for the movements. This was commented on to Peter and he further observed:

Peter: "Such characteristics do develop because these "elementals" are very primitive; and they like to be outstanding and to have characteristics of their own, but this is a subject that can best be dealt with elsewhere."

Question: "Can you indicate the amount of force that can be exercised? Is it considerable?"

Peter: "It does not matter what the weight is provided we can see the content. If we can see the content, then by rarefaction there is no limit to the weight that can be used.

"The more we adjust the weight the more inert does matter become. That is the sum total of matter—inertia—the lack of desire for the thing to move. But once get it started and it would want the same power to stop it. If you could make the etheric vacuum around the circle complete, we would have all the sitters without appreciable weight.

"Thus, movement is the directing of things by regulating its content; within, as one might say, a form of 'rarefied atmosphere'. It is as if we were holding back the pressure to keep the article stationary. It requires only a little operation to make things float—these could then be directed as one can direct a feather or a light piece of paper. The weight goes when you remove the pressure of gravity. It has no weight when gravity is removed."

CHAPTER XIV

APPORTATION

"APPORTATION" is the producing at a given place of an object from a distance. The object may be composed of any material and be of any size. The distance from which it is brought may vary from a few yards to thousands of miles.

While it is contended that the phenomena and teachings reported in this book proves the case for survival, apporting lends weighty support to this conclusion.

Apport mediumship is one of the rarest forms of mediumship. The number of authenticated reports of apporting is very limited, some of the most notable being those associated with Charles Bailey of Australia, Count Rossi, Maria Silbert, Estelle Roberts, Jack Webber and Arnold Clare.

It is noteworthy that all these mediumships are of comparatively recent times; and this may indicate that either earlier apporting may not have been recorded, or that it denotes an advance in the knowledge and adaptability of the spirit operators in the use of their human instruments. Yet we are told by Peter that where such mediumship can function, apporting is a relatively simple performance.

While the act of apporting, or its opposite "asporting" (that is, when an object is taken away from a séance room), may be a simple one to the spirit operators, yet these acts appear incomprehensible to the human mind. It means that an object, say a stone, a piece of glass, metal or a vegetable product, is taken from a distant place and produced in an instant of time within the four walls of the séance room. To achieve this the physical state of the object is transformed into another state, so permitting its instantaneous transportation and passage through solid objects such as walls, doors, etc., with greater ease than sound or electrical energy can penetrate such obstacles.

No wonder that "scientists" have so far frowned upon this form of phenomena, for it appears so demonstrably impossible. It is this apparent "impossibility" that must argue the presence and action of discarnate minds to accomplish it; the fact of its performance strengthens the case for survival, otherwise how can one explain the presence of the operators?

As a rule, a condition of darkness is necessary for apporting, though cases are reported of the act being performed in light. I have witnessed the arrival of two apports (with J.W.) in a red light sufficiently strong to show clearly the bound medium and all sitters; and, more noteworthy, a recent apport was received through Mr Clare in bright white light. On this occasion the four people present (including the medium, in trance) stood upright with all hands linked.

The apport which fell into their midst was a large and heavy copper coin. The light on this occasion was a 100-watt white electric lamp.

While other forms of phenomena have been tentatively accepted by some scientific faculties, apporting has not yet been accepted. In the realm of spirit activity, the scientific mind has always lagged behind knowledge gained in the séance room, but doubtless the time will arrive when the seeming "miracle" of apporting will be accepted.

It may be said that there is no form of physical mediumship that is so open to fraudulent deception as that of apportation. Short of the most intimate search of the medium and indeed all sitters—probably by X-rays, it is difficult to conceive precautions that would satisfy an investigating commission. Incidentally, it is not easy to obtain the services of an investigating commission composed of persons whose authority is unquestioned. Even if it were, it might well be that the unusually severe conditions imposed would be so restrictive and artificial that, coupled with the strained mental attitude of the sitters focused upon a set result, the sitting would be rendered abortive. True, we have succeeded in obtaining an infra-red photograph of the act of an apport being re-materialised in ectoplasm (through J. W.), but even this might be said to have been "framed", despite the twenty independent sitters present on that occasion. Similarly, to have an object passed into a locked and sealed box in the darkness of a séance room would have to meet the charge of its being a conjuring trick. The time will doubtless come when the spirit operators will be able to devise a test that will be indisputable; and until this occurs, we shall have to be content with the reports of sitters and investigators. It need only be added, once more, that in recent years our scientists have been able to produce results that would have been totally rejected a decade ago.

There is a further aspect of this question that may command some weight, and that is the process of apporting is but a part of the general phenomena associated with physical mediumship. It is illogical to believe that a medium in the trance condition necessary for phenomena would be able to return to normality consciously to commit a fraudulent action. Yet for apporting to be fraudulent this absurd contention would need to be maintained.

No medium of repute would jeopardise his or her mediumship by such artificial means. He or she would know it would be to invite exposure, and to destroy the confidence of friends and others in their mediumship. Finally, it is exceedingly doubtful whether the Guides would continue to work with such a medium. Therefore, apporting should be considered with the rest of accepted activity.

The detailed happenings respecting apporting through Mr Clare's mediumship reported in the first part are eloquent of the act; and the reports independently subscribed by a number of writers testify to the similarity of procedure and result. My report of the séance on July 20, 1940, tells not only of the apporting of nearly a pound of metal in varied forms, but also of the apporting of four lion claws which arose from an unrehearsed conversation. For the conversation to have been anticipated is beyond credulity; whilst for the medium or his friends to have secreted the objects and produced them by the methods reported, movement and actions would have been necessary, and these must have been discerned by myself and the other experienced sitters present.

In passing, it may be stressed that those accustomed to the work of dark physical circles develop an extra-perceptive sense. This results from their being so familiar with activity in the dark that eyes, ears and mind become tensely alert. Even the most insignificant rustle of clothing in movement is noted, and it would be most difficult, if not impossible, for anyone to rise up from a chair without being observed.

Peter, in his quiet way, has given us in the explanation that follows the procedure adopted, within the measure of our understanding. He leads us further to the contemplation of a form of life that has its nearest parallel in the fairies of our childhood. This form of life (which he calls the "little people") is as a link in the chain of life's evolution and progression. Failing more definite evidence of their existence, we can only accept the "little people" as one of the "wonders" of Peter's revelations. Some of these revelations are provable, many more—when related to authenticated evidence are most probable; and it may serve, for the time being, to receive his story of the "little people" as knowledge "in reserve" in our pursuit of truth and wisdom.

Peter commenced by saying:

Peter: "No better start could be made than to consider an article that is intended for use as an apport. In normal apporting simple articles, such as stone, metal, dried grasses, wood and soil, are most easily apported, and the range proper would be things composed of these materials. New articles such as jewellery, handkerchiefs and animal life should be considered as freak apports and can only be produced under very special conditions. You see, I am not quite satisfied with the procedure we are adopting—we are not going right down to the facts, to the nature of the intelligentsia who deal with this activity. Now, an article which is to be apported must normally have rested in its hiding place (I do not mean it is hidden) for a considerable period before it can be used. This is not a normal qualification but one of becoming steeped in its local environment. The reason is that it must not of itself set up individual radiation, otherwise there would be a disturbance within the ether at that point. This would prevent the successful construction of the etheric vacuum around the object to be transported. To explain this etheric vacuum, one might say that it compares, which is as near as one can get, to an egg, with all the possibilities it contains of life, and even to its 'shape'. Perhaps now you can see how we get back to the beginning of life, and how the life first reached the earth through an etheric vacuum."

Question: "What is an etheric vacuum? Are we right in assuming an etheric vacuum describes a condition in which there is no ether?"

Peter: "In your vacuum ether still exists. In our vacuum ether also exists when the air has been excluded therefrom. With your vacuum you change the character of the ether because you have removed the bound ether associated with that air. An etheric vacuum is precisely the same. The ether within is different from that without. The character has been taken out of the ether within the vacuum."

Question: "Did life originate in this vacuum?"

Peter: "You see, we are carrying out the reverse action by placing the object into an etheric state, and what is to prevent us carrying it further into a spiritual state, by the same means of working in reverse? Now you can see how fish can be in a pool that has never had any spawn in it. I warned you that in dealing with this matter we were dealing with primal powers that were responsible for the beginning of life."

Question: "Could I call it, or would you consider it as a sealed birth?"

Peter: "We will talk about that question later, comparing it with the birth and growth of things. Remember we have spoken of these things as being primitive.

"Here is a passing thought. Our globule or egg. Is it not remarkable how nature manifests itself?—always forming new life and possibilities within spheres and ovals; I mean in shape.

"Now studying the etheric vacuum in relation to an egg simplifies the process of explanation. Within the egg you have all the potentialities of life awaiting only the opportunity which will transform it from potential energy into pulsating active life. The same takes place within the etheric vacuum, only in the reverse way. You have something which has life, in so far as shape and quality goes, which is just awaiting the opportunity for the change to be brought about. Now we come to the roads where we start to lose you again. Like the egg, the conditions within the etheric shell of the vacuum are not the same as those without; and through the directive play of attractive etheric forces (corresponding to heat, as in the case of the egg) life (in the case of the object to be apported) is speeded up, so that the atomic structures change. When this occurs, the speed becomes so great that all physical semblance disappears. This is just the reverse of that of the egg, where the fluids become solidified and take on its form according to the germ implanted therein."

Question: "Is the action of change automatic as soon as the necessary condition is created around the object?"

Peter: "It is automatic. Now this is a point which will interest you. The sympathy between that object at a remote distance and the medium does not pertain, as is generally supposed, but where the sympathy or harmony does exist is between the operators and the medium. It is there and not with the distant object. It is a natural sympathetic understanding between the soul in human form and, for want of a better name, the 'nature spirits' which serve."

Question: "You state it is the sympathy between the soul and the 'nature spirits'. How does this operate?"

Peter: "They, the 'nature spirits', are unconscious of the directive mind of the medium: They are directly associated only with the soul of an incarnate human being. Any direction that is passed on to these 'little people' is via the medium himself or through his aura. I am speaking chiefly of apports now. Look—you have a pretty fable, *Gulliver's Travels*, where you have one giant amongst a crowd of diminutive people. It is very similar to that, but they cluster around the human being who has a physical body. That is absolute."

Question: "Does that apply to any human being?"

Peter: "Yes. The harmony may be not so complete, but I cannot go into that now. Have you ever heard of the expression 'Green Fingers'? They can resuscitate plants. Well, it is the same sympathy or harmony which exists between these little people."

Question: "The point which is puzzling is the direction that the little people get in a séance in order to obtain apports."

Peter: "The fact of the medium sitting shows that he is giving his consent for others—that is the controls—to give the direction. Now it is necessary for this work that there must be a Control who is as near to them in sympathy as it is possible to get. Hence, in this case, the employment of our friend Simba. You see, the Control works within the aura of the medium and is, for the moment, using the medium's authority for that direction. If the medium were to employ the same powers consciously, then he could 'receive food from the ravens in the wilderness', but as that is not possible, he must have an assistant, which is the same thing."

Question: "Do the little people create the etheric vacuum?"

Peter: "Yes; but mark you, it is confined always to simple things. They cannot rise above that."

Question: "Does not that require a great amount of knowledge on the part of the little people?"

Peter: "No, that is the hod in which they carry their stones. They are using their everyday means for the production of what you would consider the miracle, but to them it is simpler than the eating of your meal. The difficulty arises not in the construction of the etheric egg and the dematerialisation of the object within it, but in returning it to its normal physical state within the circle. That is the real difficulty. Observe, in the first instance, I have stated the ideal conditions are those wherein the object must have rested in its position so long as to absorb its environment. In bringing it to the circle, they have created deliberately just those conditions which they would normally avoid. That is the difficulty. That is why oft-times an object will come to you with condensation upon it, or extremes of temperature."

Question: "Can you tell us the method of transportation?"

Peter: "Transportation is very simple once the article is rendered into its etheric components (you appreciate that)—it is no more than moving it in its material shape one small fraction of an inch, because, you see, space does not exist. It is hard for you to imagine, I know."

Question: "I can imagine its passage through obstacles, but I cannot conceive the method by which it is directed from one place to another."

Peter: "Well, there is no need. For instance, to you Africa is a long way, and the lion's claw which your lady wears was brought from there to your own residence in less than an instant of time. Well, space is only a sign of your limitation. Africa is no farther away to us, in fact is not so far, as is your hand from your face, otherwise if that were not so radio impulse would take time to travel the earth. It is of the same realm, only quicker. There is an appreciable time lag so far as radio is concerned, but not in the finer ethers in which they and we would work."

Question: "Are you able to hold up the reforming of the object?"

Peter: "Very simple. Once we have achieved the initial dematerialisation and, of course, conditions being equal within the circle itself, it does not matter how long it is before it is reformed. We could almost bring a large supply, although depending always upon circumstances relative to your physical state. It depends upon that."

Question: "Do the natural elements make any difference—thunder, etc.?"

Peter: "Not directly—only in so far as they affect the medium. If he is affected by it, then, of course, that is passed throughout the whole system, physical, etheric and mental as well."

Question: "Is apporting possible while the medium is not sitting?"

Peter: "Yes. You will laugh at this perhaps. It is not necessary for the soul to be occupying the same seat, or any position as the body at any time during the day when you are working, much less when you are sleeping, because distance is no object. That is why you have often heard of cases where one has been thinking deeply of another and that other has been seen at a distance from his or her body. So you can appreciate that when you become etherically unconscious you can think without the limitations of distance, time and space. The man who keeps an open mind all the time is likely to meet more wonders than he who keeps the door shut."

Question: "Apporting a lance, for example. Would that give any particular difficulty?"

Peter: "No. We could bring you a couple of elephants if you wished. That is quite 'on the cards'. Size is no difficulty."

Reference was made to the photograph received of the materialisation of an apport with J.W. in the following question.

Question: "Is it possible, according to your line of reasoning, for an apport to be produced via the medium's body?"

Peter: "It is not impossible, but it is not normal. Can you see any reason why it should be?"

Comment: "It was said that it was produced via the body."

Peter: "Well, it might have been the place where it was rebuilt. I should hardly say it was brought via the body. It is not normal and I would not say impossible; but it is unnecessary. It may have been necessary to rematerialize close to the medium, more especially if it was not a branch with which this medium was associated. The Guide knows nothing about it. He is powerless to produce one little thing. He is responsible for the well-being of the medium and, to a lesser extent, the sitters within the environment. Like many others, however, the Guides must qualify for the work—to know how it is done. It is like a man who has control of a vast concern. He may not be able to carry out each operation necessary for the production of an article, but he knows how it is done and he owes his position to his organising ability and his power of vision for the future. That, in regard to the work of development, is very necessary. A man might be able to design aircraft but never be able to fly one himself."

Question: "In view of what has been said concerning the construction of matter, can you give us any idea of the condition into which an article is changed for the purpose of apporting? Does it still retain its atomic form?"

Peter: "Yes, only it has become speeded up, or, in other words, has had its frequency increased; it ceases to be matter temporarily, although it is not exactly disintegrated; for it retains its form in an invisible state. In your science I think you will find that some materials readily give off, under condensation, electronic forces or streams. What happens then is what would be termed 'ionisation'. You employ it in your radio valve. You encourage this electronic flow by introducing within the construction of the valve's filament a coating of material or a substance (I believe you call it thorium) which under heat from a local battery of some sort creates a cascade; this rises out of the filament and falls back again—like balls on a water fountain. But as soon as you introduce a positive potential, the flow ceases to be a disorganised cascade, and becomes a direct path from the filament to the positively charged conductor. A similar kind of process is employed in regard to the article. That is the best analogy I can give. Moreover, and this is important, before you can obtain these conditions in regard to this radio valve, you must create for it its own vacuum similar to the etheric vacuum."

CHAPTER XV

THE MECHANICS OF VOICE PRODUCTION

PERHAPS the most puzzling of all phenomena from the investigators' point of view is that termed the "direct voice".

This is the phenomenon of voices produced through mediumship by other means than that of human vocal organs.

Associated with "direct voice" is that termed "independent voice". The difference between the two is that the former is manifested through a cone or a trumpet, while the latter manifests independently of any humanly constructed mechanism.

The voices purport to be from spirit people, and there is overwhelming evidence to support this view. The words and language must be of spirit origin, because of the very nature, characterisation and information of the communications.

Two examples are sufficient to give force to this contention. The first through the mediumship of Valiantine (see later) and secondly through Jack Webber, an unlettered collier, through whom conversations were carried on between sitters and spirit communicants in French, Portuguese, Swedish and Latin, without any hesitation in the speech or a trace of an accent foreign to those tongues.

So many volumes of authenticated records of direct voice communications have been published that the reality of this manner of communication is now generally accepted. What has not so far been established is the method and means by which these voices speak. The object of this chapter is to provide a thesis for the mechanics of this phenomenon.

The following are examples of attested evidence of direct voice phenomena; and are eloquent in their proof that the mind direction for such evidence must have been from a discarnate entity.

Professor J. Hysop investigated the voice phenomena of Mrs Eliz. Blake and his report covers over 200 pages of U.S.A. *S.P.R. Proceedings*. In it he says:

> "The loudness of the sound in some cases excludes the supposition that the voices are conveyed from the vocal chords to the trumpet. I have heard them 20 feet away and Mrs Blake's lips did not move."

Mr H. Dennis Bradley, in his book (1928) entitled *The Reality of Physical Phenomena*:

> "Dr. Whynant is a great linguist speaking thirty languages and a very considerable number of dialects. He was for many years lecturer on Chinese at Oxford University. He is not a Spiritualist. . . . At a series of sittings held in New York at the residence of Judge W. M. Cannon, a famous and wealthy lawyer of the highest credentials, under the mediumship of George Valiantine, a voice was heard speaking in Chinese, etc. In my opinion these conversations in Archaic Chinese represent perhaps one of the greatest tests ever made in psychical research and spirit-voice communication.
>
> Full significance must be given to the various languages spoken and the intonation and accents of the 'voices' I have heard 'voices' speaking in German, French, Italian, Russian, Spanish, Chinese, Japanese and idiomatic Welsh; and I have heard during the same conversation the language suddenly change into French, and the replies from the spirit 'voices' have come through with unhesitating fluency.
>
> During Dr. Whynant's sittings in New York with Valiantine, Portuguese, Basque, Arabic, Sanscrit and Hindustani were spoken."

In 1927, Valiantine came to this country for a series of experiments with Lord Charles Hope and Mr Dennis Bradley, which are fully described in the latter's books *Towards the Stars* and T*he Wisdom of the Gods*. There are two incidents reported that are pertinent to the aspects of voice phenomena with which we are more interested here. The first is that Valiantine was quite normal while the voices were speaking, and that he would engage upon conversations himself with some sitters, while the spirit voices were conversing with other sitters. The second was the recording of these voices on gramophone records. The recording was carried out by the Columbia Company, a telephone wire being taken from Lord Charles Hope's study, where the séance was held, to the recording studio.

Record No. 412-4. Confucius speaking in ancient Chinese.

Record No. 412-5. Chung Wei speaking and singing in Chinese.

Record No. 412-6. Maharajah of Manobe spoke in ancient Indian language and Sanscrit.

In *The Mediumship of Jack Webber* I have reported the speaking by spirit communicators in Swedish, Portuguese, Latin, French and Spanish—and it must be remembered that this medium was an unlettered collier. Reference is also made to the very loud singing of the control, Rueben, as being of full loud-speaker strength and penetrating to houses in the next street through the closed doors of the séance room. Rueben's singing was at times maintained for over an hour continuously. The words were clearly and perfectly enunciated— the aperture at the small end of the trumpet used at the time being less than half an inch and generally closed up.*

These extracts do not take into account the great mass of intimate personal evidence which could only be obtained from a spirit communicator. Notable examples of such communications can be found in Dennis Bradley's *Towards the Stars* and Gwendoline Hack's *Modern Psychic Mysteries*, to cite but two out of a large number of records.

Throughout the history of voice mediumship there have been many references to "voice-boxes". This term (invariably used by the spirit operators associated with each voice medium) has been cloaked in further ambiguity, when questions of a pertinent nature have been asked by sitters. For example, when a spirit operator has been asked to "tell us how the voices are produced", the reply has been usually given like this: "we build a voice-box, that we can speak through", or, "we construct a cabinet with a voice-box therein, just like one of your telephone boxes", or "we fit an ectoplasmic mould over the spirit's face", etc.

---

* At a séance held at the studios of the Decca Record Co., Ltd., a recording of the spirit voice of Rueben was secured, singing "Lead, kindly Light" and "There's a Land". The ten-inch double-sided record can be supplied for 5s. 6d. from Harry Edwards, Balham Psychic Research Society, II Childebert Road, Balham, London, S.W.17. All the proceeds from the sale of records are devoted to the "Jack Webber Memorial Fund". (Original footnote entry and not available in 2019)

The lack of substantive data in such replies is obvious, yet we should be deeply sensible of the great difficulties the Guides have had to face, when asked to explain this or that.

In the chapter on the "Development of Mediumship" reference is made to the difficulty the Guides must experience in giving reasoned explanations, through the limited mental equipment of their mediums. Providing in advance theses which we are incapable of comprehending must present a further difficulty.

Further, not every medium and every Guide has been willing to sit time and time again to give us instruction as Mr Clare and Peter have done. Peter's explanations on voice phenomena alone occupied at least six evenings in order to produce a reasoned statement.

In fairness to the Guides of physical mediums in the past. it should be re-emphasised that we did not then possess the knowledge of acoustics, radio science, and the science of applying and relating electrical energy to sound as we do now. We can only appreciate that which we can understand. Our knowledge of law-governed forces and effects limits our comprehension. To explain any thesis beyond these limits is to embark on a dissertation that would be meaningless—even assuming our vocabulary permitted the attempt. To illustrate this point—to have used a generation ago such present every-day terms as a "moving-coil loud speaker" or "radio oscillations" would have meant precisely nothing and would have been discounted as meaningless.

It should therefore be stressed that no Guide of past days should be reproached for failure to impart information or to gently satisfy his hearers of those times by obscure references. It is obvious that until we are in a position to understand, or approach understanding intelligently, an entirely new conception, it would be a waste of time for any Guide to discourse upon it. Also, we must still recognise our present limitations, and be satisfied, for the moment, if we are only dimly able to perceive a little light.

By the means of infra-red photography and other cruder methods of photography (as with Margery), pictures have been secured of an ectoplasmic mass, closely associated to and connected with the medium by ectoplasmic connections. The Guides of those mediums have informed us that these formations were "voice-boxes" or "talking apparatus".

When those Guides have been questioned about these photographs (and this applies also to Guides of other voice mediums where photographs have not been secured) they have told us that these voice-boxes contain a "replica of the medium's vocal organs" through the agency of which the spirit people speak.

I refer again to U.S.A. *S.P.R. Proceedings*, Vol. II, 1926-27. The Margery Mediumship, in which Walter's speaking mechanism is described as follows:

"There is a mass which may be either grey or white, about 4 x 2 x 2 inches, resembling the size and shape of a potato. Its contour is irregular. At times, as we look at it, it seems to simulate a small face much like the dried heads of the head hunters of the South Seas, heads from which the bones have been removed. To the top of this structure from the right ear there is a white cord one-sixth to a quarter of an inch in diameter smooth. From the little mouth, as it were, of the potato-like face there comes a structure much like the human umbilical cord, one-fourth to one-half of an inch in diameter, twisted, and eight to twelve inches long. This enters the right nostril of the Psychic. The white ear cord and the twisted cord to the nose are long enough to allow the central mass to rest on the Psychic's right shoulder, or her chest or her face or her left shoulder. We have many photographs of this structure and the photographs confirm what our eyes see. . . We have handled the mass and find it like the other teleplasmic masses, cold and yet vibrant with life. The fact that this structure is attached to the nose explains probably why any and every sitter is not allowed to put a hand over the Psychic's mouth whenever he chooses, as a test of the independence of the voice. . .

"At the end of the phenomena the mass from the ear takes two to four minutes to disappear. On exposure to red light of the masses of every origin there is immediately seen a kind of shrinking as if the light was inimical to it, or similar to that of meat suddenly exposed to a very hot fire or cautery-iron."

Peter's thesis cuts right across the view that the ectoplasmic mass contains any kind of vocal chords; and here again the suggestion is made that in the light of Peter's explanations those statements were merely the refuge of Guides from the more intricate and truer facts of the case.

In my book on Jack Webber's mediumship I adopted the safe course of avoiding theorising, except on one occasion, when I made some observations on the method of voice production; and I did this because there appeared evidential circumstances to support my contentions.

I supported the view that the voice-box must have contained a sound-producing mechanism, because I have heard on a number of occasions three voices simultaneously in being.

(1) The Guide speaking through the medium's vocal organs;

(2) A voice in "miniature" close to the medium; and

(3) The miniature voice being simultaneously reproduced in volume, through a trumpet levitated in the air some six to eight feet away from the medium.

In view of the explanations of Peter, I am forced to the conclusion that the ectoplasmic structure does not contain sound-producing mechanism, as we have been previously led to believe.

Some of the improbabilities of the original contention are worthy of consideration, if only to illustrate the human error of building up a thesis without foundations in reason or fact. In my own defence I have stated these improbabilities before, and now do so again so that the position may be better appreciated.

For a voice-box, like those we have photographed (opposite), to contain a voice-producing apparatus, it would be necessary to have not only a "replica of a human throat" but also a replica of the mouth shape, palate, tongue, lips, teeth, and air bellows (lungs), to produce the perfect syllabic sounds. Further, all of these—chords, throat, palate, tongue, lips, air pressure—would have to be controlled by some muscular action, mind-controlled.

For all of these essentials to be contained within the ectoplasmic mass is not feasible; and that a spirit communicant, whether Guide, relative or friend, in their spirit condition could operate all these physical essentials, is not feasible either.

A further point in this connection. At times "direct" voice possesses characteristics of the medium's speech—not always, but frequently— and this has been explained by the reasoning that, if the voice-box is a replica of the medium's vocal organs, it is reasonable that the voice

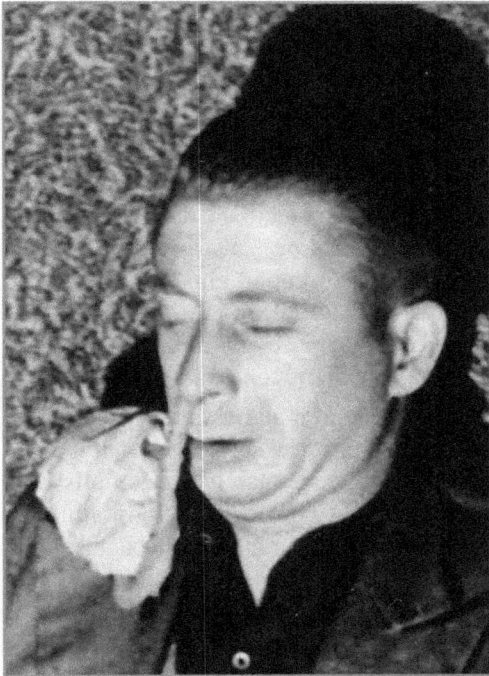

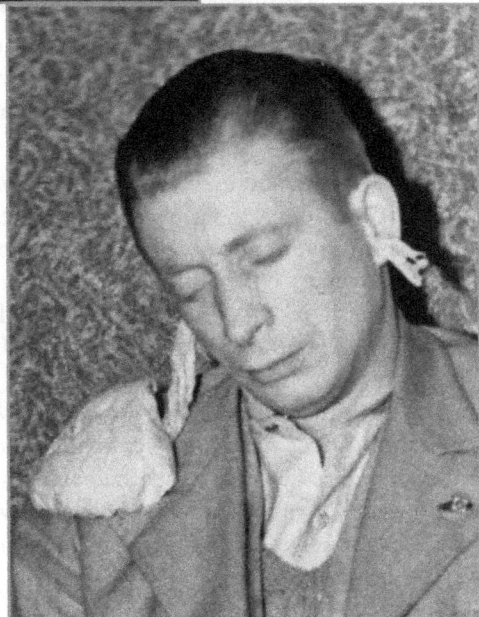

PLATE 15
"Voice box"
Grade 1, crude ectoplasm
emerging from nostril.
(see Chap XII)

Infra-red photograph by
Harry Edwards

PLATE 16

"Voice box"

Grade 1, crude ectoplasm
emerging from both ears.
(see Chap XII)

Infra-red photograph by
Leon Isaacs

produced would bear some resemblance. This reasoning naturally enforced support for the previous contention, but here again Peter's thesis provides a stronger reason why such similarity may, at times, exist.

No tone was ever created except by means of an instrument, which means that no sound has ever been borne of space or of free ether. Further, the instrument used must correspond to the nature of the tone to be produced, i.e. the instrument must be constructed of suitable materials such as wood, wires, metals, diaphragms, to receive and transmit physical voice sound waves via a telephone, loud speaker, or other voice instrument. Therefore, an etheric instrument is required for the receiving and transmitting of etheric tones.

What is more difficult to comprehend is the manner whereby the etheric sound waves are changed into physical sound waves. It is again worthy of recall that through radio science man has accomplished a similar transformation. The mind that considers it impossible for etheric sound waves to be transmitted by an etheric mechanism and then transformed into physical sounds through a delicate human receiving set—as the medium is—is the same type of mind which deemed it impossible thirty years ago to send a voice through the ether and to hear it in millions of homes almost simultaneously,

Another good parallel is provided by the telephone, where the speaker is talking from a distance; the sound waves so created travel in a new formation along the wires to be re-translated back into physical sounds.

It has been conclusively proved beyond all possible doubt, particularly through the Margery experiments, that the voice sounds of the spirit communicator are quite independent of the medium. It was so proved by either filling the medium's mouth with water or by having an inflated balloon placed in the medium's mouth which would whistle if air was allowed to pass out of it. Under such tests the control, Walter, would speak and whistle tunes some distance from the medium. With Jack Webber it was proved by hearing two, and sometimes three, conversations taking place at the same time. With Valiantine, Mrs Perriman and others, voices maintaining conversation would come from parts of the room far away from the medium, and would continue whilst the medium, in both normal and trance states, was also speaking.

The report of the sitting on November 17, 1940, when one of Mr Clare's controls spoke clearly through a trumpet with the mouth effectively blocked, provides further supporting evidence. The assumption has been that, as it has been proved that the actual physical sound is heard externally to the medium, the origin of the sound waves has also been external. This has appeared as a natural and reasonable assumption—yet according to Peter it is not so.

Peter says that the production of speech has its origin within the medium's etheric body and not in any external mechanism. Here are Peter's words:

Peter: "As a general rule there is no external mechanism for the creation of physical sound. Sounds are produced through the physical and etheric bodies of the medium. This, in itself, is a work of considerable enterprise. There is co-operative effort between the physical, sound-producing organs and the etheric counterpart, which uses the principles of electrical force." (Stress should be laid on the word "principles" to avoid the conclusion that it is the force of electricity alone that is the responsible agent.) "The muscles of the throat can be felt in action when a spirit voice is heard, but not the slightest sound is evidenced from the medium. The sound waves are etherically created via the medium's vocal organs and the respiratory system.

"These etheric sound waves are transmitted through an ectoplasmic and insulated tubular connection."

While this statement does not explain how two or more voices can be heard at the same time (these may well come under a varied or different process applicable to "independent" voice), it does provide a reasonable basis upon which an explanation of direct voice can be built. The Margery experiments referred to fall into line as being practical under this thesis: they also explain the essential presence of all those factors that must contribute to the creation of syllabic and dialectical words.

Following upon a number of questions relating to the above statement, Peter amplified his remarks in the statement which follows. In this second statement is given an explanation of the term "etheric sound waves". This is breaking new ground, entering into a new field of learning. One must allow here for Peter's apparent difficulty in giving a detailed explanation which must, of necessity, command the employment of new words and meanings. I am not attempting to apologise for Peter, but to provide what is surely a reasonable explanation for Peter's difficulties.

His second statement was:

Peter: "The voice emanates from the etheric and physical bodies of the medium. That cannot be disputed. I emphasise that . . . The external fitments (the 'voice-box'), etc., are arrangements whereby the etheric sound vibration as opposed to physical sound vibration, passes through a system of conductors, sometimes to an external etheric amplifier which you have previously termed a 'voice-box'; while that term is apt, it tends to confusion. It does not contain chords, or anything like that. It owes its peculiarity, as an amplifier, to its shape. Within that amplifier, which is the 'voice-box', there are etheric whorls for the amplification or refining of etheric acoustics. This about which we are talking is no different to sound, only it is not within your ability to comprehend it just how; words do not exist in your vocabulary which would describe it, and yet be within your capacity of understanding. It is an amplifier —as, is a trumpet to physical sound—but here, you see, we are dealing with inaudible sounds, that is, etheric sound. The voice-box, to use other words, is an amplifier of etheric sounds. You see, I have to use words which you apply to your physical vocal terms in order to explain non-physical substances and action.

"After the etheric sound waves have passed through the amplifier and refiner, it is necessary to convert them into sound—audible sound. They pass down an etheric tube—they have gained power or amplification, etherically, and have come to the trumpet.

"When the etheric sound waves enter the trumpet they leave the conductor tube, which has hitherto been sent into the free ether, as is general within the circle. The change is effected by a series of explosions; actually they are little flashes of light which you cannot see. Their transformation into audibility depends upon the vibrations, which are small explosions striking the air in the atmosphere around the diaphragm. The quality of speech or music is solely dependent on the diaphragm through which, in the case of the trumpet, the atmosphere and the ether give a cushion effect, just where the etheric wave merges and enters the trumpet. This is a series of explosions such as you get on the diaphragm of a loud speaker."

Here we have the supporting reason referred to above.

As the voice is created from the medium's physical and etheric voice-speaking organisms, it is natural that at times the characteristics of his voice should be transmitted through this process of spirit-voice production.

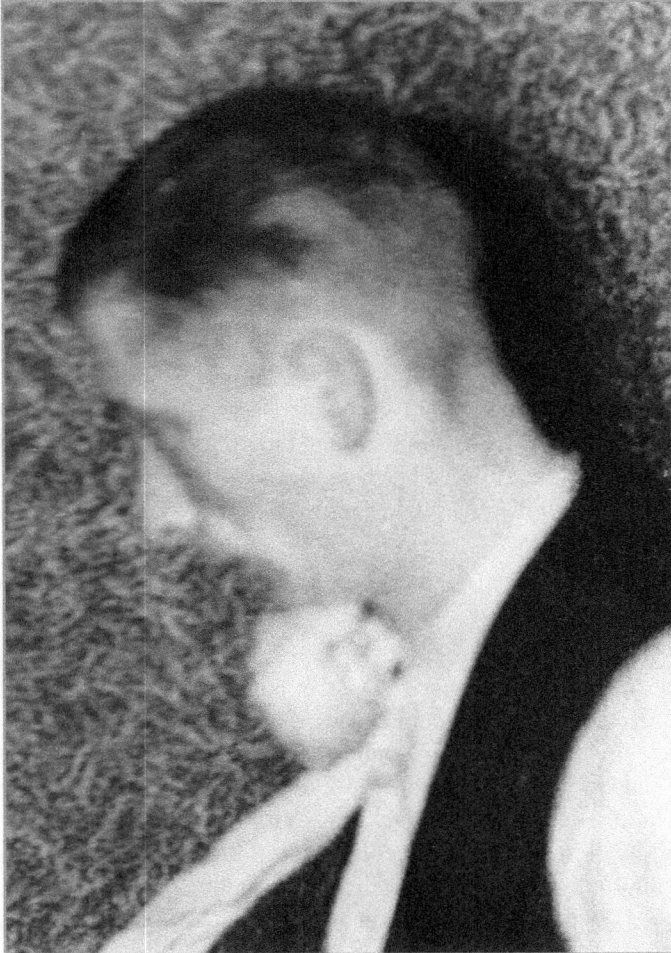

PLATE 17

Ectoplasmic formation, Grade 2, previously described as a "voice-box" with 'cable' leading to trumpet. (See opposite.)

Infra-red photograph by J. McCulloch.

On a further occasion Peter stressed afresh, as in the next statement, that the voice-box is not a sound-producing agent, and defines its function.

Peter: "When you read your notes you will see that I have referred to the amplifier or voice-box. What I wished to give you was the fact that there is no sound creation in the voice-box, and no physical sound from the vocal chords or the throat. The sound-box has no characteristic of vocal chords, but its purpose is that of amplification. It is an artificial means of stimulation where a voice may be weak. Its use is not always necessary. In the case of a strong voice you would get distortion, unless it was refined within this apparatus. It does not become necessary where the voice is just right. Voice-sounds come through the vocal chords—but not in the physical sense."

Question: "Are respiratory sounds produced through the vocal chords of the medium?"

Peter: "No, they are not. This is oft-times produced to convey something of importance. You can simulate anything by the method of which I have spoken, but in most cases it is purely the result of those explosions I have mentioned. Also note that these explosions generate heat, and heat you will feel in the air that comes from the trumpet. Though it is not always present, heat, such as breath, will be evident sometimes."

Question: "You said, 'the voice-box owes its peculiarity to its shape'?"

Peter: "Particularly true. Its substance being adaptable to shape, it can be modified. It depends on the conditions prevailing at the particular time, its shape being adapted thereto. It can be modified to produce the right volume of sound for the right occasion. There is no fixed shape for it. You can have it like a trumpet, or like a sea-shell, the whole idea being that they are, more or less, vibrations to the conditions without. The shape determines the whorls set up to give the right volume or pressure to the resultant voice."

Question: "You speak of a diaphragm being necessary to convert the etheric sound waves into audibility. What is this diaphragm?"

Peter: "It is an extremely thin, web-like substance that is connected very delicately from the end of the tube—the etheric tube—to the mouth of the trumpet. It is of great strength and its tension is enormous; so much so that it can make loud popping sounds, but it has a skin-like form of physical existence very much like the ordinary ectoplasm."

Question: "Is it reasonably possible to get a diaphragm left in a trumpet?"

Peter: "No. It is hardly possible unless you left the whole thing."

Question: "Is it possible to simulate a sound not associated with the voice, the creak of a door, etc.?"

Peter: "It is not impossible to make a deep sigh or anything like that, and, of course, the creak of a door is not an impossibility either; it could be even the song of a bird if the operator were skilled enough."

Question: Peter was asked whether the construction of physical sound waves bore any resemblance to etheric sound waves.

Peter: "Yes, it is very similar. There is one thing you do not appreciate, and that is that the physical sound that travels along the conductor is actually not within the conductor itself but within the surrounding ether. You see, it travels along the ether owing to the etheric conditions within the conductor being not quite the same as they are without; actually because you are energising that area by the passage of an electric current. Now the same conditions appertain within our etheric tube-bound ether which enable us to create within that insulation conditions similar to your copper conductors. The insulation that we have created may vary in diameter as it is purely for the purpose of creating conditions of potentiality within the ether. When the free ether outside the insulation is too dense it would be absorbed too much: the sound travels along this conductor. If we were using a range of frequencies similar to those used by your radio, which is a form of brute force, we should have to bring it down into the denser etheric conditions nearer the earth; the principles that we utilise go far beyond your known laws of frequencies. When we use the term 'insulating' in this case, we refer to the isolation of the conditions within the etheric tubular construction from that without the tube. An explanation of that is that the etheric condition within the tube is of our making, and it differs from the free ether outside in so far as it responds to our directive thought, or anyone's directive thought who is manifesting. It is nothing more or less than an etheric conductor, the same as you have your copper wire surrounded by rubber to isolate it from conducting surfaces which might be brought into its proximity." (See Plate No. 2, which illustrates this mechanism.)

Question: Peter was asked, "Does a communicating spirit personality other than a Guide usually possessed the knowledge of how to use the mechanism created?"

Peter: "Much depends upon the conditions that are created for him, and his ability to use it. It is very similar to your use of a telephone; you might be quite well understood at the distant end, yet someone else who is not able to use a telephone—and there are many—might be, if not inaudible, at least not clear. That is the same principle. They are the only limits. Perhaps you would like it this way . . . Once upon a time they found means of carrying great weights for greater distances by using circular pieces cut from tree trunks which were placed underneath the object to be moved but look what a far cry it is from those days to now. Is it not possible that the same applies to your psychic queries? But here, you see, we are employing purely natural forces, of which there is a close parallel between your known laws of radio activity and those we are trying to propound here. You utilise your known laws, through their manifestation, from the material at hand. That is the only difference."

Question: "Do you and the other spirit operators associated with you have to create actual 'machinery' of a definite kind for voice phenomena?"

Peter: "Yes, of course, that is true, but you must not have visions of wheels. The principle is the same except that etherically we do not have to employ cumbersome things, because, you understand, we are working with a common substance—ether. And that is all there is to it. Free ether and employed ether—that is the secret of it. It is very similar. to your damming a stream so as to make it flow another way and turn a mill-wheel."

Question: "Can you tell us more of how the spirit personality is able to enter into communication?"

Peter: "Yes, of course—you have conditions created for manifestation of voice. You have the medium in a state of preparation for that voice. The medium has a quality a tonal quality—which has been built up partly by himself and partly by the assistance of the Guides. There must be harmony between the Guides and the medium, and this is reflected within the etheric extension. This etheric extension has a peculiar quality of its own which in itself is not only a protection but is also the gateway. Any communicant attempting to approach through it must have a tonal quality almost identical to it. There you have harmony again. When one comes to communicate and he has not the necessary tonal qualifications then we help him to raise or lower it, as necessary. In the last extreme, if neither is successful, we can transmit, or allow to be transmitted, all its characteristics of voice quality. In addition, we are able to pass through all the things that are characteristic of the communicant, which, to you, is one and the same thing."

Question: "Your communicant is speaking to a friend. The friend asks a question and you get the reply. Can you tell us the means by which the communicant is able to receive the thought expressed by the sitter?"

Peter: "Only by thought. The expression of it helps him to do so because most people on earth cannot express thought by just thinking but only by asking aloud. Actually, it is not the voice that conveys the question but the thought accompanying it."

Question: "Is there any method of controlling who should so speak? Is there a compére?"

Peter: "No. I have partly answered that question. Those who wish to speak must have the qualifications necessary to make his thought (the communicant's thought) register upon the etheric extension of the medium. Where possible we help him or her to communicate, but always with an eye to what I have told you in the last answer but one. That is the governing factor."

Question: "Is a spirit communicant able to give speech by direct contact with the medium?"

Peter: "The communicant contacts part of the medium's auric extension—any part of the etheric field—and by so doing is able to use the conditions created, to communicate."

Question: "How is it that a childish or feminine voice is heard when using a masculine vocal etheric instrument?"

Peter: "The necessary physical sounds are first produced etherically via the human chords. The qualities of the etheric sounds are not limited in tone, as they are by physical chords."

Question: "Is there any other method of controlling who should so speak?"

Peter: "That is our responsibility. We are not responsible for the phenomena, but we are responsible for the medium and, indirectly, for everyone else. We cannot do more than provide the means—because that is our responsibility. Anything else must come as the result of patience and, unfortunately, conditions over which we have no control. There is this fact and this alone—so long as we are vested by you with the authority to control, all will be well. We hold the lever that cuts off the power, but when we are usurped from our position we cannot control."

Question: "For independent voice—do you have to create a similar mechanism?"

Peter: "Yes. It is not 'vocal'. While the terms we are compelled to use are very elementary, the principle of amplifying is sound. The voices are created via a form of etheric trumpet within the sphere of which the conditions are controllable. The voices are produced in that way."

Question: "We have heard the independent voice in white light. Therefore, white light does not prevent the mechanism being constructed?"

Peter: "You will find that the light has allowed for dark places. It is, of course, when conditions are good. I remember we have had the voice with a light in our circle under similar circumstances."

Question: "Authentic evidence has been recorded that spirit voices have been heard in various parts of a room; with and without trumpet, through the mediumship of Valiantine. The medium at this time has been normal and engaged upon conversation with a sitter—consequently his physical larynx has been in use when the spirit voices have also been audible. Does the same voice productive mechanism operate in this case as that you have described as produced via the medium's physical and etheric larynx?"

Peter: "No, that is not so. In cases like that it is a form which is not of physical mediumship at all. It is a form of mediumship wherein the conditions so combine themselves that the entities, in association with the medium, can produce directly their own voice from the rarefied ether, neither directly using the medium himself nor any part of his economy. But that is very rare."

Question: "Voice production. Would it be possible to take away the side of one of these 'voice-boxes' or amplifiers—that is, to take away the ectoplasm?"

Peter: "Yes, but you would not learn anything, because its shape would be constantly altering. It would have no construction that you could understand. It would not be related to truth or permanency."

CHAPTER XVI

MATERIALISATION

ONE of the highest developments of spirit activity through human mediumship is the materialisation of a person, who was known to the sitters during his earthly life, whereby this person is able, for a brief period, to rehabilitate himself in physical form, to be clearly recognised and to converse with his friends and relatives. There can be no weightier evidence to demonstrate the truth of survival.

The history of physical mediumship presents an accumulated mass of evidence relative to this phenomenon; and the primary conclusion from the study of the evidence is that this phenomenon is only produced in association with physical mediumship. It cannot be produced in a laboratory or by chemical or instrumental means. This conclusion not only applies to the full-length materialisations but also to its associated phenomena.

Materialisations are not hallucinations or the result of mass hypnotism; for not only do all the sitters present witness the phenomena, but from time to time they have been recorded by the camera.

As ectoplasmic structures and their development into living formations possess similar characteristics, so are there similarities governing the building-up of materialisations, their functions and dissolution.

Study of the records associated with the names of investigators such as Sir William Crookes, Baron von Schrenk-Notzing, Professor Charles Richet, S.P.R. Proceedings of Great Britain, the U.S.A., and the Institut General Psychologique of France, as well as the many other published accredited records, gives complete confirmation that the principles governing this phenomenon are the same. In no record has there been shown any fundamental departure from the general method of its creation, movement, activity, and dissolution.

In studying the records, it is noteworthy to recall, that when a medium has been found to possess the faculty for this phenomenon and has been reported on by an accredited observer, further investigations have invariably followed by other competent investigators or national psychic research societies.

In most cases the phenomenon with its characteristics has been confirmed by the various commissions, no matter is what country it has taken place. The importance of this in obvious, when critics assume that a person may fraudulently produce effects in his own home by artificial means.

It is beyond credulity that any deception would be possible in the séance rooms chosen by the investigators. Also, the medium is under continual close scrutiny during his stay with the investigating commission and his body is subject to particular search immediately prior to any sitting.

One of the conditions necessary for this phenomenon is that the process of building-up of the materialisation must take place in darkness. When built up it may be viewed in a degree of light and has at times been photographed by electric and magnesium light.

A further characteristic is that the built-up form is generally shrouded in ectoplasm, which appears to the eye as a voluminous white or shining drapery.

These two characteristics have led sceptics to assert that there must be trickery. They instance the darkness and suggest that some fabric must be hidden in the darkened portion of the room where the medium sits. They suppose collusion on the part of a confederate, or that the medium secretes material in or about his person.

The stringent restrictions and searchings that always accompany reports of investigations refute the sceptics assertions. It should be obvious that the keen minds of the investigators, who are aware of the methods of fraudulent practice, would take every precaution against such crude attempts to deceive. Indeed, the history of the evidence shows that the precautions taken have been extreme.

Mediums after external search of their bodies; and being kept under the close scrutiny of an attendant for some hours prior to the sitting, are then draped in a single garment provided by the commission, or have sat nude. In Schrenk-Notzing's work there are hundreds of photographs of structures and materialised forms and it is further reported how, on occasion, the medium would be hypnotised, taken into another room, undressed, and whilst in a nude state the emanation of ectoplasm and its evolvement would be observed—the emanation coming from various parts of the body.

Happily, such drastic conditions imposed upon mediums fifty years ago are now being replaced by more enlightened and understanding methods of control. It is asserted here, that if investigators will abandon their crude methods of restriction and search and will co-operate with the controlling intelligence in a friendly way, the operators will produce phenomena in such a way that the most critical mind will be convinced of the supernormality.

Sir William Crookes succeeded in obtaining photographs of the materialised Katie King, showing the entranced medium in the same picture. His testimony goes to prove the above assertion; for he obtained not only the confidence of the medium but also that of the operators and Katie herself: also he was permitted to walk arm in arm with her, take her pulse and temperature; and to be with her at her building up and dissolution.

Schrenk-Notzing secured a number of photographs of full-length materialised forms standing by the side of the nude medium. With Jack Webber, the narrator ("with witnesses") saw in a reasonable degree of red light—which was gradually increased by a rheostat, until there was sufficient brilliance to see clearly each sitter and the roped medium—the materialisation of his control, Rueben. From an ectoplasmic-mist associated with the medium, by a process of contraction or solidification, Rueben emerged; and the records state how he took hold of the author's hand with his and passed the former over his face so that the texture, smooth and clean-feeling, could be felt; how he repeated this with other sitters, and spoke for a number of minutes in a deep resonant voice. It is further related how he elevated his entire form to the red electric globe some nine feet high to illumine his face all the more clearly, then descended, shrinking downwards towards the floor, just as a snow man would disintegrate in a strong heat, and finally disappeared—the process of disappearance taking but two seconds.

Quite often the materialisations of heads are appreciably smaller than normal, yet are perfect three dimensional heads subject to muscular control, with movement of eyes and lips through which comes articulated speech.

One can watch at times the building up of these heads. At first there appears, over the illuminated plaque, a mist of indeterminate shape but oval in general appearance, which, when seen sideways, looks like a disc of bluish dim light. As second follows second the shape of the head appears within the mist, forming first the outline, then the features, gradually becoming stronger until perfect and often recognisable. A fairly good simile is that of focusing a camera or a picture on a screen. From a haze of light there first appears the blurred indefinite image, which leads to the precise features as the picture is brought into correct focus.

On occasion, the author has noted that if the visiting entity possessed a moustache or beard, these would be the last to form and has noticed at times that they were white, as if there was an absence of colouring pigment. On other occasions the hair would be of full colour, brown, black or red.

That the heads are three-dimensional is proved by the showing of the head in profile; and if plaques are used to illumine the manifestation, the Guide will have the plaque moved to illustrate this.

Heads are more commonly formed; as they take less power and preparation than full forms.

The records of materialisations with Mr Clare's mediumship in the first section of this book are eloquent of this type of phenomena, particularly of the occasion when Jack Webber was able to return for a short time. He materialised at two other sittings (not reported) about that time.

The appearance of the smaller forms of children three or four feet high, or of forms larger and taller than normal, certainly smaller or larger than the medium, are often seen. Sometimes one sees two or three forms simultaneously. Peter explained the reason why some forms appear so large.

Peter tells us that the creation of hands, claws or similar formations may be produced by a different process from that of materialising a discarnate entity; and such phenomena should not always be associated with materialisations.

As already stated, the building up of materialisations invariably takes place in total darkness. When the medium sits in the circle—that is, not within a cabinet—as does Mr Clare, complete darkness is an essential. The more general practice is for the medium to be seated either in a cabinet with curtains in front of the opening or in a curtained recess to a room that permits the shutting out of all light. In either case the room may be illumined by a subdued light, though the usual practice is to illumine the materialisations by means of a plaque.

No strict laws govern physical work of a psychic nature; and there have been occasions when witnesses have been able to see the building up of the form, as with Jack Webber, or the presence of a form, as described by Colin Evans, in the light of an electric fire.

Due to this necessary condition of darkness, records of materialisations generally commence with the appearance of the built-up form emerging through the curtains or by the pulling apart of the curtains.

The French physiologist, Professor Charles Richet, described the building up of a materialised form as follows:

> "I see something like a white luminous ball of undetermined outline suspended above the floor. Then suddenly there appears emerging from this white orb of light, as from a trap door, the phantom 'Bien Boa'. It is of moderate height. He is halting and lame in his walk. One cannot say whether he walks or glides. . . Without opening the curtain he suddenly collapses and vanishes on the floor. . . Three or four minutes afterwards the same white orb appears in the opening of the curtain, above the floor, then a body is seen quickly rising straight up and attaining the height of an adult, and then it collapses on the floor."

Richet adds:

> "Before my eyes outside the curtain, a living body has been formed, which emerged from the floor and vanished into the floor."

Similar phenomena were witnessed through the mediumship of Eusapia Paladino, as with a number of other mediums of her time, like Home, Slade and Eglington.

In more recent times we have had the records of materialisations with Estelle Roberts, Jack Webber and Arnold Clare. In no case where observations have been possible has there been any variance in the general principles of the method of building up, the creation of ectoplasmic drapery, the gliding or floating movements and the dissolution.

It was recorded by Sir William Crookes how on one occasion the materialisation of Katie King cut off portions of her ectoplasmic "garment" and gave portions to those present.

She then passed another part of the drapery over the gaps and they were immediately made whole. Despite the very closest investigation Crookes was unable to find the place from whence the pieces had been cut (there was no seam).

For the first time it is believed, Peter explains, the source from whence the special quality of ectoplasm for materialisations comes, and the purpose of the "ectoplasmic drapery".

It will be seen that the thesis he presents is in harmony with the experiences recorded.

The gliding or floating movement of the form is another general characteristic. As they move across a room, the motion is invariably described as floating or gliding along. This may signify that the legs and feet have not been physically formed and it is believed that the extremities are the last to be built up. It is fairly positive that the forms do not touch the floor.

The Guide of Jack Webber once asked that the floor space within the circle should be covered with white powder. This was done, and a number of forms were seen to build up and cross the space in red light—the white floor space showing up very plainly. There were no marks of footprints nor was there any disturbance of the powder.

This does not signify that not on any occasion are the legs and feet materialised: it should be as easy for them to be solidified as a hand or a head. Indeed, if evidence of a personality can be given this way it is done. An example of this is . . . when Pedro, one of the controls associated with Mr Clare's group of spirit people, makes his presence known. He manifests with a wooden "peg leg", and one hears the sounds of one foot and the stump, as he walks around the circle.

In order to save the medium from strain and to conserve energy, only sufficient of a spirit body is materialised to satisfy the immediate purpose. If the visitor is a foreigner who comes back to his relatives and speaks to them in his own voice, dialect, and tongue then the respiratory and vocal organs would be built up. Another example might be one whose identity would be absolute by showing a scar upon the face or a deformed hand. Then the effort would be concentrated to this purpose and it may be, as Peter says, the voice may be produced by other means. The author has witnessed the movements of the lips of materialised spirit people consonant with the words being spoken and which do come from the mouth of the visitor (this has been confirmed by a number of independent witnesses, including critical journalists).

Geley says:

"To build up in a few seconds an organ or an organism biologically complete—to create life—is a metapsychical feat which can rarely produce a perfect result. That is why the great majority of materialisations are incomplete, fragmentary, defective, and show lacunae in their structure."

A warning about this work is also given by Peter, who says the Guide has to exercise care, in regard to the extent to which the visitor is permitted to reassume physical life.

Peter opened his observations upon this phenomenon by saying:

Peter: "The first condition essential for materialisation is complete darkness within the immediate vicinity of its formation.

"After the materialisation is formed according to the conditions prevailing, it may, in given circumstances, be exposed to indirect light rays. This condition is the exception rather than the general rule. That provides a summary with which to begin.

"This is a condition which cannot be broken away from.

"Now what is a materialisation?

"It may be the birth of a thought, or it may be a complete birth of an entity, except that its birth has not been carried to its material or physical completeness.

"For a complete materialisation, under normal conditions, it takes about nine minutes in your time.

"First of all, there is formed for it an ovoid, matrix or mould. This is very similar to the etheric envelope of which we have spoken in our talk on apportation. Within this ether-tight matrix the manifesting entity commences to draw about himself particles from the ether, the special ether, that is, within the mould. They can only form to his personality and not to any other. As he gains greater proficiency so does his density become more pronounced.

"Within the limits of the ovoid the form is dressed about with a material of different character and is what you call ectoplasm. That is the part which you have referred to as 'spirit robes' but it is not primarily for the purpose of dressing the entity but of protecting it from the etheric bombardment without. It is, I agree, quite often draped around the form as a sort of robe, but that is more to complete the picture which is oft-times, in itself, very imperfect.

"Now what is the relationship between the now materialised form and the medium? It is this. Take, for example, the complete materialisation—by complete I mean one that has all the members associated with the body: heart, lungs, hands and feet, which have been constructed by the same means. To give forms of this nature complete action there is a corresponding link-up with the medium's physical organism; all the functions of his body are projected into that of the materialised form.

"This transfer is carried out over a network of etheric nerve cords which passes from the medium's solar plexus to that of the manifesting entity. I will carry this perfect case a step further and say that if this entity were so empowered as to be able to extract from the ether atomic particles to build up his form, it could become a three-dimensional being as solid as you are yourself; the only difficulty in this instance being that it and the medium could not both live at the same time. That shows how vital it is for the existence of a perfect control between the spirit operators associated with the medium and this particular phenomenon.

"It is, in effect, an accelerated process of bringing to birth an entity which is only one stage removed from the physical, actually it is closely allied to the earlier stages of the natural period of conception but is very much speeded up. In the normal birth of a child the incoming soul must pass through the several forms of birth, entering, as it were, one lock at a time before passing down into the next stratum, each deeper and denser than the previous one."

Question: "That is from strata to strata or plane to plane, but from whence?"

Peter: "That does not matter, because if it did we should have to go into very deep things. Let the question remain and perhaps it will form a basis for something else. It is all very well to say 'from whence' but you would still have to justify that by explaining 'why' and I am afraid that would be beyond me for the present.

"Now at the beginning I said the materialisation could be of a thought or the person of an entity.

"In the case of the materialisation of a thought this is not a true materialisation. For instance, a person who has passed over to the other side of life may not be able, for various reasons, to accomplish a complete materialisation but only able to build around the thought something that would express sufficient of his character and personality to make it recognisable. In such a case it would be just a head and a feature; and you can always recognise this phenomenon by the fact that it has no life or animation. It would be like a sculptured head, oft-times dimensional, at other times cloudy with just a faint suggestion of the eyes and nose and mouth. Now these may or may not be true expressions and do not constitute the proof of survival that you see, but it is interesting in so far as it is not of your world. Now where can I proceed from there?"

Question: "Has the thought formation a similar linking up to the medium's solar plexus?"

Peter: "Not necessarily."

Question: "It may be built up from ectoplasm emerging from another part of the body?"

Peter: "Yes."

Question: "Can you tell us how the thought formation is able to build? You spoke of the visiting entity gathering unto himself qualities to enable him to materialise. Is the thought materialisation created by a different process?"

Peter: "Yes, slightly different, in that the formation does not have lifelike qualities. It is moulded from the ordinary ectoplasmic substances of a slightly different quality. It is formed from that; and, of course, may vary considerably in size, being smaller or larger according to the governing factors at the time."

Question: "Do the controls have any work to do in regard to materialisations?"

Peter: "Yes, but not upon the forming of the figure. They maintain the right etheric conditions and help with the processes associated with the medium—always directly with the medium—which enable him to withstand etheric shocks. You might term the latter, voltages. These would, without our assistance, nearly reduce him to a wreck. We direct the forces and currents through him to provide the conditions necessary for the building-up of the materialised form. That is where our operation commences and ceases. We have our hands upon the taps that control the flow."

Question: "We have been told from other sources, that materialisations are created by the controls moulding ectoplasm around the astral body of the entity. From your explanation that is incorrect?"

Peter: "No. You see, I cannot say that that is impossible, but it is not the way it is normally done."

Question: "You stated that the visiting entity gathers to himself particles from the ether. That presumes sufficient willpower on the part of the entity to permit him to materialise. Is that all he has to have, or does he have to possess technical knowledge as well?"

Peter: "He has to have knowledge . . . he must have knowledge. I would rather not take up that subject because it has to do with a qualifying form of development of the entities.

"This I will tell you, as it may stimulate your interest. People who have lived on earth and were born with a physical defect are often provided with the opportunity, when conditions are right, to materialise. You are thinking 'why'— of course the eternal 'why'. For this reason! They are born oft-times—not always—imperfect in their body, indicating an imperfection within the soul. That imperfection is a lack of wisdom, and so they are given opportunities to build perfectly, down to the stage where the next step would be the physical. We cannot escape it, we are going to come to it sooner or later because they will have to come again."

NOTE: The foregoing statement implies reincarnation.

Question: "You have said the materialisation was three dimensional. We have felt their hands . . . they must possess weight. Could one be weighed?"

Peter: "Yes, but you must remember that they are not solid right through. It is often an incrustation, a veneer."

Question: "Yet the lungs must work?"

Peter: "Yes, but they can get to work in the same way as the lips move when 'a man pulls the strings'."

Question: "Can you give us the relationship of the materialised form to the spirit entity himself?"

Peter: "The spirit entity is always; and for ever, seeking knowledge, and he can gain it that way; but it is the soul of the one who is manifesting which is responsible for the work. The spirit is the observer, as it were, for the soul. The purpose is served by the experiences gained in the handling of the various potentials of the realm in which he finds himself. He desires to build a body if only of an etheric nature. In that way there is a gaining of wisdom, because it is the most difficult work there is to do."

Question: "Is the materialised form the soul body of the person or an astral shell?"

Peter: "It is he who has returned in reality. You have spoken of an astral shell but this is a term we do not like and you should find a better one to supplant it. But there are such things, just the same as when you have no further use for the physical shells they are laid in the ground. So the astral shell, when the soul has no further use for it, just remains a shell with no animation. They are oft-times perceived by the undeveloped clairvoyant, but it is a graveyard of 'astral bones' and they always appear to your mental vision grey and lifeless. It is a place unattractive and desolate."

Question: "You spoke of the transference of functions from the medium to the materialised form. Does that imply that for a materialised form to walk or give speech that the directing thought emanates from the medium and not from the entity?"

Peter: "The moving and speech is that of the entity, but the means whereby it is achieved is taken from the medium and travels via his nerve trunk."

Question: "So the nerve trunk provides the power for animation?"

Peter: "Yes, and though the organs are complete within the materialisation they have not quite the same character as that of the normal physical body, but are more or less copies. They carry out the functions, though mark you, they are not entirely necessary to the form that is materialising; but to give it a vitality of its own it must be more or less complete."

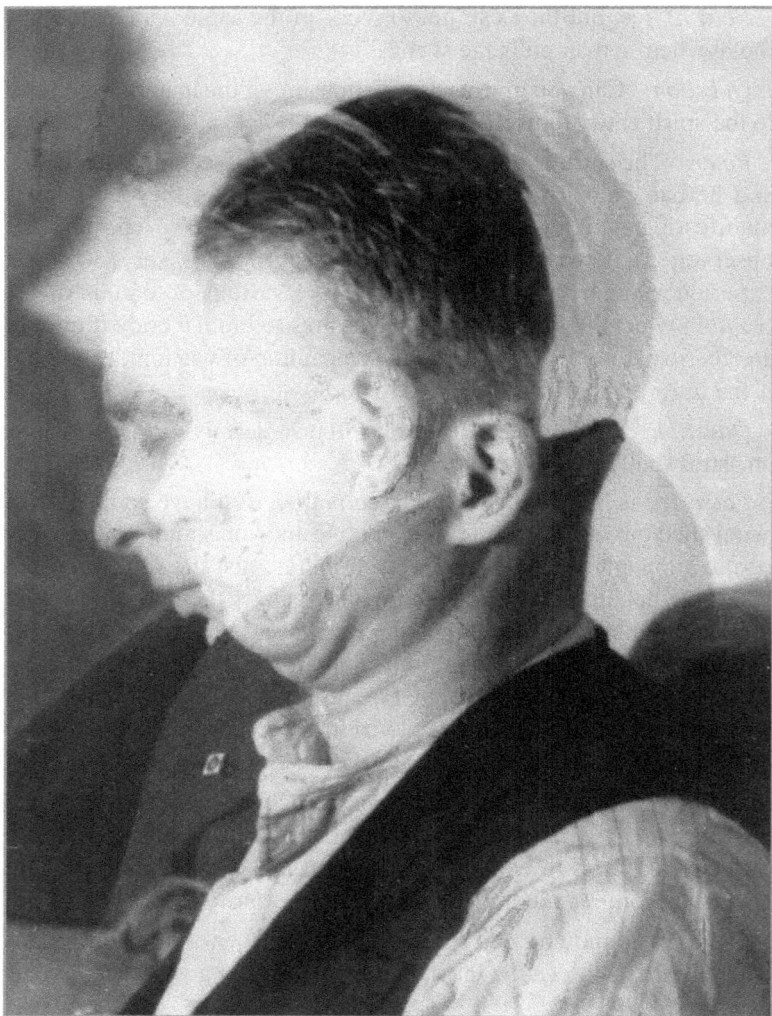

PLATE 18

This photograph shows the manner of dematerialization. The coat is shown in semi-density. The face of the medium's soul body has been recorded with the inner face strongly transfigured by the Guide. Note the harmony in the partial densities of both heads and coat. Full density is where the two heads merge. The different alignment between the eyes, nose, mouth and the ear and rear of head indicate that a rotary movement is necessary to bring both heads into alignment—indicating that both heads are three-dimensional.

Infra-red photograph by W. Clayton

Question: "If that entity had the power could it draw from the medium sufficient life as to become physical again? Might it be possible, if the control was not on guard, for the form to take on renewed physical life again?"

Peter: "Yes, but the organs are not complete. The Guides have their hands on the taps and there are therefore limits to which the form can be permitted to build. That is why you seldom find a complete materialisation."

Question: "You have spoken of the etheric qualities which are used for materialisations. Is there any special characteristic denoting these? Are they different from other atomic structures known to us? Is there anything particular about them which permits their use for the special purpose?"

Peter: "No difference that I can mention worthy of note. It is only the looseness, the polarising agency that makes the difference—the agency of nature which materialises concrete things. The largest star in your system is still half formed. It owes its size to them, yet it exists materially. It is measured; therefore, it is three dimensional, yet it is not as solid as your earth. As it solidifies so it becomes smaller. That is a parallel to the answer to your materialisation, and that is why most materialised forms seem so tall.

They even have to bend for you to see them. That is why you are often asked to stand."

CHAPTER XVII

DISCUSSION ON PLATES NOS. 2, 3, 4 AND FIG. 8

THESE three photographs are typical of "light formations" received through psychic photography. Hitherto no explanation has been given to account for, or explain, their meaning.

Certain conclusions can, however, be stated with confidence, as follows:

(1) Photographs of this nature, while not abundant, are not rare.

(2) They possess similar characteristics, of formation, convolution and construction.

(3) On two appear a central well-defined and perfect sphere of activity.

(4) They are only obtained when spirit forces are present, in the presence of a medium.

(5) They cannot be obtained by normal photographic process.

Professional photographers cannot explain them, yet they are definite results obtained under certain given conditions. The "given conditions" being, a plate exposed in a camera in the presence of a person (or persons) possessing mediumistic powers. Therefore, such photographs can only be the result of psychic forces expressed through mediumship.

The cameras and plates used were of the normal kind. Time exposures of varying periods were made in each case; therefore, no set exposure time governs the result. The probability is that the formations were only momentarily in being (photographically).

A short description as to the manner in which they were received by the persons concerned follows.

Plate No.2 was secured by Mr R. F. Bounsall, of Worthing. Mr Bounsall, senior, states that the photograph was secured by his sixteen-year-old son, at a home circle consisting of his wife, son and himself.

The plate was partially exposed in normal light before the sitting commenced, so that the image of the room was first recorded. The trumpet on the table appears transparent; this was due to the trumpet being placed on the table during this first exposure. The lens was closed. The sitters took their seats; the light was extinguished, and the lens opened again. The medium, Mrs Bounsall, sat in the chair on the right-hand side, where the formation commences. There is a distinct "cable" running from where the medium sat, throughout the whole length of the formation through an "insulation" to where it reaches the trumpet. The trumpet appears to have other effects (light or ectoplasm) on it.

PLATE 2

By means of the double exposure, we are able to see the directive action of the phenomenon. One other point should be mentioned: behind the screen is a bowl of water; though whether this has any significance is not known.

Peter tells us what this formation is; and it is pertinent that Mrs Bounsall was sitting for the development of voice mediumship.

Plate No.3 was secured by Mr S. J. Spiller, of the Ewell (Surrey) Spiritualist Society. It was taken at a sitting of a home developing circle. The exposure was approximately ten minutes in white electric light—a shaded 100-watt electric bulb.

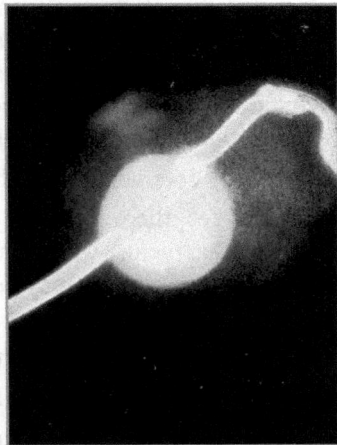

PLATE 3

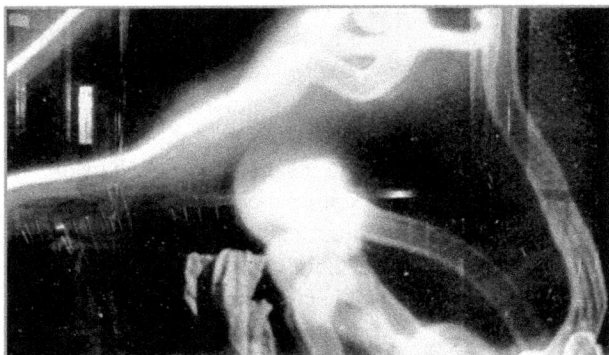

PLATE 4

Plate No. 4 was taken by Mr O. MacKinnon Charles, B.Sc., leader of the Merton Park Spiritualist Church. Exposure approximately eight minutes in darkness.

Peter's observations on these three photographs followed the question:

Question: "Regarding the photographs I have shown your medium tonight, can you tell us whether there is any connection between them and what you have told us concerning voice production, or whether they give a picture of any etheric energy about which you have spoken?"

Peter: [Plate No.2.] "The structure proceeds to what appears to be a trumpet. Now that is a pretty good example of the etheric sound conductor, though it is not completely organised, of course. You see, there is a knot in it. If you could straighten that out, you would have the voice right away. This does not, of course, illustrate the power of levitation. It has regard to voice alone, and would only be responsible for the production of voice. It has no power to levitate."

Question: "We understand that there are two distinct processes?"

Peter: "Yes, there must be, but for perfect working the formation shown on that picture would have to be much more concentrated. That is to say, not so wide. It may be that for the purpose of demonstration they have widened it to give a clearer idea of its formation."

Question: "Is the shaded part what you have called the insulation?"

Peter: "Yes, and the centre line is the conductor or the conveyor."

Question: "The insulation appears to commence where it would leave the medium's body?"

Peter: "That is right. Whilst that is not a true picture, it is useful as an example or illustration. It had to start from somewhere and the commencement, in this instance, is on the right of the photograph: then it is gradually built up and developed as it proceeds towards the trumpet. There you have as complete a plan of the principle of voice production as you can be shown. But mark you this, somewhere along the length of the conveyor, according to conditions, there would develop a bulge, a mixing chamber you might say, or your beloved 'voice-box'. This may be near to the medium, or to the source of emergence; or it may be further along towards the trumpet. In the case of independent voice, when no trumpet would be used, the 'voice-box' would be almost solid—that is dense ectoplasm."

Question: "Now can you give me any reason why the plate would receive that formation in the dark?"

Peter: "There is no evidence that they exposed the plate in the dark. You are relying upon people's good faith."

Question: "Their story is, that they exposed the plate in the darkness?"

Peter: "If that is so, I cannot tell you. There is no reason why they should not so expose it, but I cannot say yes in this instance, because I do not know."

Question: "The photograph [Plate 3] was received in ordinary electric light?"

Peter: "Why not? There you have a picture of etheric energy, but completely disorganised. It may be due to several reasons. There were people present who were about to sit for a circle, that is, conditions were being built up preparatory to the sitting; and it is, more or less, a radiation from the sitters. If you could get a good photograph of a circle complete you would not have that ribbon formation wandering aimlessly around like a wisp of silk in a breeze; you would have it linking up perfectly with each sitter."

Question: "That lacy appearance within the ribbon of light [Plate No. 3], does that indicate any particular characteristic?"

Peter: "That just happens to be etheric ripples in the substance; yet it is not substance (it is difficult to find words with true meaning). It is a slight luminosity beyond the range of human vision. It could be made tangible by a little more organisation. Do you follow?"

214

Reply: "Yes, except that I do not know the purpose for which it is used."

Peter: "It is not used for any purpose. In the photograph it is disorganised: it should be linked with each sitter."

Question: "That implies that it would be the work of the Guides or Controls to control the formation?"

Peter: "That is right. It is the rim of the bowl that links each sitter; and from that upwards would rise the ribs or the points of contact. I cannot quite explain it in your language."

Question: "In two photographs we have what looks like a ball or a sphere of light. Has this any special significance?" [Plates Nos. 3 and 4.]

Peter: "It is the ball or sphere so common in nature and science which contains the possibility of any form of phenomena."

Question: "Do you mean, like the etheric egg that would bring an apport?"

Peter: "Yes, of course; but it is exaggerated in comparison to the size of the exposure. It looks very large, but there again, it is because of its lack of organisation."

Question: "Then the actual size of such a formation would be very small?"

Peter: "Quite; in fact, the more perfect it is, the smaller it would appear."

Question: "That drawing I made—[Fig. 8]. Does this give any indication of the appearance of the 'bowsing' of the auric field?"

Peter: "It is very good, but you cannot impart to it the tenseness. I do not think it is possible for you to do that. Still, I should use it, as it gives an impression. The rim of the pull would be at the base of the line linking each sitter. The sitters would not be subscribing necessarily to it, but it would be the point of contact."

Question. "You are referring to the ribbon of light?" [Plates 3 and 4]

Peter: "Yes. When it becomes organised, it links each sitter. It is a protective ring which brings them within the influence of the tent. It is the rim of the umbrella."

Question: "Can you give us any technical reason which permits these formations, which are invisible to our eyes, to be picked up by the lens of the camera?"

Peter: "The receiving of such pictures does not depend on any particular plate, but rather on the peculiar properties of the lens; and the conditions governing the objective which enable it to be received by the lens at that moment. It is purely a matter of . . . " (here Peter hesitated) . "There is no word which I can use that will describe the peculiar property in the lens that permits it to receive this activity in the formation about which we are speaking. It collects, under some peculiar conditions, light. Light is an etheric radiation; and light exists even where it is dark to you. It is discernible to an extra sensory perception which has a degree of recording ability. The lens, by chance, might be so set, at such an angle and at such a focus from the activity, that it combines a set of circumstances permitting it to record itself with the sufficiency of light existing at the time. Actually, it is a combination of circumstances, a combination of lens and plate. So that really you cannot lay down any fixed rule except this: that where persons have been successful in obtaining such photographic results, they should always set their camera at the same angle as in the first instance and then their success is more sure."

Question: "Do you know whether the luminosity of the activity comes within the field of the unknown light ray as distinct from the ultra-violet ray or the infra-red?"

Peter: "Not necessarily so. You do not know of the light characteristics then employed because they have not yet any purpose that would be of service to you."

Question: "Even though a room may appear dark to us, it does retain some light?"

Peter: "Yes, though it is darkness to you, it is probably not dark at all. The whole thing hinges upon the ability to receive the existing properties within the lens."

THE phenomena recorded in Part I and the explanations in Part II would be purposeless were it not for the motive behind it all. In this section an effort is made to show the purpose behind spirit activity.

PART III

CHAPTER XVIII

INTRODUCTION TO PART III

Spiritualists are often asked: What is the purpose of phenomena? Why should it be necessary to lift a table or play a tambourine? What is there spiritual in such elementary activity? How do these actions imply survival?

While a distinction can be drawn, as Peter points out, between the psychic activity of brute force carried out by primitive spirit agencies and the purposeful phenomena of far more enlightened intelligences, both "brute-psychic" and "spiritually-psychic" activities imply operation by discarnate minds.

We are here concerned with the point of view advanced by Peter. We can surely recognise that the simple act of levitating an object is but a method of communication, a way of attracting our attention by unusual means. It is a planned act, deliberately performed in such a manner that it intrigues man by its supernormal character. The act of lifting an object is in itself of no importance: but the manner of its performance must impel man to think and, in thinking, draw the only possible conclusion, that it is the result of forces applied by a living discarnate intelligence.

This intelligence is capable of effecting an organised result by methods unknown to man. Therefore, the intelligence operating must belong to a different state of being to that of man in the mould of matter. Direct voice communications and materialisations force this conclusion home, for here there is the evidence of individuality.

One of the main fundamental reasons that distinguishes man from the animal realm is that he is conscious of unrest and discontent. He possesses an irresistible urge to over-come difficulties, to give pleasure to his senses and to see progression towards a more perfect state—both physically and ethically.

Man is a spiritual being animated by spirit. From the earliest times when he became a conscious personality he has ever striven towards an ideal—towards perfection—as he is doing today. As consciousness quickened and perception developed, so did his ideology likewise evolve.

It is shown that as we enter into the new sphere of activity after transition, we carry with us the experiences of our earth life . . . vice and virtue . . . character, good and bad, developed or undeveloped.

With this purposeful progression of life from phase to phase, we see how the interest and activity of the spirit realm is intimately woven into a fabric of which our earth life forms an important part.

It follows, that as both earthly and spirit progression are bound up in each other, spirit intelligences who are able to communicate in any way through a human medium will do so for the purpose of influencing us for good. So we have Guides, like Peter, serving as missionaries for the progression of spirit through the enlightenment of mankind. Their activity will, in the end, bring all mankind together and give each individual truer appreciation of his place and function in the purpose of life, quickening his evolution from grossness to spirituality.

To convince man of survival is to assure him of his own spirituality. Convince him of the purpose of life, of which he is a part; and also, of the part he has yet to play in ageless time to be; and, beyond all doubt, he will so order his life here on earth and influence that of his fellows. It will become an existence of preparation for the greater life and thereby the negation of his animalistic existence today, which is motivated by greed and selfish profit.

In these days of war, when millions of men are engaged in destroying one another and the might of nations is organised for mass destruction, the one great hope of all mankind is that out of Armageddon a new order will evolve in which peace and brotherhood will endure.

Upon what does that depend? Not treaties, conventions, partitions or armaments, but upon the building up of a great impelling moral and spiritual force within the very heart of man.

We can take courage from lessons of the past. In those days man suffered for ideals which then seemed so remote, but which are now part of our accepted life. They came not by legislation, but through the enlightenment of man's consciousness and a change in the heart of humankind.

It is the age-old story of human progression, and if we, in our generation, are to make a worthy contribution to the future, we must turn our thoughts to the method whereby it may be attained. We must ask ourselves by what means can an enduring peace be secured and upon what foundation can we establish a code of enlightened conduct.

Can the churches of today provide the urge and enthusiasm for a great and permanent spiritual uplift? Their ritual has lost its appeal. Their doctrinarian philosophies have fallen far behind the times. Their legendary sophistries no longer are accepted as truths. Virile youth, so rudely jerked out of complacency by war demands and education, no longer accepts teaching simply because it is preached to them by pseudo-authority or because their parents subscribed to it. The decline in churchgoers indicates there is but little confidence in the church as it stands today.

On the other hand, we can no longer rely upon the efforts of statesmen. After the experiences of these times we cannot pin our faith on treaties, conventions and protocols: neither have we any reason for believing that peace can be secured by legislation, national or international, so generally based upon sectional and vested interests.

What else is there?

Before this question is answered, let us see what has happened within a lifetime. We have seen the birth and growth of modern Spiritualism succeed against the greatest of odds. Founded in the humblest of circumstances in poverty and without leadership, it has had to face the opposition of the Church, the law, and the ridicule of the press. Every man's hand was turned against it. Public opinion was prejudiced by charges of the fraudulence of mediums, and that Spiritualist practices were unclean and the works of the devil. Yet, in spite of all this it has grown until today its churches are numbered by the thousand and its home circles by the scores of thousands. It has received the support of some of our greatest scientists and thinkers.

The investigation carried out officially for the Church of England by a commission of the Archbishop of Canterbury's choosing has not led to a published report. The Archbishop has banned its publication. Why? Because the majority of the commission, after two years' investigation, found that the case for survival as expressed by Spiritualism was proved.

The literature of Spiritualism is prolific. Impartial psychical research societies, backed by men of the highest integrity, have been established in all great countries. They have investigated phenomena most meticulously; and their proceedings have added weighty testimonies to the ever-accumulating mass of evidence.

Spiritualism has penetrated most countries, particularly this country, America, Sweden, France and Germany (where it is now forbidden by the German Government). The national life of Britain and America, in particular, reflects its teachings; and its implications are found in general literature, the stage, films, sermons, the radio, etc.

One of our national Sunday newspapers computed the number of Spiritualists in Great Britain as 3,000000 and just prior to the outbreak of war the finest tonic for a newspaper's circulation was an investigation into Spiritualism.

These investigations were carried out fairly and frankly by experienced hard-headed journalists who invariably added their testimonies to the truth of survival.

In peacetime, every large meeting-place in central London was booked for Sunday services.

All this has been achieved in eighty years, and most of it since 1920.

What, then, of the future?

Is it beyond reason to assume that in these days of war, and particularly in the days to come, when peace is with us again, the peoples of all nations will be demanding a new concept of enlightened philosophy? The progress of awakening the peoples to the implications of survival will be so great that the spiritualisation of mankind will come within the bounds of probability.

The truth of survival with individual responsibility is not an ephemeral thing; it is capable of being proven over and over again. The great majority of Spiritualists today are Spiritualists only because they have received personal proof of the continued existence of their loved ones.

Here then is the foundation of the future. Here is a movement that will be ever new and cannot grow old. Here is a field for science, the possibilities of which transcend every other avenue of research. Here is a dynamic living truth that can influence the whole conduct of human affairs.

This is the answer to those who ask —"What is the purpose of spirit activity?"

In this section, Peter goes further than these generalisations: he tells us of the relationship of the spirit to ourselves; and gives us a new thesis of life.

In this year, 1942, the author's fervent hope is that the Spiritualist movement in general will be able to cope with the demands the future will make upon it. That mankind will learn from the bitter experiences of these days to provide for the children of tomorrow a better heritage than that through which we are now passing.

CHAPTER XIX

THE BIRTH OF THE SOUL

MAN possesses his physical body, his soul body and his spirit.

At the physical transition he dispenses with his physical body, the soul body motivated by the spirit continuing on.

The soul body is most closely allied to our present state of being. Peter has explained several times its functions and its relation to the physical body.

In the past there has been much confusion between the meaning of the soul and the spirit and if we accept Peter's definition it certainly puts the relationship of one to the other in order. Religious denominations of all kinds have failed to provide any reasonable explanation of what the soul body really is. They refer to it in the most ambiguous of terms and have never been able to define it.

According to Spiritualist reasoning in general, and Peter's in particular, the soul body is a functioning organism, the repository of experience, the propellent to the physical.

That each person possesses a soul body is proved through the act of spirit communication—there can be no other, there is no other, alternative.

We know how all things in the universe are subject to determined laws; and of course, this applies equally to the soul body. It cannot be either an intangible, incomprehensible, abstract force, form or thing, it is definitely positive. Every lesson we have learnt from nature speaks of an evolving process; and the soul body is likewise subject to ordered law-governed change.

This view is not a conception, it is cold, hard, materialistic reason. The infinite wondrousness of the evolution of the individual soul provides a far more spiritual vista than the blind, unreasoned, superstitious views of the past.

As we so regard our own soul body, so should we give it its rightful place in our individual scheme. Its culture and development should become our main incentive. It is immeasurably more important than acquiring possessions, wealth or power.

An enduring philosophy for the right government of human conduct, individually and communally, must rest upon established and demonstrable truths. The implications that follow the proven fact of survival provide this.

In the following chapters Peter not only satisfies the reasoning mind of the functions of the soul body but engages in an effort to give us more understanding of the laws that govern it.

We know the soul body leaves the physical at transition—Peter tells us how. He also describes its relationship to the spirit and the way it first contacts its human counterpart.

Peter's explanations arose out of our question as to the way the spirit contacts the physical body. He said:

Peter: "I think we will start by calling it the birth of the soul because we cannot deal with soul and omit the spirit, nor can we omit the spirit and deal wholly with the soul.

"I do not intend to go into the initial stages where conditions are created for the formation of the physical part. It may be little understood that the order of birth into the physical realm of an individual's spirit is strictly controlled. Further, it may not be generally realised that whilst the spirit has a choice of parentage, it has not the choice of the time of birth. That is fixed and irrevocable.

"You will ask, why does the spirit have choice of parentage? The answer is that in such manner it is enabled to choose the correct environment in which to function and to provide the necessary experience for its own development.

"We are not now considering the earthward travel of the spirit through its many planes of earlier existence but only its last phase, that of physical birth.

"The spirit itself stands apart from the actual development of the form it will subsequently activate.

"The soul has complete control in the formation and the development of the child within its mother's womb . . . the building from the materials provided by the first act . . . moulding and forming according to its own wisdom, begotten by long experience.

"When it has attained a certain degree of development, a more positive association between the soul and body commences. That is the period termed the 'quickening'. A further period of development from close association with the body takes place before the child is born.

"During the time of the first period the soul of the child is closely linked to that of the mother. That is why changes in her outlook, tastes and, oft-times, temperament are so noticeable; for it is through the soul body of the mother that the soul works until a period of four and a half months has elapsed. It then has a little soul. It is full of wisdom, as it is today. The soul is closely associated with the child's development and growth in its post-natal days until approximately seven years of age.

"During that period there is little or no close association with its spirit. That is why a child up to this age is nothing more than a healthy animal, driven only by its primitive desires.

"Having reached the approximate age of seven, a change takes place. The spirit, instead of brooding, one might say, over the young form now becomes definitely and positively linked through the soul to the body.

"That is when the child changes from the 'me want' stage to the 'I want' stage. It has then realised intuitively its own individuality as expressed in the word 'I'. It is not the result of education, it comes naturally and as a matter of course.

This period is sometimes accelerated—it might be five years or it might be retarded according to the individual condition.

"Now I feel that this brief description will be sufficient to create some measure of controversy; but viewed reasonably there can be no young spirits, for spirit cannot be created; and the universal anvil from which the sparks were struck originally can only be struck but once.

"The spirit, by the way, holds dominating control over the body through its contact direct with the blood stream. It requires wisdom to control the rhythmic beating of the heart so that the spirit which animates it may become attuned to it. Now you see the processes whereby knowledge of spiritual worth and value passes down almost without let or hindrance. Now you can appreciate why we have stressed the importance of the rhythmic system of breathing, to bring the heart of the individual into the rhythm and pulsation of its universe.

"All spirit is the same whether it is polarised, as it is with a human being, or contained in the vastness that fills eternity—if you can appreciate that expression.

"The spirit of man is a part of that universe, flawless, filled with beauty, with power unlimited; but it is the soul that stands between man as the spirit and man as the physical counterpart.

"The soul carries with it the characteristics portrayed by the young life in its first four to seven years of earth life. That period is activated by three things—to eat, to live and to possess all the things that he sees, at the expense of anything that would oppose him.

"I cannot say any more in your all too few words, but that is briefly how it is. The soul is the screen that passes on the deep rays of the eternal sun of the spirit."

Question: "Then the spirit attached to one person is not individualised?"

Peter: "Yes, it is. Through its association with the soul and the body it naturally has an individuality, the totality of which is from the reactions between the three.

"It is the same with the ether, the free ether, and that which is bound or individualised. Its nature is essentially the same. It is its performance which makes the difference. It has the same potentials plus its individuality.

"You can appreciate that if all things are perfect there can be no attainment of greater perfection; and perfection in one direction may not be perfection in another. We are speaking in the one sense of the universal spirit; you must remember that you who are part of the universe proper, are still confined to a spiritual orbit within a solar system which too has its own individuality."

Question: "If the soul that comes to a new being is full of wisdom, are we to understand that it has been in existence a long time?"

Peter: "That is right. I said that the soul was full of wisdom, taking it for granted that the one who read those words would also remember that I had said the soul belongs to the natural world, having, thereby, only primitive instincts. Its wisdom therefore can only be in relation to its experiences through its own development from the mineral kingdom, the plant kingdom and the animal realm.

"All the forms and processes of growth and development have fitted it out for its development and evolution to the status of man.

"You might say to me when you come to ponder that point—that pertains to the birth of a soul, but what happens when it ceases to animate the body at its physical separation, called death? Without the body, can that soul remain individualised?

"The answer is 'yes'. So long as the spirit animates the soul for the collection of the experiences received during its sojourn on earth; and for the further working out of the many problems that it could not complete during the school hours of the earthly life.

"You are thinking, what happens when the problems are solved?

"Death—so called—takes place again . . . there is a severance, or a rupture, of the points of contact between that which is called the soul body and that which is spirit. Like the physical body, the soul body, too, gradually breaks up. It is re-absorbed into the stream of the substance of which it is made, in the same way that your physical body breaks up in your earthly conditions.

"A questioner would say: 'How is it that the soul of a man who has passed on a long number of years ago still manifests?'

"The spirit, if it wishes to make its presence known to a man still on earth, can, with ease, gather about itself particles of the several realms through which it may have to pass to get back to earth conditions, until finally it clothes itself, temporarily, with an ether. It materialises down as far as the ether realm, and dissolves when the thought that gave it birth, or the spirit which animates it, has no further use for it.

"Remember, all the consciousness of the spirit is focused and contained in its inferior member (the soul body). One must die, either permanently or temporarily, just as man dies now before the known superior (again the soul body). Neither can have full sway.

"It is like your own body, the whole of your consciousness is concentrated within an aching member be it tooth or foot; because it is where the greatest action is taking place.

"The physical body is but a limb of the spirit. It is no more perhaps than a little finger or toe, but how infinitely important.

"You might say that you are part of the universal one you call God.

"The difficulty is that, what you now consider as reality is but the shadow. What you consider as the cause is but the effect. That is the difficulty. It is a reversal. It explains itself in what I have said. The inferior plane is always the seat of consciousness and activity, and that is why the realm you live in is apparently the only one.

"There is no past, no present and no future. Life is a slow unfolding of the plan.

"Is the setting out of the details, growing and expanding all the time, just for you to return to spirit, do you think? No. For a time yes, while there is work to do; but not work to fill you with dread because of the humdrum existence of earth life. One Man gave you the answer once: 'I must be about my Father's business', and that is about as good an answer as anyone can give."

CHAPTER XX

TRANSITION

ON the next occasion we met we asked Peter if he would carry on, from "The Birth of a Soul" to the next stage.

Peter commenced by saying:

Peter: "One of your playwrights said 'All the world's a stage', and it is across the stage that you act your part and then pass out and are clapped or booed as pleases the audience. Life is very similar to that.

"My opening words on this phase of the relationship are these: Life does not commence where you of the earth apprehend it, nor can it cease when it passes from your ken.

"Life is as a mysterious stream ever flowing onward, bearing all creation with it. Life as manifested in man is the advance of evolution. It is, broadly speaking, the cosmic experiment wherein the spirit is polarised and allowed to function, having, in certain measure, the quality of free will.

"It is only in man that you find spirit segregated and individualised from the rest of life which is spirit. When man begins his earth life, it is as if man, meaning spirit (that is the meaning of the term), begins the descent of a ladder, each rung of which represents a different phase of existence; until finally he emerges in the physical realm—in this case your earth.

"After having completed this life, the spirit of man leaves by the same ladder to which has been added another rung.

"That is a crude illustration that will appeal to any ordinary reader.

"At the death of the physical, the first to leave the association of the body is the spirit. It is like the extinguishing of a flame. The soul, however, has much to do and is not really dissociated from the body completely until after a lapse of two to three days, seldom more.

228

"The spirit has direct control in the matter of life and death only. Mark that, it is important. In no other bodily function has the spirit any authority, but the way of the birth and the precise second of physical death are factors directly controlled by the spirit.

"Now you would say to me, 'But how is this accomplished?'

"You have been taught that the spirit, through the soul, is linked to the physical body by a silver cord. That is true. We have been trying to separate (though wrongly so in the sense of the word 'separation') the spirit from the soul. There is a distinct difference; but then, you cannot understand the difference without presuming a separation, so remember I am discussing at the moment the spirit.

"The spirit's control over the manner of life and death is in connection with the heart. The association of the blood with spirit can be easily seen as having something in common; for as the blood stream is to the body, so is spirit (the life stream) to the universal body. To permit the spirit to escape easily, it is only necessary to raise the bodily temperature, through heart action, to find an easy means of exit. A man is termed 'hot blooded' when he is not controlled by the spirit of reason. That is why a child is so unreasonable, for a child lives on the borrowed blood until he is between five and seven years old. The spirit enters the blood stream of the child when he realises his own individuality and uses the word 'I' instead of 'me'.

"I have spoken already about the spirit and soul of the child. Now we have to take it in the reverse order because we are talking of the exit. When the spirit withdraws its control from the blood stream, the soul cannot for long maintain its hold upon the physical body. It is like an engine with the governor gone, it races and slows up, finally tearing itself to bits. Right. The soul body is above all things instinctive; the desire to manifest in the world of fact—the physical world—is so overpoweringly strong, that it will cling to the body for two or three days. It is this power, or lack of power in controlling the blood action, the heart action, that subsequently defeats him.

"Then you have the severance of the silver cord which is the point of contact between the physical and the soul body.

"Now a word about the etheric body! I will remind you that the etheric body has no characteristics—that is, personality or temperament. It has no reactions similar to that of the soul. It is purely bound ether that might be likened unto an expanding bag

(Little Peter says 'rubber balloon') taking the outline of the physical body. It appears to be the same viewed from whatever angle; never reaching more than about three inches from the body, when the person is normal in health and is well-fed and rested. It varies according to the vitality of the individual; the aura is beyond that. The etheric body has no colour change. It is ever the same—more or less, a misty silvery colour. We will talk about the aura by and by.

"The etheric body gradually loses its shape, which is the only characteristic it does have (the outline of the physical), as decomposition sets in, and is always associated with the body until decay is complete. That is why the modern idea of destruction by fire is excellent, provided always that three days have elapsed. If you could witness the place where you bury these bodies, you would find there is present an etheric mist made up from the etheric odours from decaying bodies. It is equally as dangerous as if you left the bodies where they died. I will speak one day about destruction by fire. Now that is briefly the procedure of the exit."

CHAPTER XXI

THE PURPOSE

Question: "As many people say to us, 'What is the purpose of phenomena?' would you give us a lead on the reasons for your work?"

Peter: "That is the only logical point to which we can influence anything. Cast your mind back to the early days of Christianity, or perhaps I should say pre-Christian days. Christ showed marvels and wonders through the working of so-called miracles. In that, you saw every phase of the phenomena that have been witnessed in the séance rooms of today.

"You have seen also the miracle of healing and the materialised form in comparison with that of Christ.

"If you will ask yourself this question, which has lived longest in man's mind and what has been responsible for influencing thoughts along spiritual lines since His day? Was it the record of His miracles or was it the beautiful philosophy that He taught?

"We today are in almost the same position. We have to produce something out of the ordinary to indicate in an objective way operations beyond the normal range of man's understanding.

"Perhaps it is a forlorn hope that man, of his own initiative, will strive to follow the lead given him in all these manifestations until it guides him further and further away from the realm material. But unfortunately, in the great majority of cases he has gone just the opposite way by bringing it down to purely physiological limits. We intend that man should follow the other way, to find the link between himself and the realm of spirit.

"It was not intended that the phenomena of the séance room should be given such a place of importance within our scheme; but we are helpless, as Christ was. We cannot go beyond man's understanding or give a greater illumination than that which can be received by the minds of the people who gather within the range of our voice and operations. In itself the work of the séance room is unimportant, in so far as that those who witness it fail to understand or to realise the immense possibilities that it has.

"It is, in fact, the harnessing of natural forces under the guidance of a directive mind or intelligence. Those same forces could be utilised by the minds of carnate man in the setting-up of conditions of great value to the human family; and, of course, in the reverse sense also.

"Today, it is the mission and the plan of the superior spiritual intelligences to create again opportunities upon earth, much the same as they did years ago when man first attained to spiritual freedom. I will tell you for the first time that there will be given another John the Baptist. I mean, in the same sense. Indeed, there is in the world today one such as he; and he is calling in the wilderness.

"This movement of spiritual forces found in manifestations is a counter to the forces of evil now rampant throughout the earth and the spheres adjacent thereto.

"It is only through the power of the spirit, weak as it may appear to be, that an antidote can be provided to save the rapid dissolution of the moral fabric of humanity.

"We have to find many ways in which to manifest to you; and we oft-times do not have to be too particular what channels we use.

"The day is soon to come, I mean soon, when our voice shall be heard in no uncertain volume; and at the right moment when spiritual leadership is needed.

"All this has had and will have its inception within the séance room. It has already succeeded in focusing man's mind beyond the realm of the purely physical and has made him more aware of some force without himself; that is all we can expect to achieve at the moment.

"In that upper room 2,000 years ago, the man Jesus did manifest behind the locked doors. It required His almost physical presence to convince the founder members of Christianity of the reality of life beyond death: but having once had that proved to them, they were more than ready to carry out the instructions they had received from their risen Leader. Instructions, mark you, that no man today knows about. He had so increased their spiritual consciousness that they were minor reflections of their Master and Leader. Can you see?"

Question: "They have not given us any such communication?"

Peter: "No, they could not do that any more than I can give you instructions how to achieve certain things. But if I could gather about me men of the same calibre and with the same readiness to appreciate spiritual unfoldment as Christ did, then I could confer (through contact) the same powers of Spiritual awareness that we have through years of patient toil been able to confer upon the medium; but, of course, to a far lesser degree than that enjoyed or borne by the Master Jesus. You understand that.

"You employ the same methods today. The medium gathers friends about himself and, through patience, develops similar gifts. It is by using the medium as a focal point; that these powers are quickened. It is similar to the magnetisation of a piece of steel by bringing it into contact with a magnet of greater permanency. It is the same law. By signs and wonders we try to attract and retain the interest of those witnessing such things; so that a few, who are thus impressed to pursue it further, may gradually be led into the understanding of our way; and so that we may send them out into the highways and byways, doing and living the way of life that we always try to inculcate.

"It is very important: because consciously, or unconsciously, they are all linked together today; and they spread the seeds of spirituality within the souls and the minds of those they contact, both subjectively and objectively. So the way is prepared; and one day you will see the small growth of the tender plant. Then almost before you realise it that plant will flower and be of great strength and of wondrous beauty.

"We do not come to tear down the ancient fabrics of your Christianity, but we come to fill the gap whilst the present Church lies gasping because of its antiquity in the spiritual sense. We have come to imbue it with new life and with a fresh power; a power which is dictated by the common standards of spiritual valuation, which is directed towards the lives of all and not to the lives of the few. To replace outworn dogmas and creeds. To give the power of spiritual interpretation to those suited to dispense it. To remove the Church from the rut worn so deeply and to give it a place again within the lives and the homes of all children: to make it a constitution, and not an institution. A place where all may come to derive spiritual sustenance, rather than to receive the cold comfort of the literal interpretation of the life of one man; a man who can only live in the spirit and who can only be interpreted within the soul. By no other means can His power to influence be felt within your life, except it be through service in a like manner. That is the next step from the séance room. That is our place of commencement."

Question: "You agree with the view that today we have great need of spiritualising humanity, by knowledge and understanding of the things about which you have been speaking to us?"

Peter: "Yes, that is true: but knowledge and understanding cannot come except that it be with the realisation of all that it implies. You have to regard it as a leavening power, rather than as a science of angles and views; and it is only by stimulating that, that the purpose can be achieved. If it shall be by the path of knowledge, then by that path it must be accomplished. But a slow and painful job it will be where the minds of certain individuals arc so blinded by the tradition of scientific knowledge that spiritually they are deaf. Whereas a more humble individual, knowing nothing of the law and the mathematics of science, can achieve in one stride the secret of the knowledge we try to teach. That is our difficulty."

Question: "The view is held that spiritual development will arise from the demonstration of survival after death?"

Peter: "That is the difficulty. The demonstration of survival is the least part of our difficulty. It is its implications that are important. What a difference it can make, knowing as a fact that life proceeds unbroken; what an effect, too, the accumulation of experience here and hereafter will have upon your own life and the lives for whom you are responsible. There is a purpose behind all things if you could but see it. For instance, the production of this book . . . It will be produced. You have found the channel for its launching, and you may think you have done it yourself; but have you ever considered whether it was your own idea or how much you are being made the instrument of forces without yourself? And the same illustration can be used for most things in the ordinary individual's life. Why should anyone take a step forward or a step backward at a precise time for apparently no reason at all? Yet in the next instant his or her life has been saved or destroyed physically by taking such action. These are little problems, little pointers worthy of consideration."

Mr Hart here interposed with a question: "It is difficult to distinguish between natural laws, mental laws, and spiritual laws?"

Peter: "You have got a little mixed. The question is now: 'What is the spiritual and what is the mental?' I do not want to launch out upon a discussion tonight upon the mental processes of man, because it would bring us again into that realm of strata; and the mind itself has layers and certain frequencies that can respond only to certain stimuli. The mental processes are played upon by other forces, the spiritual on the one hand and the etheric on the other; both radiate from other minds and from the very house of the soul itself. And you must understand, too, that spiritual pain and suffering mean nothing. Pain and suffering are only things experienced by the soul. You cannot quite appreciate that. It is a very important factor because that is a part of the natural life, not of the spiritual; and it is where you will become confused by saying that natural law is spiritual law. It is not. One is a reflection of the other. Both operate in harmony, although to you oft-times they appear in apparent disharmony. And that is why man today is such a puzzle to himself; because whilst the evolutionary process is proceeding there is a grafting process going on—the spirit of man is trying to graft himself upon the flesh of the beast. Do you remember a picture of that figure 'Centaur', where you have part man and part animal? There is more in that figure, interpreted spiritually, than at first sight may be apparent to you. There is another symbol pictured by the ancient painting of two children called 'The Twins'. I believe it is marked in the Heavens as Gemini. You might consider that as a superstition, but that too has its story. Those pictures are symbols containing within their stories the history and evolution of man; and illustrate his emergence from the animalistic stage and his entry into the spiritual stage. Everything has a meaning and a purpose, and the desire within you is to come into harmony with the spirit. As your mind demands so can the spirit satisfy; but we cannot progress one step with our teaching until you are able to receive."

Peter went on: . . . "Why do we bother to speak to you? Why do we make it our concern, aching and burning to help? Because we understand the true meaning of 'Brotherhood'. You have often heard me say that 'All life is one unity', therefore I am of your life. Your life is my life; and so long as there is one member of the whole body that aches or suffers, the whole body suffers with it."

"Now for a preliminary, I think we have covered some good ground."

THE END